GERMAN MEDIEVAL TALES

The German Library: Volume 4

Volkmar Sander, General Editor

GERMAN MEDIEVAL TALES

Edited by Francis G. Gentry

Foreword by Thomas Berger

CONTINUUM · NEW YORK

G 3732

1983

The Continuum Publishing Company
575 Lexington Avenue, New York, NY 10022

Copyright © 1982 by The Continuum Publishing Company

Foreword © 1982 by Thomas Berger
Introduction © 1982 by Francis G. Gentry

Printed in the United States of America

Library of Congress Cataloging in Publication Data

Main entry under title:

German medieval tales.

(The German library ; v. 4)
1. German literature—Middle High German, 1050–1500—
Translations into English. 2. English literature—
Translations from German. 3. Tales—Germany—Trans-
lations into English. 4. Tales—Translations from
German. I. Gentry, Francis G. II. Series.
PT1384.G47   1983   830'.8'002   82-22050
ISBN 0-8264-0272-0
ISBN 0-8264-0273-9 (pbk.)

Acknowledgments will be found on page 213
which constitutes an extension of the copyright page.

Contents

Foreword

"Middle Ages" is as imprecise a term as the most feckless rhetorician could devise, encompassing a thousand years: more indeed than Western civilization has enjoyed, or endured, since Columbus discovered America and so brought to an end the epoch that had begun when Rome fell in A.D. 476. But "medieval" in the conventional view applies most appropriately to the later centuries of that millennium, those of which the tales in the volume at hand are products.

If awakened in the wee hours by the Culture Police and required to depict a typical *mise en scène* of the later Middle Ages, might not one helplessly say, "A fair!"? populated by jugglers, buffoons, mountebanks, and clerical confidence men duping the halfwitted populace in the interests of a corrupt Pope. The armorplated nobility jousts in the adjacent meadow; in the damp dungeons of the castle nearby is an unfortunate peasant who was caught pinching walnuts from the baron's tree; and in a crepuscular laboratory, before a seething alembic, stands the white-bearded alchemist, trying foolishly to turn baser metals into gold.

The quaintness has been supplied by later ages. Medieval people were practical enough to make consistent use of buttons for the first time in history, to introduce clothing that conformed to the body (hence the need for buttons), and to eat with a fork, then a new implement. For that matter, the old alchemist has been vindicated by his twentieth-century heirs, who have succeeded in bringing about the Transmutation of Elements by nuclear fission: would that the result had been merely a surfeit of gold! As to the rest of the personnel at our imagined fair, are not they, or their modern counterparts—chicane politicians having replaced the monkish indulgence-peddlers—still with us?

How then, except in surface matters such as styles of clothing and abode, and all that was obvious and subtle in the feudal social arrangement—which for the purposes of literature can be said to be halfway between pictorial accident and moral essence—are we to distinguish medieval tales from those told only yesterday? An immediate and not altogether droll answer might be: in *our* stories the heroes can often be easily identified as the kind of characters the reader of the Middle Ages would have thought not worth creating: the weakling, the hypochondriac, the sniveler, *et al.* Our tolerance for human frailty would probably seem to the medieval man rather the approbation of that which should be deplored. *His* hero is exemplary, even when damnable, like Dr. Faustus.

Medieval narratives are not devious in their means or uncertain in their moral focus. The principal personages are clearly named at the outset, their predicaments are forthrightly indicated, their responses specified: for example, Hartmann von Aue's poor Heinrich, who when he "first began to realize that the world found him repugnant . . . behaved as most people in a similar situation do. . . . Repeatedly he cursed and damned the day of his birth." Dr. Faustus is immediately shown as an ungodly young man despite his upbringing by devout parents and sponsors. In the Arthurian tales the reader is seldom in doubt as to the virtues, or lack thereof, of the principal figures: Sir Galahad is not secretly a rascal, nor is Mordred, underneath it all, a decent chap whose only problem consists in being misunderstood by his father the king.

Sudden changes of fortune occur without a hint of the preparation we have come to expect in the literature of more recent times. In *Duke Ernst,* after a few perfunctory objections, the emperor comes readily to believe the wicked count's slanders against the most admirable stepson a sovereign ever had and proceeds to lay waste to Ernst's lands and drive him into exile. At which point an even more remarkable change takes place in the very stuff of the tale, which until now has been told as standard realism with respect to its place and time: the wandering Ernst and his companions in exile reach a city of wondrous splendor, which is populated by "handsome, stately people, except that their necks and heads were like those of cranes," and this beaked folk is only the

first in a succession of fantastic tribes or breeds or races encountered by our hero, a spiritual descendant of Ulysses and a forebear
of Gulliver: griffins and giants and midgets and a species of human beings who have the feet of swans. Ernst prevails over his
extraordinary adversaries and survives his extravagant adventures,
including a war in Ethiopia and visits to Egypt and the Holy Land,
returning eventually to be pardoned by the emperor who had victimized *him,* the justice of which exchange would certainly be
questioned by us, but neither hero nor author finds it worth a
note: it's simply the way things go between persons of unequal
power. And indeed, for all our questions, do we not here recognize an ecumenical truth that spans all eras?

What would seem peculiarly medieval is the absence of resentment. So too with Dr. Faustus, who does not seek to evade fulfilling to the letter his part of the infernal agreement, "having no
other expectation but that he must absolve his debt and contract
with his skin."

"I know," says Faustus, "that the Devil will have his due." The
principle so enunciated has been generally out of fashion since the
end of the Middle Ages. One might even see the Renaissance as
the beginning of a massive effort (which is still underway) to cheat
the Devil, beat him at his own game. Though it has been forcefully
maintained that God has been dead time out of mind, no one is
so reckless as to suggest that the Fiend is not as healthy as ever.
But to admit what is owed him would be another matter. A sense
of honor is not exclusive to the Middle Ages, but it has certainly
become less robust in the years since.

Another fetching quality to be found in medieval literature, or
perhaps it is but another phase of the same candor with which the
characters state their cases, might be called ingenuous audacity.
Unprecedented events are related as though they were commonplace, and no doubt they might be accepted as such by readers
who presumably believed in dragons and unicorns without ever
encountering a living example of either. In *Duke Ernst,* again, the
author at one point steps to the front of the stage and addresses
the audience, inviting anyone who questions the truth of his tale
to come visit him in Bamberg and be reassured. "Moreover," says
he (with a straight face?), "it has been written down in Latin and
is therefore a true story with no lies."

What remains, in these notes by a storyteller of the nineteen-eighties on his forebears of the twelfth-to-fifteenth centuries, is, for the record, to ask: Why read the work of these extinct pens? The classic answers to the always implicit *ur*-question, Why read anything?, are applicable: yes, as in all literature worthy of the name we encounter truths about what it is conventional to call the human condition—though in medieval narratives, with God and the Devil, there is often the superhuman dimension as well. We are fascinated, refreshed, and yes, though nowadays we are especially suspicious of the didactic, even edified. The tales in this volume, a representative selection of the available wealth from medieval Germany (which culture, in the heart of Middle Europe, has always seemed to me that which most typified the spirit of the Middle Ages) are still eloquent.

The roguish, cynical comedy of *Reinhart the Fox* is as up to the minute as it is beyond time: "The world then was just as it is now, and many men overcame their difficulties with deceit better than those who acted uprightly." In *Unfortunate Lord Henry,* a product of the late twelfth century, can be found sufficient sexual suggestion to cause the eyebrows of the contemporary reader, trained by the psychoanalytic movement to recognize such clues, "to travel all the way to the back of his bald head" (in the felicitous phrasing of Nabokov's Humbert Humbert): Heinrich, a leper, can be cured only if he can locate a virgin who is willing to die for his sake. The one who offers herself is eleven years old, and she does not flinch when she is assured that the unique treatment that will heal *him* requires *her* to be stripped, bound to a table, and mutilated with a knife!

But the last point to be made is the first in importance. These tales satisfy the only altogether serious requirement that can be imposed upon a work of literary art: they are simply delightful to read.

Thomas Berger

Introduction

That there should be four of 100 planned volumes of THE GERMAN LIBRARY devoted exclusively to the literature of the Middle Ages is a welcome phenomenon in the late twentieth century, a time when individuals are so caught up in themselves and the "now" that it is difficult to conceive of an epoch when society and the welfare of one's fellow man played as important a role as one's individual fortune. And yet it is this aspect which unites medieval German literature from the eleventh through the fourteenth century. The greatest medieval German lyricist, Walther von der Vogelweide (ca. 1170–ca. 1230), probably summed up the problem best in his poem, *"Ich saz ûf eime steine"* ("I was sitting on a rock"), so much so that it would not be out of place to reproduce the poem here:

Ich saz ûf eime steine,	I was sitting on a rock
und dahte bein mit beine	and put one leg over the other
dar ûf satzt ich den ellenbogen:	upon which I put my elbow.
ich hete in mîne hant gesmogen	In my hand I nestled
daz kinne und ein mîn wange.	my chin and one of my cheeks.
dô dâhte ich mir vil ange	I considered most seriously
wie man zer welte solte leben:	how one is to live in this world.
deheinen rât kond ich gegeben,	I could find no answer
wie man driu dinc erwurbe,	as to how one could gain three things
der keines niht verdurbe.	so that not one of them would perish.
diu zwei sint êre und varnde guot,	Two of them are worldly honor and wealth—
daz dicke ein ander schaden tuot:	which often do injury to each other.

daz dritte ist gotes hulde,	The third is the favor of God
der zweier übergulde.	which is worth more than the other two.
die wolte ich gerne in einen schrîn.	Those I wanted to have *all* together.
jâ leider desn mac niht gesîn,	Unfortunately it will never be possible
daz guot und weltlich êre	that wealth and worldly honor
und gotes hulde mêre	along with the favor of God
zesamene in ein herze komen.	ever meet in one and the same heart.
stîg und wege sint in benomen:	Paths and trails have been closed to them:
untriuwe ist in der sâze	Deceit lurks in ambush (and)
gewalt vert ûf der strâze:	brute force parades openly.
vride und reht sint sêre wunt.	Peace and justice have been dealt a death blow.
diu driu enhabent geleites niht, diu	If the three do not receive safe conduct,
zwei enwerden ê gesunt.	the two will not recover in time.

It is, of course, possible to read Walther's poem as an expression of distress at the conditions prevailing in Germany at that time (early thirteenth century) when the nation was engaged in a civil war between the followers of the Hohenstaufen Phillip, who was Regent for the young Frederick II, and those of the Guelph Otto of Brunswick. Obviously Walther is referring to the depredations of unscrupulous members of the nobility who are utilizing the unstable situation to increase their holdings and their standing in the world, but, as he also indicates, at the cost of God's favor. Their actions have brought about a condition that medieval German writers, both before and after Walther, often lamented—the loss of peace and justice, a loss that threatened the very foundation of their society. Indeed, well over a century earlier, the *Annolied* poet inserts a description of the unrest in the German Empire brought about by the conflict between the Empire and the Papacy:

Dar nâh vîng sich ane der ubile strît	Then began the evil conflict
des manig man virlôs den lîph,	in which many a man lost his life.
duo demi vierden Heinrîche	At the time of Henry IV
virworrin wart diz rîche.	the Empire was brought into total disarray.
mort, roub unti brant	Murder, robbery and arson
civûrtin kirichin unti lant	devastated churches and lands

von Tenemarc unz in Apuliam,	from Denmark to Apulia,
van Kerlingin unz an Ungerin.	from France to Hungary,
den nîman nimohte widir sten,	which no one could withstand
obi si woltin mit trûwin unsamit	even if they wished to keep faith
gên,	with each other.
die stiftin heriverte grôze	They organized great military campaigns
wider nevin unti hûsgenôze.	against relatives and countrymen.
diz rîche alliz bikêrte sîn gewêfine	The entire empire turned its weapons
in sîn eigin inâdere.	into its own innards.
mit siginuftlîcher ceswe	With a victorious hand
ubirwant iz sich selbe,	it overcame itself
daz dî gidouftin lîchamin	so that the cadavers of the baptized
umbigravin ciworfin lâgin	lay scattered and unburied—
ci âse den bellindin,	as carrion for the baying
den grâwin walthundin.	gray wolves.

While the *Annolied* poet is certainly more graphic in his description of the results of the war, probably due to the fact that the two major supports of medieval society, the Papacy and the Monarchy, were locked in an unparalleled struggle for supremacy, a struggle that would prove to have fateful consequences for Germany, the similarities between his concerns and Walther's are obvious: When the protectors of society, the nobles, do not fulfill their function, chaos and injustice will result. Because human society since the Fall of Man was perceived as being fragile and imperfect under the best of circumstances, the medieval poets, as members of this society, were sensitive to the necessity of all working together to bring about the condition which would enable all to fulfill their duties and to ensure that each received his due.

As is obvious from the above, the Middle Ages were anything but idyllic. Even in the best of times it was a period of unrelieved hardship for the larger part of the population, a period when ninety-five percent of the population supported the other five percent through hard physical labor. It was this five percent, in turn, which supported literary production, a time-consuming and expensive process. Thus, medieval literature is, in a sense, the literature of the elite, paid for and consumed by a small fraction of medieval society. But as pointed out above, the issues addressed by the literature, while played out against the background of the concerns of the feudal nobility, must also be viewed in a more global manner, namely the concerns of the Christian living in an age in which the Church was the arbiter of social practice and moral behavior. As a result, whether or not the Church as institution appears in medieval works, the moral theology of the Christian religion, which defines correct action, is present. The stress, as is to be expected, is on the correct action and sense of justice of the ruler or, more generally, those in power. For while those in power have more authority and wealth, they are more susceptible to the allures of the world and are thus in greater danger of losing their immortal souls. Most of the tales selected for this volume have the above as a main theme.

As is often the case with medieval writers, so little is known about them—many times even their identities are in doubt—that it is virtually impossible to construct a biography. With Hartmann von Aue, however, there is—relatively speaking—an embarrassment of riches. In the prologue of the *Unfortunate Lord Henry* Hartmann identifies himself by name, indicates that he could read, which would imply Latin and probably some French, and designates himself as a ministerial of the House of Au. Further, he states that he was seeking a tale to relate that would relieve the tedium of his idle hours. In other words, Hartmann is intimating that he did not consider writing to be his main profession, a not uncommon position among early and high courtly medieval poets and one which may account for the large number of anonymous works from this period. Hartmann wrote several other works, including two Arthurian romances, *Erec* and *Iwein,* based on the like-named tales of Chrétien de Troyes; *Gregorius,* a Saint's *Vita; Das Büchlein,* a tract dealing with courtly love; and several courtly love songs. He was, apparently, highly esteemed among his contemporaries for his poetic skills as Gottfried von Straßburg indicates in his *Tristan:*

Hartmann der Ouwaere	Hartmann von Au
ahî wie der diu maere	ah! How he dyes and adorns his tales
beide ûzen unde innen	—both outside and within—
mit worten und mit sinnen	with words and with sense

durchverwet und durchzieret!	through and through!
wie er mit rede figieret	How eloquently he establishes
der âventiure meine!	his story's meaning!
wie lûter und wie reine	How clear and transparent
sîniu cristallînen wörtelîn	his crystal words
beidiu sint und iemer müezen sîn!	are and ever must remain!

What Gottfried is praising in Hartmann is his ability to render his sources correctly and intelligibly to his listeners. Important for the medieval mind was not so much the newness of a tale, but rather how well an already known tale was recounted. Hartmann, according to Gottfried, is a master of the arts of rhetoric. Above all, the poet must have a source and he may even basically translate his source as long as he does it in a manner understandable to his audience. The medieval German courtly poet's main task was to interpret his source. Thus it is no accident that Hartmann states in the beginning lines of *Unfortunate Lord Henry* that he found a tale that was written down somewhere and will now begin to interpret it.

The story that Hartmann wishes to interpret concerns a decent and just nobleman who, at the height of his prosperity and power, is stricken with leprosy. Although it is never quite clear at the beginning why Lord Henry is so grievously afflicted, as the poem progresses we learn that he had forgotten to render sufficient thanks to God for his good fortune. What saves him in the end are the realization that his punishment was just and his willingness to submit to God's will. By an act of supreme selflessness he prevents the peasant girl from sacrificing herself for him and thus evinces the great virtue of Christian charity, which is enough to cleanse his body of the disease. Noteworthy is the fact that the noble himself effects his own salvation, not another party. And by so doing Lord Henry evinces those qualities expected of the powerful and is therefore worthy of salvation. Also of interest in this tale is the subsequent marriage between Lord Henry and the peasant girl, something that would have been highly unusual. But the girl is the daughter of a *free* peasant and thus shares the same status as the Lord Henry, which would then ensure that their children would also be free. It has been suggested that Hartmann was referring to an incident that had taken place in the family history of the lord

of Au whom he served, but without the presence of any supporting material all explanations must be viewed as pure speculation.

The unique tale of *Helmbrecht* was probably composed between 1250 and 1280 by someone who identifies himself as Wernher der Gartenaere and about whom nothing else is known. The
story of Helmbrecht, the peasant's son who left his rightful place
in society to become a robber in the company of a knight, has
received much attention in modern scholarship and has been in-
terpreted as an example of an ideology that made the desire for
upward mobility of the peasantry a criminal offense or as a work
that criticized the territorial ambitions of the Hapsburgs, who
armed peasants and used them in their campaigns. Actually, it is
not necessary either to impose a modern ideology on the work or
to try to pinpoint a specific historical event as the stimulus for the
writing of the work. Rather, Wernher is attacking the ambitions
of both those peasants and those knights who are abandoning their
proper place within medieval society, their "order," and, as a result, bring about chaos. Several times within the work Wernher
laments that the knights of his day are not like those of old, and
he also has the elder Helmbrecht admonish his son repeatedly that
he belongs "behind the plow." In other words, Wernher is viewing
the instability of his times as due to the failure of members of
society to fulfill their proper functions, either to protect the peasants (nobles) or to plant and grow food for society, for without
the peasant, as the elder Helmbrecht remarks, there would be no
noble existence since the nobles depend upon the work of the
peasantry to keep up their style of life. Of interest in *Helmbrecht,*
and fully consonant with the concerns found in didactic literature
of the late thirteenth and fourteenth centuries, is the inclusion of
individuals other than nobles in the grand scheme of things. Both
peasants and nobles are depicted as having important functions in
society, something which less than one hundred years previous
would have been unthinkable in the literature.

The tale of *Reinhart the Fox* was probably composed around
1190 but exists only in fragments and two later redactions of the
German text. In spite of the moments of—mostly low—comedy it
is a cynical work that not only calls the concept of courtly love
into question, but also attacks the concept of kingship itself. Reinhart, the evil servant, actually the upwardly mobile servant, emerges

as the hero after having destroyed the court and committed regicide. Nothing is known of the poet, Heinrich der Gleisner (Heinrich the Hypocrite), not even his status. It is felt that the work was written in the service of a reactionary member of the Free Nobility who strongly disapproved of the policies of the Hohenstaufen regarding the position of the ministerials, who were formerly members of an unfree class and who were, under the Hohenstaufen, being allowed to assume positions of authority and influence in the empire, often to the detriment of members of the free nobility. Because of its theme and early date of composition, *Reinhart the Fox* occupies a special place within German literature of the courtly period, combining as it does the biting satire of Heinrich von Melk and the didactic concerns of late medieval poetry.

The legend of *Duke Ernst* is preserved in fragments from around 1187 and a later version from around 1210. There were also many later German versions, including one in prose, as well as three Latin versions, both in prose and verse. It is doubtless one of the most popular tales of the German Middle Ages. The story of the powerful Bavarian noble banned by the emperor must have a historical basis: it could refer to the revolt of Liudolf against his father, Otto I (953) which would fit within the time-frame of the work. But it could also be a comment on the banning of Henry the Lion of Bavaria by Frederick Barbarossa, a much more immediate concern of the period. It would not at all be unusual to camouflage a political statement by removing the event to the distant past, especially if a convenient parallel could be found. In any event, it is quite obvious that the sympathy of the—unknown— poet lies with Ernst. His banishment is viewed as unjust and due solely to the machinations of a jealous advisor to the emperor. The loyalty of Ernst to Otto is stressed and the hope of reconciliation is ever present. Unlike the case of *Reynard the Fox* the integrity of kingship is not placed in question; indeed just the opposite. The king of the Crane-Beaks is portrayed as evil and ruthless because of his unprovoked wars of conquest and kidnapping of the princess of India, whereas the king of the Cyclops, who only wishes to protect his land against aggression, is depicted as a noble and just ruler. The ultimate reconciliation of Ernst and Otto doubtless represents the wish of the poet, if indeed the work may be viewed as referring to the rivalry between Henry the Lion and Barbarossa, that the German empire be strengthened through the cooperation of the emperor and the territorial princes. For where this harmony exists, order and peace exist as well. In this way a connection with the concerns found in the other tales can be discerned.

The two tales composed by Konrad of Würzburg are minor literary masterpieces and give a hint of his range. The beauty of the language of the *Tale of the Hearts* compares favorably with Gottfried von Straßburg, and the *Reward of the World* is a jewel of allegorical didactic poetry. Interpretation is not necessary since the "message" in both is quite straightforward. They were composed in the latter half of the thirteenth century.

The Faust legend is, of course, part of world literature and *The History of Dr. Johann Faustus* does not need to be further expounded upon here. The version in this volume is based on the oldest surviving manuscript of the Faust book, written down around 1580, which probably best represents the content of the original.

With the exception of the *History of Dr. Johann Faustus* the tales chosen for this volume represent a generic and thematic selection from the twelfth and thirteenth centuries. Most are not well-known—or known at all for that matter—to English speakers and it is hoped that these translations, most done especially for this volume and all completed within the past four years, will provide readers with an insight into the artistic variety and beauty of medieval German literature.

F.G.G.

Der arme Heinrich

Ein ritter sô gelêret was
daz er an den buochen las
swaz er dar an geschriben vant;
der was Hartman genant.
dienstman was er zOuwe.
er nam im manege schouwe
an mislîchen buochen.
dar an begunde er suochen,
ob er iht des funde
dâ mite er swære stunde
möhte senfter machen,
und von sô gewanten sachen
daz gotes êren töhte
und dâ mite er sich möhte
gelieben den liuten.
nu beginnet er iu diuten
ein rede die er geschriben vant.
dar umbe hât er sich genant,
daz er sîner arbeit
die er dar an hât geleit
iht âne lôn belîbe,
und swer nâch sînem lîbe
sî hœre sagen ode lese,
daz er im bitende wese
der sêle heiles hin ze gote.
man giht, er sî sîn selbes bote
unde erlœse sich dâ mite,
swer umb des andern schulde bite.

The Unfortunate Lord Henry

Hartmann von Aue

There was a knight so learned
that he read in books
whatever he found written there.
His name was Hartmann and
he was a vassal of the House of Aue.
He began searching around
in various kinds of books,
looking through them to see
whether he might find something
with which he could make
oppressive hours more pleasant,
things of such a nature
which would do honor to God
and with which he could
endear himself to his fellow men.
Now he will begin to interpret for you
a tale which he found written.
It is for this reason that he has mentioned his name
so that he would not be
without reward for the work
which he has expended on it
and so that whoever might hear it recited or might read it
after his [Hartmann's] death
might pray
to God for the salvation of his soul.
One says that he is his own intercessor
and redeems himself thereby
who intercedes for the sins of another.

1

The story which he read tells of a lord living in Swabia in whom no quality was lacking that a knight in the flower of manhood should have to win full esteem. No one in all those lands was regarded so highly. He had at his disposal lineage as well as power and wealth. Also, he possessed capabilities in many areas. However sufficient his possessions were, however flawless his ancestry, which was doubtless comparable to that of princes, still he was not nearly so rich by reason of birth and possessions as he was because of his sense of dignity and noble attitude.

His name was very well known. He was called Lord Heinrich and was born of the House of Aue. His heart had foresworn duplicity and ill-breeding, and he kept this oath with constancy to the end of his days. His honor and conduct were without the slightest fault. That abundance of worldly honors one could rightly wish for had been lavished upon him. And he knew how to increase these honors through his many sterling qualities. He was a flower of young manhood, a mirror of the joy of the world, a diamond of constant loyalty, a full crown of courtly behavior. He was a refuge to those in need, a shield of protection for his kin. His generosity weighed the amount to be given against the need. Both excess and lack were foreign to him. He carried the wearisome burden of honors upon his back. He was a bridge stretching forth help and was well-versed in singing of courtly love. Thus he knew how to gain the honor and glory of the world. He embodied all the qualities of the courtly gentleman and showed mature wisdom.

When Lord Heinrich had thus attained the enjoyment of honor, possessions, a happy heart, and earthly joy—he was praised and esteemed as the first among his kinfolk—his lofty existence was turned into a life of utter humiliation. In his case, as also with Absalom was made clear, as Holy Scripture has told us, the empty crown of wordly sweetness falls from its place of highest esteem into dust under foot. There it says, *media vita in morte sumus,* which means we are hovering in the midst of death when we think we are living to the fullest.

The stability of this world, its constant and best wealth, power, and majesty can be mastered by no one. We can see a true picture of that happening with the candle which turns to ashes in the act of giving forth light. We are made of fragile stuff. Just look how our joy dissolves in tears. Life's sweetness is mixed with bitter gall. Our blossom must fall just when it seems to be thriving best. Heinrich's fate made very evident that he who lives on this earth in great esteem is despised in the sight of God. Through God's command he plunged from his esteemed position into a despicable state of misery: he fell victim to leprosy. When the grave chastisement became evident on his body, he was repulsive to everyone. However pleasant all the world found him before, now he was so repulsive that people avoided looking at him. The noble and wealthy Job met with this fate, too. In the midst of good fortune he piteously found himself on a dung heap.

When poor Heinrich first began to realize that the world found him repugnant, he behaved as most people in a similar situation do. His reaction to his bitterly felt anguish differed greatly from the patience of Job. The good man Job suffered with patient bearing all the afflictions that came his way so that his soul might find joy. The disease and tribulations which he suffered from the world were occasions for him to praise God and he was happy. Alas, poor Heinrich did not at all react in this manner. He was gloomy and dejected. His soaring heart sank, his buoyant joy went under. His self-esteem tumbled. Honey turned to gall. A sudden dark thunderclap shattered his noontime. A cloud, thick and sullen, enveloped the radiance of his sun. Many a sigh escaped him at the thought of having to leave such honor behind. Repeatedly he cursed and damned the day of his birth.

And yet a little joy was left to him. He still had one consolation. He had often heard that there were several different strains of the

disease and some of them were curable. Hence his hopes and
thoughts were quite mixed. He thought that he could perhaps be
cured, and so he hurried off to Montpellier to seek medical advice.
Here he quickly found nothing but the sad news that he would
never recover. He received the news with disappointment and rode
off toward Salerno and here also sought the skills of experienced
doctors in the hope of being cured.

The best physician whom he found there immediately gave him
a strange answer: he was curable and yet he would never be cured.
"How can that be?" asked Heinrich. "What you are saying is quite
impossible. If I am curable, then I'll recover. And whatever is imposed upon me in the way of a fee or however strenuous the treatment might be, I'm quite confident that I can accomplish it." "Give
up your hopes," the doctor replied. "I'll tell you the nature of
your sickness, although my explanation won't do you any good.
For a cure a certain medicine is all that is necessary. Hence you
are curable. However, no one is so wealthy or has such keen in-
tellectual powers that he can attain it. Thus you will forever remain uncured, unless God wishes to be your physician."

"Why are you trying to discourage me?" asked poor Heinrich.
"I have a great amount of wealth at my disposal. Unless you want
to act contrary to your medical skills and medical ethics, not to
mention that you would be turning down my silver and gold, I'll
make you so favorably disposed toward me that you will quite
readily heal me." "It's not that my good will is lacking," replied
the doctor. "And if the medicine were of such a kind that one
could find it for sale or that one could acquire it by any means, I
would not let you languish. But that is unfortunately not the case.
Hence you must of necessity remain without my help. You would
have to find a virgin of marriageable age who would be willing to
suffer death for your sake. Now it is not the usual state of affairs
among people that someone freely takes such an act upon himself.
Nothing else is necessary for a cure than the blood from the heart
of such a girl. This would be a cure for your disease."

Now poor Heinrich saw clearly that it would be impossible for
anyone to find a person who would willingly die for him. Thus
the one consolation which had made him undertake the journey
was taken from him. And from this time on, he had no hope left
concerning his recovery. Because of this the pain of his heart was

so great and strong that it infuriated him most of all that he should go on living. He journeyed home and began distributing his lands as well as his personal effects according to his own feelings and the judicious advice of others as to where it would do the most good. With discrimination he increased the means of his poor relatives and also gave material comfort to poor people who were strangers to him so that God might have mercy on his soul. Monasteries received the rest. Thus did he free himself from all his major possessions except for a farm on cleared land. Hither he fled from people. Heinrich was not the only one to bewail his tragic affliction. In all the lands where he was known and even in foreign lands where he was known only by reputation people grieved for him.

The man who had already been farming this land for a long time was a free peasant who never had any of the great troubles which other peasants had whose lords were worse and did not spare them taxation and other fees. Whatever this farmer did willingly seemed good enough to his lord. What is more, he protected him from any violence inflicted by outside parties. Because of this no one of his class in the whole land was as well off as he. To this peasant came his lord, poor Heinrich. Whatever Heinrich had spared him earlier, how that was now repaid! How handsomely he reaped the benefits of this! The farmer was not at all bothered by what he had to do for Heinrich's sake. Out of loyalty he was determined to endure willingly the burdensome task that was now his lot because of his lord. He spared no means to make Heinrich comfortable.

God had given the peasant a good life according to his class. He was capable of strenuous physical labor, and he had a hard-working wife. In addition, he had beautiful children who really bring joy to a man's life. One of the children, as one says, was a girl, a child eight years old. Her actions revealed her real goodness. She would never budge from her lord even a foot. To gain his favor and greeting she served him constantly in every way she could with her kind attention. She had such a pleasing way about her that she could have fittingly been the child of the emperor in her loveliness.

The others were smart enough to know how to avoid him without being too obvious. But she fled to him all the time and nowhere else. She alone made the time pass quickly for him. With the pure goodness of a child she had opened her heart to her lord so she could always be found at his feet. With pleasing eagerness she attended her lord. He, in turn, tried to please her in whatever way he could. Her lord gave her in abundance whatever fitted in with her childhood games. Also in his favor was the fact that children are so easy to win over. He got for her whatever he found for sale—a mirror, hair ribbons—whatever children find nice—a belt and a ring. By means of these attentions he brought things to the point that she became so close to him that he called her his bride. The dear child never let him remain alone. She thought of him as a completely healthy person. However strongly she was influenced by the gifts and playthings, still it was before all else a sweet disposition, a gift of God, which made this way of acting please her. Her devotion manifested great kindness.

Once, when the unfortunate Heinrich had already spent three years there and God had tormented him with great bodily suffering, the peasant, his wife, and the girl I have already mentioned were one day sitting together with him as they worked. They were lamenting over the sufferings of their lord, and they had every reason to be sad. For they feared that his death would work great harm for them in that they might lose their good standing and their property, and that a different lord would be much more severe with them. These thoughts kept running through their minds until the peasant thus began to inquire, saying, "My dear lord, I would like to ask a question, if I may do so with your favor. There are so many doctors of medicine in Salerno. Why is it that none of them was able to find help for you with his skill? Sir, that is what surprises me." Poor Heinrich emitted a sigh of bitter anguish from the bottom of his heart. Such was the sadness with which he spoke that sobs punctuated his speech: "I deserved this shameful humiliation at God's hands. For you saw very well how formerly my gate stood wide open to wordly joy and that no one among his family and relatives had his wish fulfilled better than I. This was impossible since I always had my way completely. During this time I took very little notice of Him who in His goodness had given me this life. My attitude was that of all fools of this world who are persuaded that they can have honor and possessions without God. Thus did my foolish notion deceive me. For I very seldom looked to Him from whose favor many honors and possessions came my way. When, then, the Heavenly Gatekeeper had enough of my arrogance, He closed the gates of happiness to me. Now I'll never enter there! My foolish attitude spoiled that for me. As punishment God imposed an infirmity upon me of such a nature that no one can free me of it. Now I have become repugnant to the common people. Those of prominence take no notice of me. However lowly the man who looks at me, I am still more lowly than he. He shows me his contempt by casting his eyes from me. Now the loyalty in you really becomes evident for the first time—that you let me stay with you in my wretched condition and that you do not in the least flee from me. But although you do not shun me, although I am loved by you, if by no one else, and however much you have me to thank for your prosperity, still you would easily resign yourself to my death. Who in the world was ever so worthless and so wretched? I used to be your lord, now I am your suppliant. Dear friend, by keeping me here in my sickness you are earning for yourself, your wife, and my bride life everlasting.

"I'll gladly tell you what you asked me. In Salerno I was not able to find a doctor who dared or wanted to take me into his charge. For the means by which I was to recover from my sickness was to be of such a kind that no one in the world is at all able to gain it. I was told nothing else but that I would have to find a virgin fully able to marry who would be willing to suffer death for my sake, that the doctor would cut her open to the heart, and that nothing else could help me than the blood from her heart. Now it is obviously impossible that any such girl would willingly suffer death for my sake. Hence I must bear shameful misery till my death. May God send it to me quickly!"

The innocent girl heard what he told her father, for the dear child had the feet of her dear lord resting in her lap. One could easily compare her childlike attitude to the goodness of the angels. She understood what he said and forgot not a word. She kept thinking about it in her heart until she went to bed that night where she lay at the feet of her father and mother as she was accustomed to do. After they had both fallen asleep, she pressed many a deep sigh from her heart. Her sadness because of the sufferings of her lord became so great that the flood from her eyes poured over the feet of her sleeping parents. Thus did the dear child awaken them.

When they felt the tears, they awoke and asked her what was the matter with her and what kind of distress it could be that caused her to weep so quietly. At first she did not want to tell them anything. But when her father repeatedly begged and threatened her saying she had to tell them, she spoke: "You could well weep with me. What can cause us more trouble about our lord but that we shall lose him and with him give up our possessions and good standing? We shall never again get a lord so good that he would treat us the way he does." They said, "Daughter, you are right, but sorrowing and lamenting are not going to help us one bit. Dear child, don't talk about it. We are just as sorry as you are. Unfortunately, we are not able to help him in the least. God is the one who has taken him from us. If anyone else had done it, we would have to curse him."

Thus did they silence her. That night as well as the whole next day she remained dejected. Whatever anyone else did, these thoughts never left her heart. Then finally everybody went to bed the following night. When she had lain down on her usual place for sleeping, she again bathed everything with the tears from her eyes, for she bore hidden in her heart the greatest amount of goodness that I ever heard of in a child. What child had ever acted as she did? One thing she was completely resolved to do: if she was still alive the next day, she would in fact give her life for her lord.

This thought made her happy and light-hearted. She had not a care in the world except for one irritating fear: when she told her lord her intention, he might back down; and if she made her plans known to all three of them, she would not find any constancy in them and they would not let her go through with it. So greatly was she disturbed about this that her mother and father were awakened by it as in the previous night. They sat up facing her and said, "Look, what is the matter with you? It is very foolish for you to take this sad situation so completely to heart since no one can do anything about it anyway. Why don't you let us sleep?" Thus did they begin to take her to task: what good did her crying do since no one could prevent or make good the misfortune? And so for a second time they thought they had silenced the dear girl. But they little realized what she had resolved to do. The girl replied to them, "As my lord told us, he is quite able to be healed. And unless you want to keep me from it, I am suitable medicine for him. I am a virgin and have the right disposition. Before I see him go to ruin, I would rather die for him." When they heard this, both mother and father became sad and troubled. The father asked his daughter to put such thoughts out of her mind and to promise her lord only what she could really carry out, for her present plan was out of the question for her. "Daughter, you are just a child and your devotion in such matters is too great. You are not able to go through with it the way you have just proclaimed. You have no idea what death is like. When it comes to such a pass that there is no way out and that you must die, then you would much prefer to go on living if you could bring it about. For you have never entered into a more deplorable pit. So, shut your mouth. If you ever in the future talk about such things again, you'll get what's good for you!" And so he thought that by pleas and intimidation he had silenced her. But he was not able to do it.

His daughter answered him, "Dear father, however young and inexperienced I may be, I still have sense enough to understand from what I've heard the harsh fact that death of the body is violent and severe. But whoever lives a long life filled with trials and hardships doesn't have it very easy either. For after a person has struggled and made it to a ripe old age through much hard work, then he still has to suffer death anyway. If he then suffers the loss of his soul, it would be better for him never to have been born. I have the opportunity, and because of it I shall always praise God, of being able to give my young body in return for eternal life. Now, you should not try to make it hard for me. I want to do the best thing for you as well as for me. I alone am able to preserve us from suffering and harm, as I shall now explain to you. We have honor and possessions. These come from the favorable disposition of my lord. For he has never spoken a command to cause us suffering, and he never took away any of our possessions. As long as he remains alive, things will go well for us. If we let him die, we shall also go to ruin. I want to keep him alive for our sakes through a well thought-out plan so that things will go well for all of us. Now let me do it, for it has to be."

When the mother saw how serious her daughter was, she began

to cry and said, "Remember, dear child, how great the hardships were that I suffered for your sake, and let me receive a better reward than the words I hear you speaking. You are going to break my heart. Make your words a little more pleasant for me to hear. You are going to forfeit salvation by God by what you are doing to us. Don't you remember his commandment? He certainly commanded and asked that one show father and mother love and honor, and as a reward he promised that the soul would be saved and one would enjoy a long life on earth. You say you want to offer your life for the joy of both of us. But you will actually be filling our lives completely with suffering. Your father and I enjoy living because of you. What good to us are life, property, earthly well-being if we have to do without you? You should not cause us to worry. My dear daughter, you ought to be a joy for the both of us, our pleasure unmixed with suffering, a bright delight for us to look upon, the cheer of our life, a flower among your kin, a staff for our old age. And if through your own fault we have to stand at your graveside, you will be forever cut off from God's favor. That is what you will earn in regard to us! Daughter, if you wish to be good to us, then for the sake of our Lord's favor, change your attitude and forget these ideas I have heard from you."

"Mother," she replied, "I give you and father full credit for how well you have provided for me, as a mother and father should provide for their child. This attention I experience from your hands day after day. From your good favor I have a soul and a beautiful body. Everyone who sees me says in praise that I'm the most beautiful child he has seen in his whole life. To whom should I attribute this favor besides God, if not to the two of you. For this reason I shall always stand ready to obey your command. How great is my obligation in this!

"Mother, wonderful woman, since I have you to thank for both body and soul, let it be with your approval that I deliver both of them from the devil that I may give myself to God. Certainly the life of this world is nothing but loss to the soul. Besides, until now worldly desires' have not touched me. I want to thank God now that he has granted me the insight, young though I am, to look with contempt upon this fragile life. I wish to deliver myself into God's dominion as pure as I am now. If I were to continue living, I'm afraid that the sweetness of the world would drag me down under foot as it has done to many whom its sweetness has also deceived. Then I must even be kept from God. To Him we should bewail the fact that I must live even till tomorrow. I don't find the world a nice place at all. Its comfort is great hardship, its pleasure great suffering, its sweet reward bitter want, its long life a sudden death. Nothing is more certain than that today's joy will be followed by tomorrow's suffering. And finally at the end is always death. That is an anguish to make you weep. Neither noble birth, nor riches, nor beauty, nor strength, nor exhilaration can protect one. Virtue and honor help one in the face of death no more than lowliness and vice. Our life and our youthful vitality have no more substance than clouds or dust. Our stability trembles like a leaf. Whether man or woman, whoever likes to fill himself with smoke is a very misguided fool who doesn't know how to think things out rightly and who simply follows the world. For over the foul dung is spread for us a silk cloth. He whom this splendor leads astray is born for hell and has lost nothing less than both body and soul. Now call to mind, dear woman, the love you as a mother owe to me and temper the sorrow which you have because of me. Then father will think things over in similar fashion. I well know he doesn't begrudge me salvation. He is a man honest enough to recognize well that you could not long enjoy having me even if I remain alive. If I were to remain here with you unmarried for two or three years, then my lord is probably dead, and we shall very likely suffer such distress from poverty that you will not be able to give any suitor a sufficient dowry on my behalf, and I would have to lead such an impoverished existence that you would rather see me dead. But let us forget about this problem for a minute. Even if nothing were causing us distress and my dear lord were to be preserved for us and went on living until I were wed to a man who was well-off and respected—this is what you want to happen—you would then think that everything had turned out for the best for me. My heart has told me otherwise. If it turns out that I love him, that would bring distress. If I find him repulsive, that is as bad as being dead. In either case my lot is one of suffering, a life filled with hardship and far from comfort with all sorts of things that cause women trouble and lead them astray from joy.

"Now put me in possession of that full abundance that never dwindles. A Free Yeoman seeks my hand to whom I give myself gladly. You should certainly give me to Him. Then my life is really well taken care of. His plow works very well for him, his farm is filled with all provisions. There neither horse nor cattle die. There one is not vexed by crying children. There it is neither too warm nor too cold. There no one grows old as the years pass: older people become younger. There one finds neither frost nor hunger. There suffering of any kind is absent. There one finds complete happiness without any hardship. To Him I wish to go and flee such fields that rain and hail destroy and floods wash away, fields with which one struggles and always has. What one is so tediously able to gain through toil in the course of a year is suddenly destroyed in half a day. These are the farm lands I wish to leave. Let them receive my curse. You love me. That is as it should be. Now I would gladly see that your love does not turn out to be the opposite. If you can come to see that I have the right understanding of the situation, and if you wish me to have possessions and honors, then let me go to our Lord Jesus Christ whose grace is so constant that it never fades, and who has as great a love for me, poor as I am, as for a queen. God willing, I shall never through my own fault lose your favor. It is certainly His commandment that I be obedient to you, for I have my life from you. This I do without regret. But at the same time I must not be disloyal to myself. I have always heard people say that whoever makes someone else happy in such a way that he himself becomes unhappy and whoever treats someone else like a king and shows only contempt for himself—that this is too much devotion. I certainly want to be obedient to you by showing you devotion, but above all else I must be true to myself! If you want to keep me from my salvation, then I would rather let you weep a bit over me than not to be clear about what I owe to myself. I constantly long to go where I shall find complete happiness. Besides, you have other children. Let them be your joy and thus console yourselves over losing me. No one can keep me from saving my lord and myself! Mother, I heard you complain just now saying it would cause your heart great pain if you should have to stand at my grave. You will most certainly be spared this. You will not stand at my grave because no one will let you see where I shall die. This will take place in Salerno. There death shall free us four from every kind of misery. Through death we shall all be saved, I much more so than you."

When they saw the child so eager for death speaking so wisely and acting in contradiction to all human norms, they began to consider that no tongue in a child's mouth could manifest such wisdom and such insight. They were convinced the Holy Spirit must be the cause of these ideas, who also was active in St. Nicholas as he lay in the cradle and taught him wisdom so he turned his childlike goodness toward God. They considered in their hearts that they did not want to and should not at all prevent her from doing what she had taken upon herself to do. The idea must have come to her from God.

The peasant and his wife turned cold with grief. They sat there in bed and for love of their child so forgot their tongue and were so out of their senses that neither of them could then speak a single word. The mother was torn by a fit of weeping in her suffering. Thus they both sat sad and dejected until they realized what little good their grieving was doing them. Since nothing was able to change her mind, the only sensible thing for them to do was to grant her wish willingly because they could never lose her in a better way. If they showed opposition to her plan, it could get them into a lot of trouble with their lord and other than that they would accomplish nothing by it. With a show of agreement they then said they were happy with her plan.

This made the innocent girl happy. When it had barely become day she went to where her lord was sleeping. His bride called to him saying, "Lord, are you asleep?" "No, I'm not, my bride, but tell me, why are you up so early today?" "Lord, my grief over your illness forces me." He said, "My bride, you show very well in the way you treat me that you are sorry. May God repay you accordingly. But there is nothing that can be done about it." "Truly, my dear lord, there is help for you. Since you can be helped, I shall not let you wait another day. Lord, you told us that if you had a virgin who would willingly suffer death on your account, you would thereby be healed. I myself want to be that girl, so help me God. Your life is more useful than mine."

The lord thanked her very much for her intentions and in sorrow his eyes filled unnoticed with tears. He said, "My bride, death is by no means a pleasant affair as you perhaps picture it to yourself. You have made it very clear to me that you would help me if you could. That is enough for me from you. I know your affectionate heart. Your intentions are pure and good. I desire nothing more from you. You are not able to carry out for me what you have just said. May God reward you for the devotion you have shown toward me. Since I have already tried several remedies, I would be the laughing stock of the people here if this didn't do any good and my disease continued as before. My bride, you act like children do when they are impulsive. They act immediately on whatever comes to mind, whether it be good or bad, and regret it afterwards. My bride, you are acting that way, too. You are convinced of what you are saying now. If, however, someone were to take you up on it so that your intention would be carried out, you would very probably regret it." He asked her to think it over a little more. "Your mother and father," he said, "cannot easily do without you. I should not desire something that would cause suffering to people who have always been good to me. Whatever the both of them advise, dear bride, that you should do." In saying this he smiled broadly for he had no idea what would then take place. Thus did the noble man speak to her.

The father and mother said, "Dear lord, you have been very good to us and shown us great respect. The only fitting response for us is to repay you in kind. Our daughter desires to suffer death for your sake. We are quite happy to give her our blessing, so completely has she convinced us. It was not a quick decision on her part. For three days now she has been constantly urging us to give our blessing to her plan. This she has now achieved. May God let you be healed through her. We are willing to give her up for your sake."

His bride was offering to die in order to deliver him from his illness, and her determination was evident. This caused much joylessness and displays of sorrow. Quite different were the worries they had, the three of them on the one hand and the girl on the other. The father and mother began to weep bitterly, and they had every right to weep over the death of their very dear child. The lord also began to think about the devotion of the child, and such sadness took hold of him that he wept much and could not at all make up his mind whether it was better to go through with it or let things be. Because of fear the girl also cried. She was afraid he would become faint-hearted and not go through with it. Thus they were all dejected and sought no cheer. Finally their lord, poor

Heinrich, pulled himself together and thanked all three of them for their loyalty and generous care. The girl was exuberant that he was willing to go along with her plan. He prepared himself as quickly as possible for the trip to Salerno. What was suitable for the girl was quickly ready. Beautiful horses and expensive clothes which she had never worn before: ermine, velvet, and the best sable one could find. These were the girl's clothes.

Now who could fully express the deep sorrow and lamenting, the bitter suffering of her mother and the misery of her father? The departure of their dear child would have been a torment for them as they sent her away healthy to her death never to be seen by them again, except that the pure goodness of God which gave the child's heart the determination to die willingly relieved their distress. It had come about without any help from them. Hence they were spared all self-incrimination and depression. For otherwise it would have been a miracle that their hearts did not break. Their sorrow turned to joy so that afterwards they suffered no distress about the child's death.

And so the girl rode off toward Salerno happily and willingly with her lord. What could now trouble her except that the journey was so long and her life was thus prolonged? And when he had finally brought her there as he had planned, he found his doctor and with great elation told him he had found the kind of girl he had told him to get. Then he let him have a look at her. This seemed unbelievable to the doctor. He said, "Child, did you reach this decision on your own or were you influenced in your plan by entreaties and threats from your lord?" The girl answered that these ideas came from her heart.

This surprised him greatly and he took her aside and begged her in all seriousness to tell him whether her lord had persuaded her by means of threats. He said, "Child, you must seriously consider the matter further and I'll tell you exactly why. If you were to die and you didn't do it willingly, then your young life would be at an end, but unfortunately it would not help us the least little bit. Now keep nothing concerning your decision from me. I'll tell you what is going to happen to you. I undress you. Then you stand there completely unclothed, and the shame that you certainly will feel as you stand there naked before me will be great indeed. Then I bind your arms and legs. If you have any regard for your physical well-being, then consider the suffering yet to come. I cut into you all the way to your heart and tear it still beating from you. Now, young lady, tell me how you feel about all this. Never has a child so suffered as you are going to suffer under my hands. That I should carry it out and witness it fills me with great trepidation. Consider how your body will be treated. And if you regret it the least little bit, then I have performed my work and you have lost your life in vain." Again he entreated her in all seriousness that unless she knew she had great determination, she should forget the whole idea.

The girl said cheerfully, for she well understood that on this day death would help her escape from worldly cares, "May God reward you, dear sir, that you have told me the complete truth. As a matter of fact, I am a little hesitant. A certain doubt has arisen in me. I want to tell you exactly what kind of doubt it is that has taken hold of me. I am afraid that our efforts will not be brought to completion because of your cowardice. You talk like a woman. You have about as much courage as a rabbit. Your qualms about my dying are excessive. It's certainly true that you are not taking care of things very well with your great skill. I am a woman and have the nerve. If you are not afraid to cut me open, I certainly have the courage to suffer it. The gruesome details of the operation which you have just explained to me—I was aware of all that apart from you. I certainly would not have come here if I didn't know that I am so firm of purpose I can easily endure it. I have lost all paleness, if you please, and the firmness of my resolve has so increased that I'm standing here about as fearful as if I were about to go dancing. For no bodily suffering that is over with in one day is so great that I should think that this one day was too high a price to pay for eternal life which never passes away. Nothing should make you uneasy concerning me since my mind is made up. If you are confident you can give my lord his health again and give me eternal life, then for heaven's sake, do it soon. Show what kind of doctor you are. He in whose name it shall be done is urging me on, and I well know for whose sake I am doing it. He gives due recognition to service and lets nothing go unrewarded. I know well that He Himself says that whoever performs great service, such a person's reward will accordingly be the greatest. Hence I shall consider this way of dying a sweet affliction because of such certain reward. It would certainly be a foolish attitude if I were to turn my back on the heavenly crown. Then I would certainly be silly, for I am of humble origin."

Now he had heard that she was completely unshakeable and he led her out again to the sick man, her lord, and said to him, "Nothing can stop us. Your girl is completely suitable. Be happy, I shall soon make you healthy." Again he led her to his private room where her lord saw nothing and closed and bolted the door to him. He did not want to let him see how her end would come about. In the room that was well supplied with suitable medicines he ordered the girl to undress immediately. This made her happy and joyful. She tore the garments at the stays. Almost at once she stood there undressed and was naked and bare, but was not the least bit ashamed.

When the doctor looked at her, he realized in his heart that a creature more beautiful than she was rare in the whole world. He felt so completely sorry for her that his heart and mind almost made him hesitate. The generous girl saw a high table standing there. He commanded her to climb upon it. He tied her to it tightly and took in his hands a sharp knife that was lying there that he used for such operations. It was long and broad, but it did not at all cut as well as he would have wished. Since she was not to survive, her suffering saddened him and he wanted to make her death as pleasant as he could. Next to him a very good whetstone was lying. He took the knife and began stroking it across the stone very carefully, thereby sharpening the knife. Poor Heinrich, who was standing there in front of the door and who disturbed her joy, heard this and it saddened him greatly that he should never see her alive again. And so he began to look around and he searched until he found a hole going through the wall. Through the crack he caught a glimpse of her bound and naked. Her body was very lovely. Then he looked at her and at himself, and a whole new attitude took hold of him. What he had thought before no longer seemed good to him. And in an instant his former attitude was transformed to one of new goodness.

As he saw her in all her beauty, he said to himself, "You are really harboring a foolish thought in that you desire to live one day apart from His approval against whom no one can accomplish anything. Since you certainly have to die, you really don't know what you are doing in not bearing with great willingness this wretched existence God has given you. Besides, you do not really know whether the child's death will cure you. Whatever God has assigned for you, that you must always let happen. I will not witness the death of the child."

He made up his mind immediately and began pounding on the wall and asked to be let in. The doctor said, "I don't have the time to open up for you." "No, doctor, I must talk to you." "Sir, I can't. Wait until this is finished." "No, doctor, we must talk before that." "Well, tell me what you want through the wall." "It's really not that sort of thing." Immediately he let him in. Then poor Heinrich went to where he saw the girl bound. He said to the doctor, "This child is so lovely. I just cannot see her die. May God's will in my regard be done. We must let her up again. I shall give you the silver in accordance with our agreement, but you must let the girl live." This the doctor of Salerno was happy to hear and he obeyed, immediately untying the girl.

When the girl realized she was not going to die, she took it with a heavy heart. She acted not at all as she usually did nor in accordance with her upbringing. She had her fill of sorrow, beat her breast, tearing and pulling at herself. No one could have looked at her without crying, so dolefully did she behave. With great bitterness she shrieked, "Woe is me, poor me! What is going to happen to me now? Have I then lost the splendid heavenly crown? It was to be given to me as my reward for this ordeal. Now I am really dead. Alas, powerful Christ, what honor has been taken from us, my lord and me! We are both bereft of the honors which were predestined for us. If this had been completed, his body would have been restored to health and I would have been eternally blessed.

Thus did she again and again ask to die. But no matter how desperately she longed for it, her pleadings were in vain. Since no one did as she wanted, she began to scold, saying, "I have to suffer because of my lord's timidity. People didn't tell me the truth. That I've found out for myself. I always heard people say you were upright and good and had the steadfastness of a man. So help me God, they lied! The world has always been deceived in you. You always were and still are a great big coward. This is obvious to me through the fact that, even though I am brave enough to suffer, you don't have the courage to permit it. Lord, what caused you to become afraid when I was being bound? After all, there was a thick wall between you and me. My lord, don't you have enough backbone to be able to stand another person's death? I can promise you explicitly nobody is going to do anything to you. And the whole affair is to your advantage.

However much she pleaded and begged and even scolded, it did not help her a bit. She still had to go on living. However much she scolded, poor Heinrich accepted it calmly and with good grace, as an able knight should who never was lacking in refinement and good breeding. After the luckless visitor had dressed the girl again and had payed the doctor as he had agreed to do, he rode straight home again to his own country although he well knew that at home he would find nothing but ridicule and sarcasm from all sides. All this he put in God's hands.

In the meantime, the dear girl had scolded and cried herself almost to death. Then He, *Cordis Speculator,* for whom the gate of the heart is never locked, saw clearly her devotion and her distress. Since He in His sweet providence had thought it best to try them both just as completely as He had tried the wealthy Job, Holy Christ made manifest how dear devotion and compassion are to Him. He freed them both from all their miseries and at that very moment cleansed Heinrich and made him completely healthy. Good Lord Heinrich improved to the extent that while still on the journey he regained full health under the treatment of God our Lord and was just as he had been at the age of twenty. When they had thus been made happy, he had it announced at home in his own country to those who he knew would in their good will and sympathy rejoice in their hearts at his good fortune. Justly they would have to be joyful because of the favors God had shown him.

Those closest to him who knew he was coming rode out or went on foot three days toward him to welcome him. They would believe no one's word, only their own eyes. They saw the mysterious working of God manifested in the handsomeness of his body. Concerning the peasant and his wife, one can certainly presume, unless one wants to do them an injustice, that they did not remain at home. The joy they experienced can never be expressed in writing, for God provided them with a tasty feast for their eyes, namely, their daughter and their lord. Never did anyone experience joy equal to theirs when they saw both of them were healthy. They did not know how to act. Their greetings were a strange assortment of unusual ways of behaving. The happiness in their hearts was so great that a rain of tears from their eyes flooded their merriment. The report is certainly true that they kissed their daughter's lips well over three times.

The Swabians received him with a splendid gift, namely, a greeting filled with good will. God knows that an honest man, who has seen them at home, has to admit that no greater good will was ever shown than when they, his countrymen, welcomed him on his journey home. What happened afterwards? What more needs be said? He was better off than before in material wealth and honor. All this he referred to God with great constancy and acted according to His commandment much more than he had previously. For this reason his honor rests on a solid foundation.

The peasant and his wife had well-earned possessions and honor for the way they had taken care of him. Nor was he so dishonest as to prevent them from having them. He gave them as their own on the spot the extensive farm, both the land and the people, where he had stayed while he was sick. His bride he treated as a courtly lady or even better, giving her all sorts of things and seeing to her pleasure. Justice demanded this of him.

At this time his counsellors began to advise him to marry and praised this institution. But their suggestions diverged. Then he told them what he planned to do. If it seemed good to them, he would send for those nearest him and bring the matter to a conclusion according to what they might advise him. He had invitations and summonses sent to whoever might be of help. When he had gotten them all there, both relatives and vassals, he explained his intentions to them. With one voice they said it was proper and opportune for him to marry. A lively dispute arose among them as they were giving their advice. One counselled in one direction, another in the opposite direction, as always happens when people are called upon to render advice. They could not agree at all.

Then Lord Heinrich spoke, "You all well know that a short time ago I was greatly repugnant and disgusting to people. Now no one shuns me. God's commandment has given me a sound body. Now tell me, in God's name, how can I repay the person whom I have to thank for the favor which God has bestowed on me; namely, that I have regained my health?" They said, "Promise that you and what you own shall ever be at this person's service." His bride was standing near by. He looked at her lovingly, and embracing her he said, "You have certainly all been told that I have this wonderful girl standing here by me to thank for having my health again. She is just as freeborn as I am. My every thought tells me to take her as my wife. May God grant that this seem fitting to you. Then I shall have her as my wife. Truly, if this cannot be, I will die without marrying, for I owe her my life and good standing. By God's grace I bid you all that this may find your favor."

All spoke at once that it would certainly be fitting. Priests were readily found who gave him to her in marriage. After a long and happy life they both gained possession of the eternal kingdom. May the same thing fall to the lot of us all at the end! May God help us to attain the reward which they received. Amen.

Translated by Frank Tobin

Duke Ernst

Now all of you listen carefully, and I'll tell you wondrous things about a noble knight. You should pay close attention, for it does one good to listen to them: many men become high-spirited wherever there is talk of brave deeds. But those who stay at home on their land and, lacking the courage to seek honor, never take part in heroic battles like the ones they hear about are greatly vexed. They have never endured danger, avoid it because they are not suited to it, and belittle accounts of it when they can. These people strongly dispute the tales, suppress them as only lies, and are without noble qualities. However, no heed is given to their protests if worthy knights are present whose boldness has often taken them on perilous journeys in foreign lands and who have known pleasure and hardship among strange peoples. They don't object to what is said, for they have experienced such things themselves.

I am speaking thus so you will be the more attentive to the story I have to tell, since I shall not conceal the perils and great troubles which Duke Ernst suffered when he was expelled from Bavaria. It is written in books that he ruled the lands of the Bavarians and protected both rich and poor: everything he did brought him high praise. The youth bravely defended the inheritance left him by his father until a monarch with all the power of the empire drove him out. This banishment caused a large number of knights to turn away from him through fear, but he departed honorably with many good warriors who chose to risk life and possessions in his company until death. Thereafter he often encountered dangers which he boldly overcame. Duke Ernst was a dauntless hero.

I shall also let you know how it happened that this noble man came to grief through the emperor. They say his father died when he was a small child and, in addition to his inheritance, left him many worthy liege knights, who brought him up. This was as it should be, because they kept him away from everything evil. His highborn young mother, Adelheid, who was renowned for her manifold virtues, had the child taught both Latin and Italian and also sent him for further training to Greece, where he met scholars of several branches of knowledge. He worked hard to master all sorts of skills and therefore became greatly respected. The boy thus spent his childhood learning foreign lands, and since his conduct was most praiseworthy, he became widely known in many kingdoms. People often spoke well of him in every way, for he was modest, loyal, and generous. This is why warriors gathered from afar to aid him in his time of need.

The boy directed all his efforts toward things worthwhile, was considered noble and upright, and could not help succeeding. He feared only reproach and scorn and, to gain fame and God's favor, shared whatever he happened to have. He was friendly toward his men and granted them many honors, so they strongly supported him later when he was in great distress. They were subject to him then wherever he led them and stood by him bravely: neither freemen nor villeins forsook him until their death. When the youth reached the age at which he wanted to bear arms, he ordered that everything needful be made ready for him and at once was given a battle steed, a riding horse, and armor. He then formally received the sword, and with him Count Wetzel—a fine young man who was never to lose courage—and other vassals who had been raised in knightly manner from childhood. Because of this honor, Wetzel was always loyal to him, never deserted him regardless of danger, and supported him valiantly to the end of his life. The two came to know many strange lands, and no perils separated them until at last they were parted by death.

After he and Count Wetzel were knighted, the duke was very powerful, and no one thought his court dull. Those who knew him could not find his equal in all the German lands. He traveled through the country with a large company of proud knights and squires, whom he treated generously, giving them money and clothing. His bounty endeared him to everyone, for he spared neither silver nor gold where his reputation was concerned. His men were therefore faithful to the lord in time of trouble. The duchess Adelheid was happy she had raised a child who brought her praise from far and near and did him honor with her ladylike manners. She was so renowned for good breeding, wisdom, and wealth that many powerful princes wanted her as a wife, but she did not wish to remarry. To their regret, she intended to remain single the rest of her life.

At the time the nobles learned this, the Holy Roman Empire was governed by a mighty emperor, Otto by name, to whom the countries of many German and Italian princes were subject and also the realms of the Wends and Frisians, which he had conquered. A great number of lands had to do him homage, and he was highly esteemed among monarchs. The emperor protected widows and orphans from all danger, strictly enforced his decrees, and made Saxony more secure within and without than it had ever been before or will be again. As is well known, the lord founded a mighty bishopric, called Magdeburg, on the Elbe for heavenly honor. He overcame the people without force of arms: the devil suffered great harm when they turned from him to receive God's favor. The bishopric was dedicated to Saint Maritius and his companions as well as to the glory of the Most High who had granted him salvation. The emperor placed people and land under its control and strengthened it by the gift of a large income from taxable property. He therefore will forever enjoy praise and esteem in the eyes of God. He also established a monastery there, because of which many voices still praise God daily.

I tell you that the monarch knew how to conduct himself in keeping with his station. He was a famous warrior by whom the empire was well protected and a noble knight who was properly compassionate toward rich and poor: he gave very willingly to all who sought his aid. In his youth he had married an Englishwoman, who had died and was buried in state in the church. The pious queen, named Ottegebe, was a fruitful vine who was obedient to God and had fully turned her heart to Him. When death came, she gained heaven and eternal joy, so that her soul is now as blessed as was her life. You must know that God showed great favor to the noble lady while she lived and, for her sake, caused many wondrous signs to appear which anyone who wishes may see even today.

The emperor therefore, as I told you, had no wife and would gladly have taken one who pleased him and was suitable as a queen for the empire. So he summoned the princes and let them know his mind. "My dear friends," he said, "if you think it proper and if it can be done with honor, then help me find a wife who is acceptable to you. You may be sure that I shall show my gratitude in any way you like." When the princes heard this, they met in council to decide how to carry out the emperor's wishes and agreed that they knew no one as suitable as the duchess Adelheid. They thought she was rightfully praised above all others, and knew nothing to her discredit: "Everyone who is wise says this, so we would be satisfied if he could win her." If the emperor should choose her, they declared, she would make a worthy queen and please them all with her ladylike manners. She was clever and noble and from childhood on had conducted herself with prudence and charm.

Being of one mind, the princes went before the emperor and told him about the excellent lady: her high birth and many virtues, her wit and youth, and her noble spirit. She well deserved to be queen of the empire, they said, for they did not know her equal among all the women of Germany. When the emperor heard their advice, he was pleased, especially because of the highborn lady's noble temperament. He delayed no longer but, with his own hand, wrote a letter which contained tender words expressed as lovingly as he knew how and sent it to Bavaria with a prince whom he considered a fitting emissary. When the nobleman arrived with the document, the lady received him with a cordial greeting, whereupon, with proper formality, he delivered to her a message from the mighty ruler of the empire who had been so friendly as to send her the letter. "In view of this," he concluded, "let me urge you to accede graciously to the request of the emperor and all his lords. You will be forever highly esteemed if you fulfill the wishes of the empire."

The good lady was very polite. Bowing, she took the letter and said, "I shall do the will of the empire, as one should." Then she had a messenger go at once for the chaplain, who was to read to her what was in it.

Listen as he begins: "Most noble duchess, this letter from the lord and governor of the empire, written by his own hand, urges you in your exemplary youth and exalted virtues to note carefully its contents. Since all my advisors have told me of your excellence, you should turn your heart to my love and let me make you queen of the entire Holy Roman Empire. Then no woman in the world will be able to compare herself with you, you will be praised ever more highly, all the princes will serve you, both rich and poor will be subject to you, and manifold honors will make you proud and happy. Much has been said to me of your goodness: dearest lady, if you could be led by me and the princes and willingly promise to marry me, you would never be disappointed as long as you live. I shall give you as much power as you please in the things which you should govern and which make you happy, and all who now think themselves your equals will serve you: you will be their queen."

Hearing this letter and also what the emissary said, the lady raised her heart to God in thanks for the great honors which He wished to bestow on her. She praised Him in spirit and offered a prayer that the matter might turn out favorably for her. Without delay she sent for her son, asking him to come and hear the message from the emperor, since it was proper that she have his advice about it. The young man hurried to his mother and was told of the proposal she had received. He was very pleased and said, "This makes me proud too. Since all the princes want you for their queen and the emperor thinks so highly of you that he wants you as his wife, my advice—as one who loves you—is that you should not refuse him, but gladly do as he asks. We shall rejoice with you, for you will never regret it." When the son declared the proposal to be suitable and advised her to accept it, the lady sent the courier back with friendly words and a message to the monarch and his vassals that she would do whatever he wished. The nobleman hurried away joyfully and did not rest day or night until he came to the emperor and told all he had heard. He received a great welcome from the princes and their lord and thanks for having served the honor of the empire so well.

The message of the beautiful lady pleased both his retinue and the monarch, who wished the wedding to take place outside the rich city of Mainz in six weeks and ordered that everyone work early and late to make all needful preparations. In high spirits he set out at once with his attendants for Bavaria to get the lady. A large number of handsome knights were present when the duchess

Adelheid was given to the emperor as his bride, and one could see that he and all his men were very happy. Many brave warriors in shining armor rode merrily along as they led the lady away, and the broad fields were sometimes too narrow for the great throngs which joined them before they reached Mainz. When they crossed the Rhine to the plain before the city where the festival should take place, they saw many beautiful tents set up on the green grass. The place where the emperor was to celebrate his marriage offered all sorts of amusement, and one could hear loud cries, singing, and various kinds of stringed music. There were a great number of such diversions as are found at festivals, and no one was sad. No finer celebration in honor of its ruler was ever held before or since throughout the Holy Roman Empire, which caused him to be praised in all the lands. He gave silver, gold, much fine silk, and mules with riding equipment to the knights and had splendid presents brought to the princes; no one can tell you how delighted everyone was. The host of wandering minstrels there also received plenty of gifts, so they too were joyous.

When the festival ended, the princes and the many provosts and bishops came before the emperor one by one to say good-bye as the large assembly departed. The loyal knights separated in a lighthearted and cordial manner and set out on different ways, while their monarch, followed by an ample retinue, rode off with his beautiful wife and brought her to the place where he planned to stay. The noble queen knew how to make him happy: her love so endeared her to him that he was fonder of her than anything else and treated her with great honor. He was always considerate toward her, and she never gave him cause for annoyance, but tried to keep his favor with womanly kindness. Whenever anything went contrary to his will, she skillfully dispelled his anger. They lived in such harmony that, for her sake, he gave up all improper conduct, which denial was good for both of them. The emperor and the queen loved each other and, since their relatives caused them no trouble, enjoyed happiness without ill will for a long time. They lived in splendor and high esteem. How could it be better for them? Under him the empire too was at peace and highly respected, for no one of that time was his equal.

The emperor was in truth very favorably disposed toward Duke Ernst because of his mother and sent him a messenger with regards and best wishes—as a lord does to his vassals—and the request that he come to visit the queen. The knight complied by riding with his attendants in a splendid cavalcade to the court, where the emperor welcomed him cordially. So too did his mother, who was delighted and presented him with all sorts of gifts. The emperor then invested him with many large fiefs, saying, "You are fortunate, my brave young man, for I shall treat you as my son as long as we two live, and enfeoff you with so much of my property that you will be forever devoted to me. You have been sent to me by God and shall be privy to all my affairs. Exercise authority over people and land and help me protect and manage the empire in such a way that everyone in it will be safe from robbery and arson. For this I shall constantly reward you." The emperor then gave so freely both to him and to his companions that they thought it too much and wanted no more. Duke Ernst knew by this generosity that the emperor was truly fond of him. Afterwards also the monarch often showed him a fatherly regard and treated him like an only child: he, his relatives, and his vassals were at all times concerned with adding to the young man's fame. He frequently summoned the duke to court for his advice, and the latter's words and manner on these occasions caused both emperor and empire to listen. His counsel was wiser than that of anyone else there, and he was in every respect an excellent knight.

The emperor therefore liked the duke, who earned his regard by service to him and the realm, and the queen was pleased to hear her son so praised at court, for his name stood above all those who had been the emperor's advisors for a long time. He repaid the monarch's good will and many large gifts of silver and gold honorably won in a great number of fearful battles and was devoted to him and at peace with him throughout the years they were together. This annoyed a certain Heinrich, and he—advised by the devil, who has led a host of others astray since then—destroyed their friendship through treachery. The rogue, a relative and counselor of the emperor, began to spend his days plotting to turn him against the knight, only because the latter enjoyed the special favor of his lord. The deceitful man of whom I speak was the count palatine of the Rhine, and he and his followers were troubled and angry because he had less standing at court than formerly. So he pondered over what to say to discredit and get the emperor to hate Duke Ernst.

The traitor went to the monarch and at once told him a lie, that the duke was only pretending to be subject to him. "Listen to the truth as I heard it myself," he said. "He wants to limit your rule so he will be your equal in might and majesty. This worries me, my lord. Your own gold is to blame, for he has used it to win the devotion of all the princes; you could lose your power. Why don't you choose a more loyal favorite? Indeed, he says openly that he wants to be considered your peer in splendor, birth, and nobility and that he ponders early and late on how to gain your inheritance and authority. This was told me as the truth, your majesty, by one who heard him say it and then secretly asked me to warn you before he takes you by surprise and seizes your power. Were he to force you out, my lord, what would happen to me? I too would be driven off. My dear lord, consider this matter in time so we can save ourselves from him. I am really afraid he would take away my authority also if he should become ruler of the empire."

Greatly startled by the news, the emperor spoke: "I can't believe he would be so hostile to me as you say. He is being accused because of envy and hate. You must know that he will never do it. He is faithful and upright, honest and truthful, and has served both the empire and me with so much love and devotion I can't accept such an evil report. I know him to be too reliable for this. He is free of all deceit and treachery, is fully loyal to me, and—as a noble warrior—has always supported me with a willing hand. If you value my friendship, don't repeat this idle talk, because you will only drive him from my service forever, and I would be very sorry to lose him thus. You are to leave him alone."

"May God have pity on poor me," cried the count, "since Duke Ernst has beguiled you into preferring him to me. I know well that I owe you great loyalty and friendship; I too have been faithful to the empire and you, and I think I am his match. I am also a highborn prince with lands and property and am acting out of duty and with good reason. Were your forces strong enough, I wouldn't be concerned, but I would never get over it if you should lose your life or throne. Had I found him here, I'd have denounced him at once for his traitorous intentions toward you. He couldn't have denied it. The man who told me is very reliable and would have sworn on pain of death to the truth of his account: you can be sure that Duke Ernst must have said this to him. I am deeply grieved at your disbelief, for you must know you are robbing yourself of life and throne. You must proceed wisely in this matter, great emperor, and guard your honor with prudence, because it will be too late when their troops ride against you from all sides. We'll have no defense then. Since the princes will support him, he will have such a mighty army that they can attack you and put the empire to the torch."

The emperor believed his relative when he told the lie, and became both angry and sad. "May God reward you, noble knight," he said, "for being concerned about my peril. He will regret this if I live. He will never raise himself so high that I can't oppose and put him down in such a manner that I shall have peace in my empire with no threat from him."

As the monarch began to rage, the treacherous man spoke: "Don't be so furious; just do as I advise, and you can easily punish him without serious harm to yourself. But tell nothing of what I said to the queen or any of your attendants, for they will warn him. You must see to it now that he pays for his crime before he learns of your intentions. One must destroy him by seizing the castles of his land: we have to fall upon him with an army ere he can make preparations for defense. His vassals will support him with many troops, and he would do great damage to the empire if he were in a position to fight. However, you can prevent that and avoid injury. You must gather an army without anyone finding out where the expedition is to go or whom you are to fight until the attack takes place. Since he can do nothing without his strongholds, I advise you, my lord, to try to win them over with gifts and promises so they will not take part in the conflict. Then the bold warrior will have to flee from your empire without a struggle."

The emperor at once took the count's advice and followed his plan—which he deeply regretted later, for it brought him misfortune. He gathered a large army that he sent against his stepson, whom he renounced with burning and pillage. The latter could do nothing but defend his castle as his devotion to the emperor was being repaid with destruction. The count did a lot of damage to the duke's strongholds and cities, many of which he captured and garrisoned with his own troops while burning the rest: all because of a monstrous lie. After Count Heinrich, with murderous hate, had caused great havoc in the land through fire and plunder, he began a fierce siege of Nuremberg. Here he found large numbers of experienced warriors who defended themselves very well and defeated the host of attackers which, from all sides, stormed the moats and the slopes before the walls: most of the carnage was at the city gate. The count, who carried the emperor's banner during the assault, knew how to urge his men on, and old and young pressed forward with such vigor that they suffered huge losses before they had to retreat to the field in front of the city and strike their tents. They barely escaped, leaving the city untaken.

I don't know for how long afterwards the count and his army continued to burn and pillage the land, destroying castles, villages, and cities without resistance. The duke knew it was done by the authority of the emperor and finally took counsel with the most important of his vassals to decide what action should be taken. One of them, Count Wetzel, spoke: "If you counterattack now and the matter comes before a court, you can't claim you did nothing against the empire, and will be found guilty. You must seek to win the emperor's favor, and if he wants to destroy you in spite of everything, all will know he is the aggressor. I advise against doing battle, for you could not withstand him with a thousand armies, and he may well make amends for the destruction if he agrees to listen to you. Let it go till then, and should he still want to drive you out, defend yourself boldly. We'll cause him a lot of trouble before you quit the empire and abandon your own land: we'll defend ourselves well and not give it up easily. In the meantime you should find out from my lady, the queen, why you are being treated so badly. That is my advice," said the knight.

The duke therefore sent a messenger to his mother to tell her the story and describe the great injury which was being done him unjustly. A worthy knight whom he fully trusted carried the message and, riding off at once, managed through wisdom and cunning to get to the queen and tell her what was happening. She wept with grief at the news and asked the secret emissary to stay overnight. Knowing where to find the emperor alone, she went there and said to him discreetly, "I beg you, exalted emperor, for the sake of almighty God and your own honor to be so kind as to hear me. My son Ernst has sent word to you and me, lamenting the injury he has suffered and the fact that he has lost your favor without cause. He doesn't know how he has lost it or why you angrily want to take his land and ruin him completely without accusation or trial. The good knight asks permission to present himself, and if anyone has heard that he has harmed you in some way, he will make such amends as the law requires. He will gladly give you whatever you want from him if you will show him good will and let him have peace until he can prove he is and always has been loyal to you without deceit or guile."

To this the emperor replied rudely and in fierce rage, "You may not ask for this, because I cannot grant it. Lady, your son has grievously insulted me and will never again come where I might be: he can be sure of that. If I live, I'll let him understand that he has wronged me. Make no mistake: I'll see to it that he gets sick of his country. I promise you that I'll be his bitter enemy to the end of my life." When the lady saw the fierce wrath of the emperor, she was greatly alarmed and dared not entreat him further, but in a stately manner at once returned to her quarters. She quickly sent the messenger back to his land with word to her son that the count had so grossly slandered him to the emperor that truly no one could help and that "he should act as befits a warrior and, whatever the situation might be, defend his country with such vigor that his honor would be preserved. The emperor is very angry and declares openly that all the duke's lands will be seized and that he will pay with his life if he does not leave the empire." This was her message to the lord.

Hearing this, the emissary rode back as fast as he could and in a short time came to Bavaria, where he found his lord at one of his castles. The duke asked if he had learned what he had done to cause the emperor to become his bitter enemy, and the brave man replied, "I'll tell you all about it. Your mother, the queen, sends her love and word that you should vindicate yourself, that you are in serious trouble, although it is not your fault, for the count palatine has secretly turned the emperor against you. She says that, as a stout warrior, you should now consider how he can be made to suffer for it, since the scoundrel wants to drive you from your land and it will be a constant sorrow for her if you do nothing. My lady told me she has heard that no one can help you with the emperor, that he intends to remain your bitter enemy. Now show that you have always been an able knight, she says, and God will aid you all the more because it is the emperor who wrongs you.

Even if he should drive you away, with God's help you must act in such a manner that people will forever say your land meant so much to you only an emperor could expel you. But she also told me this: 'I don't advise him thus just for that reason, because he is first to try something better. The emperor has sent for the princes, with whom, I think, he intends to discuss the duke. Let them know about the situation, and urge them in a friendly manner to intercede with the emperor for him. He must find out at once what is said about him there and then act accordingly.' " These were the words the queen sent to her son.

The duke then dispatched a messenger, who rode hastily to where the princes were, arriving in a single night. When he told them of the distressing state of affairs, as his lord had directed, they were very sorry about the great injury he had suffered for no fault of his, and declared they would gladly intercede for him. They came to the court early the next morning after they had attended mass and, going before the emperor, threw themselves at his feet and began their plea: "If we may entreat you, lord, then graciously let us present a request, and hear it without anger."

"Arise," said the monarch, "your petition will be granted if it is proper. Tell me what it is."

At this one of the princes said, "We beg you, noble emperor, for God's sake indeed, to change your mind and show mercy to the duke, who has been grievously maligned to you and has lost your favor without doing anything wrong or knowing why. The princes here therefore request that you deign to be gracious to him, since he asks for pardon. We shall help him make amends for any offense he has committed until we have dispelled your wrath and sorrow—however you wish, choose, or decree—to the honor of the empire. Lord, let him appear before you, and allow him to make good such wrong as he may have done you in any way you desire, and we shall forever be devoted to your service. Since he wants to gain your favor in good faith, don't let him be destroyed when he is not guilty. He is willing to place his life and possessions at your mercy, so grant him peace until we bring him to you for trial. We will be his security for anything else you may require of him until his innocence is proven."

Flying into a rage, the emperor answered quickly, "Your request is unseemly. I have sworn never to be reconciled with him

or leave him in peace and shall not change my mind. Those who
are devoted to me and to the empire and want me for a friend
should not present such a petition, for he wishes to drive me from
the throne and set himself up as my equal in nobility and power.
If I live, he'll be sorry. Either he banishes me or I him—he can
count on that. And any prince who has encouraged him to oppose
me will always be my enemy: you have my word for it." Their
fear made the princes stand and withdraw their plea. However
dear the duke had been to them and however gladly they had
supported him with arms raised high in entreaty, they now had to
swear to make war on him. They didn't dare refuse; everyone had
to renounce him. Even the duke's relatives had to bear arms against
him, so the emperor commanded. The result was that all Germany
was to suffer greatly, because the duke defended himself bravely
against the monarch for six years. He then could hold out no longer
against the forces of the emperor and his other enemies and had
to leave his land.

When the messenger returned and the duke heard what had
happened at court, he exclaimed, "May God now in his kindness
care for us and avenge me on the treacherous man who caused me
all this trouble and injury even though I've done nothing to hurt
the emperor! I tell you truly, he'll pay for the slander with which
he turned away from me my dear lord, whose fame I, in loyalty,
have never envied. Until this moment his misfortunes have always
grieved me, and now I must act to do him harm—I would be
forever happy if I could avoid it with honor. The truth is, God
knows, that I lost his favor through no folly of mine, and still he
is pitiless in his anger. But I'll share his empire for a while yet, he
can believe me, whether he likes it or not. I have so many brave
warriors, who will not let me be driven out while they live, that I
can withstand him unless much greater distress, sickness, poverty,
or death conquers me as they do hosts of other men. It won't be
so easy for him to take from me the land I inherited from my
forefathers, and it is still not certain that he can."

When the duke heard that the emperor had summoned the
princes to a council at Speyer, he thought, "No matter what happens to me, I must journey across the Rhine to the enemies who
have caused me this trouble." He picked two of his men whose
bravery he knew and rode off with them in haste. While they were

crossing the Rhine, he told his companions what he proposed to do, and they thought the plan a good one. It was very late by the time he rode into the castle courtyard. He took Count Wetzel with him and asked the other man to guard the horses well and be sure to be ready and armed when they had carried out their purpose, so they could ride off at once before they were captured. The duke then hurried quickly and in anger to the emperor's door. Two chamberlains were standing in front of it, but they were keeping a poor watch, and it was not barred. He and his companion could not have wished for better luck.

The emperor was sitting in private council with the count palatine as the bold knights came in, swiftly drew their swords, and ended the discussion in a most unfriendly manner. The emperor sprang up hastily, leaped over a bench, and barely managed to escape into a chapel: to him the brief moment seemed a long time. His vassal paid dearly for the advice he had given, as the duke struck him such a blow that his body fell in a wretched heap and his head flew across the chamber. "Damn the emperor!" cried the duke. "The one I was after got away. I surely would have killed him, and he deserved it for listening to you. You devil, what were you trying to do to me? May God punish you! I never wronged you or anyone else and therefore should have been rewarded by both you and the emperor. Now you are lying miserably in your own blood: that's what you got by it. There was no need for you to treat me as you did, and many died because of your treacherous counsel. May He who rules over all have pity on your soul!" No one had appeared yet when the duke reached the horses, and, mounting, the three bold knights galloped away before they were attacked. The dark night helped them to cross the Rhine safely. During the following years the duke defended himself bravely before withdrawing from his land.

When the duke had thus avenged himself and the emperor learned that his relative was dead and that the duke had galloped away unharmed, he was deeply pained. "For your sake, my noble warrior," he spoke, "I shall always be his enemy. He has filled my heart with bitterness. I am deeply grieved at your death and shall not be happy until I wreak such vengeance for you that people will tell of it forever. If I live till morning, I'll soon be in his land—unless all forsake me: my knights, my relatives, and my other friends. I lament to God this sorrow and disgrace and call on my friends to make the duke regret having ridden here to dishonor the council so. For the rest of my life I shall remember with pain that he dared do this shameful thing to my kinsman. No monarch ever suffered a like affront, and he can be sure that he'll pay for it. I shall always be offended by the insult I received here in the presence of all my vassals."

It was clear that the emperor was unhappy. He had the corpse laid out suitably on a bier and a night watch placed over it (as is still the custom today), and in the morning it was buried with great ceremony. Afterwards he summoned the princes to the castle and complained to all of them about the dreadful wrong done him—that Duke Ernst and Count Wetzel had attacked him so shamefully in his own castle, heaping on him dishonor and injury from which he would never be free as long as he lived: he could never forgive the duke for the death of his kinsman. Moreover, there was this grave threat to himself, for they nearly killed him: he would have lost his life if he had not fled into a chapel. "Knights," said the emperor, "you should be angry that the duke has dishonored you and the empire in this brazen manner."

They decided at once to make war on him and divest him of all his possessions, those he had inherited as well as his fiefs. "You are quite right, lord," asserted many of them. "He deserves whatever happens to him." The emperor placed Duke Ernst and his followers under the imperial ban and, before leaving the council and the Rhine, ordered a campaign of the princes against the duke's land. He summoned all the knights who were able to bear arms and got more than thirty thousand bold warriors from the German lands. The princes also came with many good knights who were ready and eager to fight. The emperor then ordered that the troops be led under his banner into Bavaria against the duke. He reached Regensburg with a great army and besieged it, which assault brought death to a host of brave warriors.

The emperor's banner was carried by strong men—as is still done before an assault—while a host of stalwart knights put on shining mail. They surrounded the city, stormed the walls on all sides in great force, and knights and foot soldiers died in large numbers. The bolder of the duke's men, who displayed green pennants, charged in squadrons out of the city gate and fell upon the emperor and his troops, who were attacking it. There were great losses when the defenders met the enemy: the two groups dashed against each other, and a furious battle began. Here bright helmets were split and battered by the swords which resounded on them; there knights were wounded and covered with blood as blow was given for blow and lives were sold for fame. Here deep gashes were struck through mail, which the proud warriors repaid in kind: they swung swords, thrust lances, and threw spears. Attackers and defenders inflicted heavy casualties: many bold men found a cool rest from strife and were carried off dead.

The battle lasted until night. Both sides fought so fiercely the defenders could not disengage from the emperor's troops before darkness separated them. They then retired to the city, while their enemies pitched camp on the plain around it, where all sorts of barracks and tents were set up. Those who had died fighting bravely and had lain on the battlefield were placed on litters and borne away. The damage to the besieging army was such that the emperor later sorely lamented it, for he had lost more than a thousand men in the attack. This grieved and angered him, but afterwards he lost still more: those who did not recover from the severe injuries received on the battlefield. They died wretchedly.

I've heard that the ones in the city also suffered casualties in dead and wounded from which it was hard to recover, but they simply had to let them go, as one often must do in a war. The emperor began a massive siege, and his opponents, manning the defenses on the towers and battlements, showed clearly that they would resist him. The order to attack was given, and the entire invading army, knights and foot soldiers alike, pressed forward from all sides almost to the wall. The carnage was terrible as sharp missiles came down from the towers and stones were hurled from the crenels of the battlements. One could see many mortally wounded, who were never to fight again, plunge into the moat, and much gleaming mail darkened by red blood. The proud young knights who strove for fame soon found here only death.

When he had besieged the city in vain for more than six months, the emperor was beside himself with rage. He was distressed beyond measure that he had suffered such great losses and would gladly have vented his anger on this renowned city. He quickly had roofed battering rams and siege towers built, and prepared for a long siege. Since he still could not force those in the city to come to terms, he brought the siege weapons, manned by bold warriors, close to the moat and mounted a fierce attack. However, in spite of the size of this army, which had been brought there from distant lands, the valiant garrison swarmed onto the battlements and defended their walls. The struggle went badly for them, and with cries of pain, they fell as thickly as snow flakes. The emperor ordered a general assault, while his catapults demolished all of the parapets within range and the missiles from the siege towers caused great distress. The defenders would have been glad for peace because of their fear of the siege weapons used against them, which had killed so many. The assault went on with fury all day, from early morning until night, and they had no relief until the enemy was driven off by darkness.

The garrison used the night to send a messenger secretly to Duke Ernst to ask him what they should do now to save themselves. With utmost effort they had been able to hold out thus far, they said, but could no longer defend the city and would die if they remained in it: there was no way to keep it. The duke sent back word that he would rather give up the city than lose a single one of them: "No matter what I may do, tell them to make such terms that they can appease the wrath of the emperor, who is so angry at me, and leave the city alive." The messenger quickly returned with this advice, and at daybreak the emperor received notice that the defenders would put themselves at his mercy if he would let them live and go back to their homes in peace. Because of their own great losses, the besiegers were heartily pleased, and when the emperor asked for the opinions of the princes, they all agreed they would like to accept these terms. "Then it shall be so," spoke the monarch.

After peace had been made, as I told you, and the emperor had extended his hand to the garrison, he ordered his banner raised on a high tower and moved into the city. Some were unhappy that he should thus take possession of it, but his army was there, and nothing could be done: they had fought long and fiercely against the emperor and could resist no more. Since they had often and bravely defended themselves, one could readily see that the noble knights were indeed not averse to combat. The emperor and all his men were very glad to get the city without further struggle and let its protectors come out alive and go wherever they wished: many orphans remained behind. Those who came with the emperor also had nothing more to fear, although some had suffered injuries from which they would never recover. Their ruler stationed a garrison of his own men in the city and left at once. Tents were taken down, barracks were burned, and the field was abandoned. One could see, gleaming afar, the bright hauberks of the host of brave warriors who followed the emperor's banner which waved above them. It was a huge and mighty army.

The powerful monarch then moved ruthlessly through the duke's land and did him much harm by looting and burning villages and breaking down his strongholds. Duke Ernst simply had to accept this, because his enemy had such a large force that nothing could withstand it. The emperor did not intend to leave anything—all was to be taken or destroyed—and vented his wrath by ruining the land, but still did not forgive the injury done him. However, he paid for it with many a warrior who never returned home alive, for the duke's men would not just submit to the ravaging of their land, but struggled bravely. They resisted as long as they had the means and the strength with which to fight.

When Duke Ernst saw his castles being seized and his land laid waste, he lamented the loss to those who were to stand by him in his need till death and help him night and day to get revenge, because he had always cared for them. He then rode into the emperor's domain, where his men, going back and forth, also ravaged large areas with fire and destroyed many castles. Whenever he gained the upper hand, he mutilated some of the emperor's vassals and killed others. He caused much grief to those who had sworn to ruin him, and intended that they should lose both life and possessions. In this manner, with raids against the emperor, the duke held out more than five years and remained in his land against the will of his enemies without their being able to drive him out by any stratagem. He knew how to maintain himself with bravery and shrewdness. His men, moreover, were devoted to him and upheld his honor until the lord, because of the demands of the war, used up and gave away all he had. Only then was he forced to leave his land.

Unable to carry on the struggle against the emperor longer, Duke Ernst acted wisely, since he had to give it up in any case. He sent for all of his knights—the finest in the land, whose courage he knew—and chose from the battle-tested warriors fifty of the very best, men who had never failed him in danger. These wanted to go with him into exile. "You are friends who have never forsaken me," he said, "but have bravely stood by me through all my troubles. And, because you have always been loyal, I would like your advice. My land has been laid waste, both plundered and ruined, and I've used up all I have. My dear helpers hope to receive something from my wealth and believe that I have a lot of gold. But the war has made me poor," continued the lord, "and the emperor and his vassals—as I have learned from good sources—are enemies who are conspiring against my honor. Now I can offer no further resistance to the emperor. Everywhere one hears how surprised people are that I have done so well and held out so long against him. This was mainly because of your valiant aid. However, I must withdraw, both because of concern for the outcome and because it is the thing to do. I tell you truly that he who swims against the current will finally go downstream, even though he may do well for a while. This has come home to us and is what I fear. Indeed, you have often heard that whoever makes war against the empire for long, although he may hold his own for a time, in the end will be the one who suffers. This can also happen to me.

"We have defended ourselves so boldly against the emperor and have done such injury to all his vassals that I can no longer stay in this land. You yourselves know, my dear friends, that we have fully destroyed everything around us, used up our own possessions, and would perish if we remained. If there were spoil to be had, as formerly when we inflicted injuries on the enemy, we would not need to starve and could protect ourselves well enough. But as things are, we would be wise to retreat from the emperor, for we have no army. I think we should journey overseas. Should you knights agree, it would be fitting for us to take the cross for the sake of God and enter the service of the holy grail. In this way we can leave with honor before we are driven out. We have opposed God's will, and it is right that we should do penance to gain his favor so he may forgive our sins. Then, if we live to see the day that we return home, everything the emperor took from us will be given back. Now I ask all of you, vassals and kin, not to let me go out of the land alone. Others will give you alms and honor for joining me, and I shall forever repay your kindness with presents and services." Thus spoke the esteemed lord.

The knights answered with one voice that they would risk their lives for him and that his idea was a godsend. They would leave their children and wives at home in God's care and in His service undertake the journey across the sea with the duke. All promised to go with him, saying that death alone could prevent them. Then he and his men waited no longer, but joyfully went to the church to receive the cross. The news quickly spread far and wide throughout the land that the valiant Ernst had taken the cross— which everyone was glad to hear—and that fifty of his knights had been chosen to go with him to serve God across the sea. Later, many others decided to make the journey. Great care was taken that the duke and his men should be well equipped with bright hauberks, iron greaves, helmets of hard steel, and sharp swords, for these fine warriors deserved the best. They left the empire with such splendid armor that truly no one anywhere, then or even now, was ever better outfitted for a crusade. No one who was not vengeful would dare to claim that the knights quit their land because of poverty. That became clear to everybody.

As they prepared for the sea voyage, many good knights who also wanted to serve God were happy they could go along, and large numbers of others throughout the German lands were pleased that the duke should undertake the crusade. To support it, his mother sent him five hundred marks, a great deal of fine cloth, splendid bedding, and clothing of silk and ermine which was neatly stitched with gold. The lord received the gift thankfully and divided it with his companions. He was in every way a noble knight and could not help it that he was driven away without cause. As long as he was in the land, he suffered such hardships that one still tells of them.

When the time drew near to set out for the sea, many troops of foreign knights who knew the duke well came and asked him for the sake of God and his own courtesy to be gracious to them and let them travel with him. They wanted to journey in his service as far as the city of Jerusalem, since he knew how to protect them from whatever danger might threaten. For their part, they would support him in everything he undertook and not fail to serve him

because of any peril, but stand by him with their lives and possessions till death. "This is how we feel," they said, "and we place
all we have at your disposal."

"I have marked your words well," answered the duke, "and
welcome you with God, dear friends. You may be sure that I shall
not forsake you as long as I live. Whatever God has given me,
great and small, will be held in common with you and shared with
you. While I am alive, you will not regret joining me in hope of
finding trustworthy aid. I gladly receive you as brothers and comrades and shall not think myself lord of any of you. You shall be
my equals during the journey and may be sure I shall protect you
at all times the best I can." The knights thanked the duke, who
was very pleased to have gotten such a large number of able men
for his expedition. He had a thousand well-equipped knights in
his band, first-rate warriors who left the land with him at this time
after having accepted him as their leader and sworn to be subject
to him.

After the lord was fitted out for the voyage in a manner suitable
to his station, said good-bye, and started on his way, there was
loud lamenting from both vassals and kin: one will never again
hear of such sorrow as they voiced on having to take leave of him.
All of his subjects were sad, because he had always faithfully cared
for them during his rule. He rode from the empire then in high
spirits, turning over castles, land, ancestral property, and vassals
to his kinfolk, to whom he wanted to leave all this in the event
that it later should not be seized. Thus the splendid lord, accompanied by gallant knights, departed from his homeland.

Duke Ernst was pleased that his band was so large, for it was a
mighty host that followed him joyfully toward the sea. He bade
Count Wetzel, a skillful warrior, take charge of the army, which
he did very ably; and they were so ready for combat as they trav-
elled along that they were left in peace. They came thus into Hungary, and when its king learned of it, the duke was indeed welcome, for the former had heard a great deal of the courage with
which he had defended himself such a long time from the emperor. After they had drawn near, the monarch greeted the lord
and his knights and invited them to his court, where he treated
them with high esteem and received their warm thanks. He prepared night quarters for them and happily gave the duke presents,

then ordered that they be conducted with honor through his land. Duke Ernst took the gifts and left very pleased. The king helped them through the forested mountains of Bulgaria, and they entered the Grecian Empire with light hearts.

As the army approached Constantinople, the duke bade his marshal ride ahead with the squires and look for quarters so those coming after them could have a place to rest. This quickly reached the ear of the empire's ruler, who insisted on having the duke and his companions as guests, for he had heard of the lord and knew he had been driven from his land without cause. He also knew how long the duke had defended himself against the emperor, while laying waste the latter's domain, and how splendid his departure had been. He gave orders that all of his people should take good care of the strangers, which was done with zeal. Whether poor or rich, they were treated very well and better than was commanded. They got whatever services they wished.

The duke was there three weeks or more before the emperor could get a vessel suitable for his guests, one which would carry food, clothing, and armor, as well as men. At last he found the right ship for the voyage and ordered that the army be taken to it and given a six month's supply of good, fresh food in addition to gold: he liked the duke for his courage. When everything was prepared for departure, the lord went before the emperor and politely asked leave to go, since he was ready and fully supplied with provisions for the expedition. "That is because of your kindness," he said, "for which we shall always be in your debt. As long as we live we shall pray that God will preserve your life. Now permit us to depart."

The emperor then ordered that he be given much more gold, which was carried to the ship, and replied, "May God let each of you journey in his service and protect you so that you may serve him in such a manner that we shall be happy with you. I wish this for you and your men." The duke thereupon left the emperor, and he and his companions joyfully boarded the ship. They had greatly pleased the Greeks, large numbers of whom sailed with them (in over fifty ships) because of their friendship and were subject to the duke. They did this in order that he and his army would get safely to the Holy Land.

After everyone said goodbye and came to the ships, the sails were hoisted, and the warriors set out for Syria with plenty of supplies and in high spirits. After five days, however, cries of distress arose among God's troops, for a violent storm came up, scattered the ships until no two were together, and quickly sank twelve of them. Those on board suffered a horrible death. The rest were in great peril on the fearful sea, and the duke's army was blown so far from the Greek host that neither ever saw the other alive again. The lord was deeply troubled at becoming separated from the Greek knights, but the wind kept driving his ship away over the sea. He had been wise enough to put all his men and the bold warriors from Germany who had joined them on the road into one vessel and was now glad that they at least were still with him. He and his men were in constant danger and could always see grim Death in front of them as they were carried off on the wild waves to distant seas where no one had ever been before or has been later. One can truly say that they were in misery: never since has a man endured such hardships as Duke Ernst suffered then.

The good knights were driven about for more than three months without sighting land and despaired of their lives because all of the provisions were gone: they had to endure in fear. But early one morning as it was becoming light, the clouds began to disperse. The danger was over. The dawn gleamed brightly, and the weather became delightful, as it does after storms. The sky became blue, the sea clear and brilliant, and the winds which had dashed them about so fiercely died down.

They saw that help was at hand when they caught sight of a beautiful land racing toward them: it was called Grippia. Filled with joy, they steered toward it and sailed into a harbor, where they cast anchor and found firm bottom. They saw a splendid city surrounded by a high wall of precious marble—yellow, green, blue, black, red, and white—which gleamed more brightly than glass. It could not have been lovelier, for the stones were carefully laid in an orderly design like a chessboard and here and there formed all sorts of pictures of familiar and strange things which one could make out and name. Around the wall was a moat through which ran a river that fully enclosed the city. The battlements were skillfully adorned inside and out with gold and jewels, large and small, all wrought with great craft. The city did not need to fear any army, for it was strongly fortified with barbicans, towers, and parapets, many-colored and artfully carved—as we know from the books in which this appears. Thanks be to him who wrote it down for us so clearly. Strange people lived in this city, whose splendor shone afar.

When the knights drew near the land, they took in the sails, lowered the small-boat, and anchored. Then Duke Ernst spoke to his friends and vassals: "Since we have little food and God has sent us to this fine land and beautiful city, I think we should buy provisions before we perish. We have lived through grave danger and have spent a long time at sea without being able to get anywhere. Now that we have found this wondrous city, I would also expect to find some people in it who are guarding it. We shall learn today whether they be heathens or Christians, and shall deal wisely with them so they will sell us food. If they are not Christians, they won't let us go unharmed. But it matters little to us if we are killed here. Since we set out in God's service, we shall not complain if we die in battle rather than starve to death on the ship."

Having heard these words, they replied, "We went forth to serve God and for no other reason," and said they would be glad to suffer death while doing his work and for him would always cheerfully accept pain as well as pleasure. The warriors eagerly put on their shining hauberks and, as soon as they were fully armed, entered the small-boat. When they came ashore, Duke Ernst tied a red banner to a spear and ordered Count Wetzel to carry it. This knight then bravely led the others, all dressed in armor and bearing weapons and shields, across the plain and took the banner to the city gate, where they halted.

The gate was open, and the knights saw no one on either the outer or inner battlements. They were very surprised, and each said to the other, "I don't know what it means. These are strange people to conceal themselves in such a manner. I believe they have hidden to protect themselves from us. They want to entice us into the city, where they can fight better: there is no other reason not to show themselves. But they had better be careful, for we could still cause them trouble. Before they kill us, we will cut some of them to pieces."

The bold Ernst then said, "Sooner then die out here, we will do what is needful to get wine, bread, and other food. We are wearing strong, bright mail and are well prepared for battle. Crowd together now, you young knights, and push over the bridge with the banner and through the gate, and we'll all fight our way in before they even think of driving us out. Sell your lives in this fortress today for such a price that they will remember us with pain and sorrow forever."

The knights thronged bravely around the banner held by the count, who then led the wanderers up to the wall and the gate. No one was there. They ran through it into the city, and still no warriors came forth to attack them. Unopposed, they went to the middle of the city and waited to see who would come. Here, in a beautiful park, they found a cool, shady courtyard at the center of which, arranged in a circle, were many chairs and tables. The chairs were elegant, and the tables were covered with silk and gold cloth trimmed with costly, finely embroidered borders. No emperor ever had as splendid a place to eat. I can tell you that the tables were well supplied: on each was bread, fish, the meat of tame and wild beasts, and wines from mulberry, honey, herbs, and grapes—the best to be found anywhere. In a land like this, one need not ask where it all came from. The cups and goblets were of gold, the dishes of finely wrought silver, and everything one could want for a feast was there in great plenty.

"Eat now," said the valiant Ernst to his knights, "but be wise and offer hearty thanks to our Lord for the rich gifts which he has sent us today." Then he went on, "Whatever we find that will serve us as food, we may take without sin. Leave all the rest, however, for perhaps God wants to test us. You must not be tempted by their gold or silver or pay any heed to the fine cloth. Just thank our Lord who has often saved our lives and now has given us this food, which we never needed so urgently. Without his aid we would have perished miserably and helplessly of starvation on the wild sea. Everyone should praise him, because he has performed a wondrous miracle for us. Now all go to the tables and eat joyfully, that you may revive yourselves, and when you have finished, follow my advice and quickly load the ship with enough food to last until God leads us to Jerusalem. We cannot stay here longer than till daybreak, so be prepared to leave then. I am sure that this city hasn't been abandoned. Its people are somewhere close by and will soon return, and we must act with that in mind."

After the knights had washed their hands, they sat down at the tables and ate and drank until their hunger was gone, for although they ate a lot, there was no lack of food. When they finished, they got up and walked about the city—the well-traveled and the novices alike—staring in wonder at the huge treasures of gold, precious stones, and beautiful ornaments. While doing so, they entered a house—as God had willed—where they found meat, wine, and bread. No one could tell you how much was stored there, but it would have been more than enough for the army of a king. They were all very pleased and quickly loaded a full supply onto the ship. Afterwards they left the splendid city, deserted with its gate open, and went to the ship to rest from their labor.

When they had lain there a while and were refreshed, Duke Ernst suddenly said to Count Wetzel, "No matter what might happen to me, I'd like to go back to the city for a closer look: it is so beautiful. Tell me at once whether you will go with me."

"To be sure I'll go with you," answered the count, "and you need have no fear that I'll die there. Now, my dear lord, you should ask all of our companions, as close friends, to be ready to help us and—for the sake of God, their honor, and their knightly breeding—to come quickly, prepared for battle, as soon as they learn we are being attacked. They should all rush bravely to our aid when they hear the noise of conflict so that they may rescue us in time. I can't believe there is no one in the city, even though, for some reason or other, they don't want to show themselves. I think they hope to learn our intentions. Now since they don't want to attack us, we must find out what they have in mind. May God protect us! But whether it hurts or helps us and whatever their plans, we'll go there just the same. We must take a better look at the place even at the risk of being captured." The knights then promised to save them from danger or die with them.

Returning to the city, they discovered many lovely works of art made of fine gold and examined, one by one, all sorts of wondrous things made from gold and precious stones. They saw stately palaces—beautiful, grand, and strangely formed—with arches and lofty doors which were more ornate than any others on earth and sparkled like stars. They saw splendid halls, and everything was artfully planned, inside and out. The city lay so close to the sea that even a mighty king with his army would have to leave it in peace, for he would be unable to harm it.

After they had looked at these wonders, they went back to the park where they had eaten and, passing through it, saw nearby a place which had a gold roof and skillfully fashioned emerald walls that gleamed bright green. In it Duke Ernst found a room which was gracefully decorated with jewels set in shining gold. They entered and saw a bed (the mattress of which rested on taut bands) that—so we are told—was beautifully trimmed with gold and decorated with pearls arranged in squares and other precious stones in strange patterns. Lions, dragons, and snakes, all skillfully wrought of gleaming gold, adorned the bedstead, and at the tops of the bedposts four large jewels shone like the sun and as if they were burning. They gleamed like a glowing fire, and Duke Ernst was pleased. On the bed were two quilts of fine and costly cloth, silk sheets, and an ermine counterpane which had an artfully stitched border of great value with many precious stones, and above it hung a canopy of glistening silk and gold fabric with an elegant, wide fringe. The two young knights thought the bed was wonderful.

In front of it they saw a large, heavy chair of white ivory which was covered with fine carvings and skillfully embossed with gold. Four huge amethysts, blood-red and worthy of high praise, rested on the knobs of the back, and a costly silk fabric covered the seat. The chair was thus well suited to the splendid bed. A four-cornered carpet, of blue velvet and adorned with a costly border, lay on the floor, and two golden goblets of the best wine in this land or any other stood close to the bed. They saw here the greatest wealth in the world—this was evident in everything—and all had carefully been made ready for some grand festivity.

When the knights had looked at the splendor of the bedroom and gone out again, they saw by the palace a large and beautiful courtyard with many green cedars. They went closer and found two streams flowing out of the courtyard side by side—one with warm, the other with cold water—and singing a charming song as they rushed along. Nearby stood a lovely bathhouse which was covered over with an arched roof of green marble strongly supported by buttresses. How could it be more beautiful! Inside gleamed two red gold vats into which water flowed through two skillfully wrought silver pipes that were cleverly arranged to supply a strong flow of either warm or cold water, whichever one wished. It drained off, so we've heard, through a bronze pipe on the other side of the vats and was conducted over the entire city, for a good reason. The streets, large and small, were of marble—some of it as green as grass—and the water was made to flow through all of them just as soon as people got up in the mornings, because they wanted the city to look nice. Every bit of dirt and rubbish was quickly swept away, and the city was washed clean. Its streets glistened like snow. I don't believe any other city on earth was ever so splendid.

Seeing these wonders, the noble Ernst spoke to his companion, "I would very much like to take a bath. We don't need to worry. As far as I can tell, there is no living thing here to harm us while we bathe. If someone enters the city, we'll hear him at once and put on our armor. We have endured such hardships on the wild sea and now, praise God, have come to a place where we can get some rest and comfort."

"Since you won't forgo it," answered the count, "I'll have to give in, but you would do without the bath if I had my way. You may be sure of that. However, since you won't take my advice about it, I too shall have a quick bath. Just keep in mind that we are in grave danger and, I am afraid, might be killed without being able to defend ourselves." Then both hurriedly took off their clothes and sat down in the vats. They had to prepare the bath themselves, so they opened up the pipes, and clear water, warm and cold, flowed in over them. They were pleased at this and bathed. As soon as they had finished, they left the bathhouse in order not to be trapped there. Seeing no one, they went through the beautiful palace and into the bedroom, where they at once lay down on the highly ornamented bed and rested after their bath. Many were later to sorrow because of that.

When the knights had rested a while, Count Wetzel spoke to his lord, "It is time we got up and went back to the ship to our companions. They may think we have been gone too long and may rightly be concerned as to what has happened to us here. Indeed, I am afraid they are angry at us. Get dressed quickly, my lord, so that we shall be ready for battle in any event. We have looked at the great wealth here and can truly say that we have never seen at home or abroad splendor such as this. The city is large and spacious, beautiful and strongly fortified, stately and imposing. No other city of like beauty and grandeur was ever built on earth or ever could be. It is the crown of all the cities seen by anyone: I shall always maintain that." The two men waited no longer, but got dressed at once. They were handsome warriors, wore very fine armor, and had often proven themselves in battle. They looked so knightly they would have graced the troops of any emperor, however mighty. Taking up their shields, they quickly left the chamber and went through the gleaming palace. It was indeed beautifully and delightfully adorned: many arches were made of precious stones, and there was no end to the wonders which had been built into it. The sun never shone on such a stately great hall.

While gazing at the rare sight, they suddenly heard a strange cry, mighty and terrible, which came from the plain outside the walls and sounded like the screeching of a huge flock of wild cranes. The din was very loud and frightening, as fierce a clamor as has ever been heard. The knights were surprised and went aside to stand under a dark vault where they felt safer. A window was there which was high above the park, and by leaning into the embrasure, they could look over the whole city, far and near, and watch whatever happened inside and outside the walls without anyone seeing them. They waited here, where no one could approach them without their knowing it. They had chosen a good place to protect themselves.

After the brave men had stood for some time by the window, looking in all directions, they caught sight of a strange throng of men and women in front of the city gate. Both young and old had well-formed hands and feet and were in every respect handsome, stately people, except that their necks and heads were like those of cranes. The watchers saw a large army of them walking and riding toward the city, armed only with shields, bows, and skillfully wrought quivers of deadly arrows. They wore clothing of satin and different kinds of fine silk which was decorated, according to each one's taste, with silk and gold trimming. Save for their long necks, no fault could be found with their bodies, which, with both men and women, were strong and beautiful.

I'll tell you more of what I have heard about these odd people. It was their city: they ruled there boldly, were proud and carefree, and had a vast wealth of silver and gold—as much as they wanted—besides large revenues. The king to whom they were subject was one of themselves. He had taken his army with many galleys to India and killed its monarch just as the latter and his wife were about to set out for one of the Indian cities: the monarch couldn't defend himself from pain and death. The king of Grippia slew him at once and sank his ship with all on board, including the queen—except their daughter, whose life was saved because of her beauty. The mighty ruler of Grippia wanted her as his wife and brought her home with festive joy. The great banquet in the park was prepared in her honor, and when those in the city heard that the galleys were approaching the shore, all of them—men, women, and children—went forth gaily to receive her. Their clothing adorned with all sorts of ornaments, the strange people then noisily escorted the bride to the city gate where everyone dismounted.

As the knights watched the wondrous sight and carefully observed these unusual beings, they were not afraid, but held them in low esteem. "I would like for us to remain here," said the duke, "where we can see all that they do. They can't harm us, and we'll easily get back to the ship whether they wish it or not. Evening is a long time off, so we can stay until we find out what they are going to do now. I have to laugh at their thin necks. I know that they will all come to this park, to the tables which hold the feast. The food was prepared for them this morning, and you can well believe that they didn't expect to suffer some loss when they left it alone."

"Sir, I am your vassal," answered the count, "and you can depend on my loyalty, for I will prove it with my life and all I have. I am sure these people cannot hold out against us, and would not fear them if their army were much larger. I will fight a thousand and more by myself, and should they match me in strength, I will still cause them a lot of grief. I'll cut a path through them with my sword and spare no one. You may be certain of that. We are well equipped for battle, and by getting in too close for their arrows, we'll quickly cause such havoc among them—unless I'm very much mistaken—that they will entirely forget about their bows. Things will go badly for them today, because many will lose their heads. Since their necks are so thin, there will be a great slaughter if they attack us."

They stood there and watched two men walk side by side in

through the gate. They wore fine tunics of a rare silk which were embroidered and trimmed with jewels and, over them, coats of another silk: the clothing made the men look quite handsome. Their leggings were slit in a courtly style and heavily trimmed with gold thread through which the linen gleamed whiter than snow. They had on gold spurs. The two belonged to the highest rank below the king and were therefore allowed to walk in front of him, which they now did with stately and measured steps. Their necks were thin and long: indeed, from head to shoulders they were just like cranes. Each wore a splendid quiver of white ivory, lined with silk and trimmed around the edges with precious stones in costly settings, and carried a well-shaped horn bow, strung with silk, and a golden shield, the boss of which was a huge garnet that—so the knights thought—could not have sparkled more brightly. After the first two, they saw another pair following, who wore silk and the best satin in the world, daintily sewn with shining gold thread and gracefully ornamented down to the legs with many pearls which gleamed in a truly splendid manner. They had bows and quivers of great value and gold-studded shields too elegant to describe, as were the lovely ornaments they wore. The knights thought their appearance and manner very praiseworthy, although they were also like cranes.

Behind these four warriors who were now entering the city walked a handsome man who seemed very happy and wore garments that shone from afar. His costly leggings were trimmed with gems large and small, set in gold, down to the tips of the shoes, to which red gold spurs were fastened. He wore a silk tunic, a gold-studded belt, and a coat of silk and gold fabric with finely sewn ribbons going from neck to wrists and splendid, broad braid which went from the shoulders down to the hem. He also had on a crown with many jewels, which showed that he was the ruler of the land. His neck and head were those of a swan! This, believe me, was the king of Grippia. Two highborn nobles walked close behind him, wearing clothes as elegant as could be found anywhere. They had been chosen by the king to lead between them the most beautiful girl ever born. Her skin was whiter than snow; her hair could reach to the ground; her form—enclosed in pure gold—was as lovely as that of any woman who has been on earth before or since; her beautiful features were those of normal people. The knights saw her walking sadly and weeping without restraint. She was protected from the heat by a canopy supported on four skillfully wrought golden poles carried by four men. As I told you before, she was born in India and taken from there by the king. She was crushed with grief over the death of her father and mother and over her own perilous situation, because of which she too was to die.

After the girl was led into the city, all of the people crowded through the gate until no one, old or young, remained outside. Uttering strange sounds, they sang one of their own melodies as the king brought her straight to the delightful enclosure with the many fine seats: the racket was deafening as the festivities began. One could see the girl's despair when she looked at everyone around her and nobody spoke to her in a language she could understand. She wept openly, and the tears fell without ceasing down to her breast, soiling her clothing. She was filled with sorrow and could not be happy. As much as they were like people, she could not comprehend either their speech or their behavior, but only heard cries like those of cranes. I too have no idea what they meant by these sounds; however, they gestured just as people do today.

The lord high steward stood in front of the table and assigned seats to the nobles by pointing out chairs with a baton. He then sent servants to all, to pour wine for them and get them whatever they wanted: there was plenty of everything one could think of. The king of Grippia walked in state to his table, and at his side the steward seated the girl, who was wretched and out of place at the festival. She and the king washed their hands in heavy gold basins, and highborn chamberlains in splendid attire, the noblest in the land, kneeled and offered them towels. Fine manners were displayed where the monarch was dining with his bride. Mead and wine were poured into many gold goblets, and silver dishes for all kinds of fare were everywhere. Then the wise and courtly steward noticed that the food was already gone, at which everyone was greatly surprised and wondered who had eaten it. The steward at once ordered servants to hurry to the kitchen and bring more. When this was done, they ceased to ask what had happened to the food, thinking their own people had eaten it. It did not occur to them that strangers were nearby in the city. However, although no one had asked them to the banquet, they had come uninvited and had even had a good bath, just as God had provided. But later this action was to bring many to the grave.

Tables were then set up in the large hall for the guests, and they were asked to go to their seats. The people proved there that they had plenty of mead and wine to offer, and also meat, cheese, and fish. Water was brought, and no one was too tired or careless to wash in a gold basin. When all had washed, they went respectfully before the king and bowed to him politely before sitting down. No one has ever heard of another banquet so deserving of praise. Servants came and, dividing the tables among themselves, brought meat, both wild and tame. All ate and drank everything they liked, except the girl, who did not want to eat. But no one should blame her for not being happy. When the king kissed her, as he often did, he pushed his beak into her mouth. In India she had known nothing about such an expression of love, but she had to endure it here in Grippia among these strange people.

One could see that the girl's eyes, once bright, were dim and red with tears, and sad to say, there was nobody to whom she could lament her deep distress. Duke Ernst and the count heard her crying and were moved with pity that the beautiful lady had no friend in all the throng to listen to her wails of bitter grief. "I'll never in my life be happy again," said the duke to his companion, "if we can't think of some way to help this lovely woman get away from here. I have seen her misery, and my heart aches that she must suffer so. Now consider how we can come to her aid. It would be strange indeed if the lady should spend her whole life in this foreign land where she doesn't even know the language. If you think it a good idea, I'd like to steal down to the hall, rush among them with drawn swords, and leave it up to God. Before either they or those in the courtyard have gotten ready to fight, we'll have caused such damage among them that they will never recover. They won't be prepared, and we'll cut them down like cattle and drown them in their own blood. They have only their arrows, which won't pierce our mail. So we'll push through until we get out to where she is sitting with the king and free her from distress. We'll kill him, rescue the lady, and get her away before they have a chance to resist. Even if they had a larger army, we could get through the city gate whether they liked it or not. Then we'll swing our swords and protect ourselves until we come to our companions. Take my advice, brave knight, and we'll dash in among them as I said. I feel sorry for this beautiful lady."

"Prince," replied the count, "I'll follow your orders no matter what happens to me, but you should do as I suggest and not act hastily. You yourself have seen that there is a large army here, and we'll need to be clever to get out alive. If we begin the fight while they are all around us, they will kill the lady right before our eyes. Rather than endure the shame of letting us escape with her, they will try somehow to take her life. We can help her far better after they have left the tables. The warriors will leave the park when the king goes into the hall to his guests. Later we can easily slip into the bedroom and kill the king there: he won't be able to save himself. If those with him resist, we'll cut many of them down, seize the lady, and take her away. We'll be outside the gate before they know it, and our comrades will rush to aid us there. We'll cover the lady with our shields and, if I'm not mistaken, bring her safely across the plain to the ship." The duke was happy with the plan.

They didn't have to wait long until the king had finished eating. Then everyone seated before him stood, and he went into the hall, where many noblemen came up to greet him. There were music and singing, courtly dancing and folk dancing, and cries like those of cranes and hawks: thus they did honor to the bride. The two knights had never heard such a clamor as arose throughout the city. The Grippian people performed all sorts of wondrous games and feats in front of the bride, but these didn't raise her spirits. Neither did the presence of the king beside her. She was so sad, that the monarch became displeased and bade the people leave, since he wanted to go to his bedroom. Those assigned to the task brought the lady after him into the beautiful chamber, accompanied by a great outburst of discordant song from the courtyard in front of the palace. Everyone in the city then parted here, each going to his own lodging, as is done at court festivals even today. When they went to their safe houses to rest, they did not foresee the trouble which was to befall them and therefore later suffered great distress.

After the people had been sent away, there remained only twelve of the king's most highborn vassals, men whom he kept with him as advisors, and they were in the chamber when the bride was to be undressed. Then one of them happened to go out of the room and walk toward the nook where the two armed knights were standing. Catching sight of them, he quickly returned to the chamber and declared loudly that he had seen two men. The Grippians thought they had been followed from India with hostile intentions and became very frightened. They seized the lady at once and avenged themselves by stabbing her in many places with their beaks. She screamed loudly, which startled, angered, and grieved the knights. "We waited too long," spoke the duke. "She is crying out in great pain: they have killed the lady in that room. But we'll get vengeance at once." And they rushed into the chamber with their bare swords gleaming. They cut down the king and his men, killing all of them except one, who just managed to escape. The one who had reported them got away in time. As soon as he heard the ring of swords, he sprang out of the room behind them without a word of farewell. After barely saving his life, the man spread the news throughout the city and aroused a loud commotion among the people.

The duke bent over the princess and spoke to her: "I am so sorry for you, beautiful lady, and will never cease to lament your fate. They'll be punished, God knows, for what they did to you. Tell me whether your life can be saved. If God grants me the favor of letting you live, you can be certain that I and the many warriors on my ship will get you home. And, if you should die, I will today take such vengeance on your enemies that they'll be unhappy the rest of their lives. Before we travel on, we strangers will give them pay that they will never forget and will lament to all their descendants."

The daughter of the king of India could only lie there sorrowfully, stained by her warm, red blood, for she was in great pain and near death. Her condition could not have been worse: she was in agony and became weaker each moment as her heart began to break. "Noble knight," she answered, "may God reward you for the trouble and danger you have taken on in this foreign land for my sake. Whatever happens to me, I praise God that he has sent me your help and comfort and that you have freed me from the many sorrows I would always have suffered in this marriage. Should it be God's will that I recover, you truly might have a good reason to be happy about it the rest of your life, for I would make you very powerful and confer on you many honors if God were to help you bring me back to India and you should then want to remain there. You would always be the peer of any king, so wealthy you could have whatever you wanted and enjoy all kinds of pleasures and amusements, a ruler over many rich lands. All this would be yours, just as I have told you.

"A host of bold knights was subject to my father, and all of them—counts and dukes among others—served him uprightly and with honor. They helped him in battle wherever he led them, and he gave them red gold in return. He was therefore liked by all, and rightly so, as long as he lived. His misfortune came from the king of Grippia, who attacked him at sea with his army and killed him, my dear mother, and all the retinue with us on the ship. No one, either nobleman or servant, was spared except me alone, whom they carried off. When he was slain, my father had no other children besides me; so none but I has a right to wear the crown: of that you may be sure. However, all that has changed. I must remain in this foreign land until doomsday, since I can live no longer. May God grant you a safe voyage home." She bowed to him, and with her last word, the soul went forth from her mouth.

The duke and his companion were deeply saddened at the death of the lovely girl and wept with grief. Then they laid her out for burial, placed over her a cover of gold cloth, and prayed that our Lord, the Creator of the world, in his kindness would be merciful to her. Filled with pity, the knights quickly went from the ill-fated chamber, out of the palace, and through the courtyard gate into the city. They held their shields up in front of them because they wanted to fight: for the sake of the beautiful lady they wished to gain fame or die in battle. Thus they advanced, protected by their shields.

By then the gates on both sides of the city were blocked, and all the streets were filled with people, so that the knights were surrounded. There was a frightful roar as they were charged by the throng. The only way to get out now was to cut a path through it. These strange people showed great courage there, for which the knights angrily rewarded them. Holding their shields before them and swinging their swords fiercely, the two sprang bravely into the crowd. The blades did not miss the long, thin necks, and the number beheaded was amazing. They spared no one who opposed them, and cut down all those in the way, even though many of the slain seemed their equals in size and strength. A host fell rather than let them pass, but still they carved out a road almost to the city gate. However, it was closed and barred, and the tireless knights had to fight on as more and more warriors died at their feet. The two put their backs against a wall to protect themselves better and, striking out at those in front and to the sides, in a short time made it a bitter day for many. Then, since the enemy could not harm the knights in any other way, they attacked them from all sides with bows and arrows. When the shields became so heavy that they could hardly hold them up, the knights cut off the arrows with their swords and trampled them under foot. They went on fighting and killed large numbers, but the danger became ever greater, and they began to fear they would not escape.

In the meantime the knights' companions on the ship, hearing the sounds of battle, hurried with their banner and sharp, heavy swords to the city gate to help them. They didn't wait there long, but hacked their way in with swords and moved toward them through the city. Their aid came just in time for the two, who would have died without it, but it brought death to many others. The duke and his men couldn't stay there long; they had to get away quickly, for some of the enemy had gone up on the parapets and were fiercely hurling down stones. The knights broke off the fight and left without any losses: the outing and the baths had cost them enough. In spite of the efforts of the Grippians, they departed and went happily down toward the sea. The brave men had survived great danger but were to suffer much worse on the way to the ship, for they were assailed by a fearful misfortune that brought death to a large number of the company.

As I have told you, the duke left the city unharmed and led his knights toward the ship; he wanted to take them out to sea again. Then they saw a mighty army of the landed nobility who were coming to see the bride: the Christians thought there were twelve thousand or more powerful and highborn warriors in the host, which stretched far and wide. They were armed with horn bows and strangely wrought quivers and shields and were riding the best steeds in the world. As the knights hurried to the ship, this force rode at them and began a fierce struggle in which many perished.

When the duke saw them coming, he said to his men, "Well now, my dear friends, today you will indeed prove that you dare to fight, for we shall meet them in battle like valiant knights. Since they have cut us off from the ship, gather around the banner and defend yourselves bravely. We'll buy our way into heaven with our lives: after all, no one wins its glory for nothing. The joys there are without end, and we shall earn them today because we shall be warring against people who are not baptized and do not worship God. If it is not my Lord's will for us to die here, then they can't drive us back further than the sea. They have a powerful army, and there is no time to delay. You should turn your hearts to the Lord in prayer that he may be merciful and help us in our need. But have no fear of death, knights, for we journeyed forth to serve God, and we shall be saved from our enemies even if they take our lives. Therefore fight boldly, relying on God, who has often saved us from distress. If they come close enough for us to use our swords, we shall kill so many of them that they'll never be able to mourn them all."

After the duke had thus urged his men on, they waited no longer, but prepared for the battle like valiant warriors. Their lord took the banner himself and led them, as the enemy, mounted on great numbers of swiftly charging war horses, began the assault. The Grippians drew their bow strings far back and let fly a cloud of arrows against which neither mail nor shield was full protection. Troop after troop attacked Duke Ernst and his men by shooting at them from a distance. Surrounded on the broad plain, the knights were unable to get at the enemy with their swords and could only try to protect themselves with their shields. They warded off the heathen who harassed them, but could not do them any harm, since they avoided close contact and never brought their fast horses near enough for them to be seized. These tactics brought losses to the knights and very much annoyed the duke, who thought it shameful that the enemy would not engage in hand-to-hand combat. When he saw how weak his defense was, he carried his banner with great effort and peril right through the huge army and down to the sea where the ship was. Five hundred knights, wounded and dead, remained behind. Like a true warrior, the duke helped the others get away. He stopped on the beach with raised shield and ordered all his men to go quickly to the ship and save their lives. Close beside him stood the count and supported him as comrades do.

The knights defended themselves while the sailors came with the small-boat, picked them up group by group, and took them to the ship. As soon as the rest were aboard, the two leaders sprang into the boat and hurried to the ship. Our Lord at once sent them a better wind than anyone else ever had, before or since, which took away their cares and made them happy. Yet, as they raised the sails and set out on the unknown sea, they grieved for those whom they had left behind. Although the wind quickly bore them far out to sea, the heathen were so enraged because of their own losses that, in a short time, they were hurrying after the poor strangers with fast galleys in an attempt to prevent them from escaping alive. But the duke and his noble knights left them behind and were soon out of sight—which was a severe blow to the pursuers, who then returned to land. When the landed nobility heard the news that the king of Grippia and many of his people lay slain, and later found their bodies, they were deeply grieved and mourned them bitterly. They quickly carried away and buried the dead and brought medicine which healed the wounded. Since death had claimed their king, they had to let him go and choose another at once. Meanwhile the strangers sailed on, resigned to God's will.

The duke and his friends, knightly pilgrims all, were nearing a much greater danger and now had to suffer mortal distress on the sea: a host of their sins were washed away at this time, as I shall tell you. On the twelfth day, so the story goes, they came close enough to land to see a large mountain, called the Loadstone, toward which the ship began to move. You can well believe that the travelers were glad to catch sight of it. Soon a whole forest of masts came into view, and the knights became lighthearted, thinking their troubles were over and that they would find cities and people there as in Grippia. While still a long way off, they could see masts like towers on the ships, as I said, standing bare and bleached white as snow by the weather. The knights did not hold back, but sailed joyfully ahead on the unknown sea in the belief that everything was turning out well for them.

However, when a strong current began to drive them toward the harbor, one of the sailors climbed to the top of their mast and with horror recognized the mountain. Sadly he called down to those in the ship, "Knights, prepare quickly for eternity, since we shall never leave this place alive. That mountain is in the Congealed Sea, and unless God saves us, we shall all die here, for we are being driven against it. You must review in your hearts whatever you have done contrary to God's will and turn to him in true repentance. I shall tell you about the power peculiar to that rock. It draws to itself in a short time any ships built with iron nails that sail within thirty leagues. This is no lie: one does not need to steer toward it, but is forced to come. There where we see the ships in front of the dark mountain, right against the rock, is where we shall starve to death, as the others who sailed here have done. We cannot change this. Therefore pray that God may be merciful, because we are already close to the rock."

Hearing this, Duke Ernst said to the knights, "My dear comrades in arms, you should earnestly entreat our Lord by his grace to receive us into his kingdom, for this rock will destroy us. Praise him now altogether with hearts and voices. We are fortunate, since if we die on this unknown sea, we shall dwell with God forever in his kingdom. Rejoice, all of you, that we have come so near him." When they heard these words, the men took them to heart and at once did as the duke counseled. They put themselves fully in God's hands and followed the command to confess and repent with the fervor which is suitable before God. In this manner they prepared themselves well.

After the homeless wanderers had finished their prayers and settled their accounts, they raised a woeful cry to God, asking their creator to care for their souls. Meanwhile they had come close enough to see the high-masted ships clearly. The rock pulled the knights faster. Then its power drove the ship with such force that the waiting vessels had to give way. It dashed toward the rock so violently that all the ships crashed against each other and their masts collided again and again: many ships were broken in two by the shocks. It was a wonder that the knights were not killed by the old, decayed masts of other vessels which plunged down onto theirs, for they crushed everything around the ship as they came down. One would not have expected it to survive, since all the others struck by falling masts sank at once. In such a way many guests had already been received who later died and never returned home. The duke and his army were greatly distressed to see fearful Death standing close before them. Yet they reached the rock alive, which showed that God had helped them.

As soon as their ship came to rest, the men did what is still done by people who have long been closely confined and want to get ashore. They all sprang from the ship without delay and went about singly to look at the curious things in the large fleet which crowded around the mountain as thickly as trees in a forest. Never before or since has anyone seen such riches as the knights found on the ships. They beheld the greatest fortune anyone on earth could have, wealth so vast that for a long time their minds could not grasp it. Indeed, no man has ever been wise enough to count or fully conceive of this treasure: the silver, gold, jewels, and manifold fine silks and satins there were beyond measure.

When they had finished viewing these things, the duke and his men left the ships and climbed the mountain to find out if they could see land anywhere. However, no eye caught sight of a single trace that might lead them to the mainland, which failure disheartened them. It was clear that the mountain was far out in the sea and that they would have to die miserably of hunger without a fight. The knights were therefore filled with care as they lived beside the rock. But they said that they would endure hardships without complaint, since God did not want to spare them any more than all those who had come and perished here before them. As they could not avoid this great trial, they would gladly suffer death to gain God's grace and would accept the misery as a punishment for their sins: both the duke and his knights had faith in the Child of the Virgin.

They spent such a long time on the ship that at last they began to feel great distress, although sound of body, for their supplies were gone: the good food they had brought from Grippia, where they had won it as warriors. At last almost everyone in the ship had starved to death, and only the duke and six men, out of the whole army, were still alive. The others were borne away by a griffin, one by one, after they died. The living did as follows: when death took a knight, they carried him up to the deck at once and left him there, and—you have often heard this told as true—griffins came and flew off with the body to their nest. It was their custom, and they had carried away corpses many times in the past. In this manner the griffins finally helped the duke and some of his men to escape to the mainland and survive, but the others became food for them and their young.

Duke Ernst was distressed to see his companions die wretchedly of hunger without his being able to aid them, and because of them, he suffered bitter grief again and again as death carried them off before his eyes, leaving him only six. These were almost starved and had only half a loaf of bread left, which they divided among themselves; sadly enough, there was no more. Then, putting body and soul in God's hands, they fell on their knees in the form of a cross and fervently prayed that our Lord would be merciful and help them in their great need, for they were much afraid of death.

When these poor men had finished their prayers—which later were answered—Count Wetzel said, "I have just thought of the best plan for us, which will save us if anything can. Before we give up, we must search carefully through the ships until we find some skins. Then we'll put on our good armor, sew each other into the skins, and lay each other up forward on the deck. The griffins will seize us and carry us off, but will not be able to get at us because of the armor, which has often protected us in the past and will do so again. As soon as we discover that the old ones have gone to look for food, we'll cut ourselves out of the skins and climb down to the ground. And if it turns out otherwise, if God does not intend us to be saved, we would still much rather die bravely there than suffer this misery." The knights all replied that God must have given him the idea, and ran at once to the other ships, where they were overjoyed to find a large number of hides. Returning, they cut one into thongs with which to sew themselves in and that evening brought together what they needed for the journey. They undertook this perilous deed with faith in our Lord, who had often delivered them before.

With everything ready, they took counsel to decide who should be the first to be sewn into the hides. "It must be my lord and I," declared the count. "I'll sew him and myself into two hides because I won't ever part from him in life or death. I'll suffer danger or distress with him, however it may be, and share his fate: either to be saved or to die by any means. Whatever comes must come to both of us together. However, you can count on this: if God sends us good fortune so that we escape from the young griffins, you too will be carried away from here, and soon. No one can tell how strong these birds are, but don't mourn for us, because if we live, we'll all get together again." He was right, for they did see each other later.

His comrades agreed with the count, and at break of day the two men got ready. They hurried to put on the armor which every knight has who wants to be protected from danger: shield, helmet, and iron greaves. They did not gird on the sword, but laid it bare beside them. Then each was sewn up into a skin. Their companions wept as they were about to carry the two onto the deck, but the duke asked them to have faith in God, entrusting themselves to his care, and sew one another into the strong hides, just as the count had proposed. Still the knights wept loudly over their lord, and the parting was very sad as they took his advice. When the sun rose, the knights carried the men, who were well hidden by the tough skins, to the deck and laid them there, as I told you. The griffins came flying again over the wide sea to the ships, as was their custom. Seeing the two, each quickly seized one of them with great force in its claws; then they bore them off to their nest and dropped them in front of their young. These tried in every way to get at the food, but at last had to give up since they could not even tear open the hides. The men cut themselves loose and climbed down the rock into the forest, where they were safe from the griffins. God had mercifully delivered them from their dire trouble, for which they offered thanks.

They were close enough to escape that they had little cause to fear as they hid in the thick trees. Meanwhile the old griffins returned to the nest with two more men, who did as the first had done. They too saved themselves from the young birds by getting out of the hides and climbing down the rock. The griffins flew a third time to the ship, where two men had already sewn themselves up firmly, but a third was too weak to do anything to help himself: his strength was gone, and he had to die on the sea. The birds brought the others as food to their young, which tried from all sides with powerful claws to reach them, but could not harm the poor wanderers. These, like their companions, were able to climb down into the forest. The duke and the count had not killed the young griffins, for a good reason. If they had done so, the old ones would not have brought anybody else to the nest: they all were alive only because the birds had carried them to their young.

Duke Ernst was heartily pleased to see his men coming and, running up to them, kissed all four: God had again performed a miracle, as he had done many times in the past. Later they obtained good food and thus escaped starvation, as God willed and decreed.

Having rejoined each other, the knights were very happy that our Lord in his great mercy had wondrously restored their lives, as he often does today. They resolved to hurry further into the forest and started out joyfully, but found nothing there to still their hunger. Pausing now and then to eat plants and whatever else turned up, the poor pilgrims went on until they came to a large, beautiful river, which was clear and had a fast current. The exiles were delighted and stopped there to eat their fill, as the river teemed with fish. They went into the water and caught enough with their hands to drive away hunger and restore their strength. Since there was wood for a fire, they broiled the fish and gave fervent thanks to God. Then the knights searched up and down the stream for a place to cross. However, they almost lost hope because they had to turn back. The way was blocked upstream by sheer cliffs and downstream by mountains so high that their peaks reached to the clouds. The broad river flowed through the mountains more swiftly than one can tell. The knights again lamented their wretched plight and thought their end was near.

Once more they cried out to God in distress, for they were afraid they would perish if they did not cross the water, which—as you have heard—was deep and wide until it shot into a narrow opening in the mountain and raced through with great force. The knights were faced with a dreadful problem and were deeply concerned. "Consider what we should do now," said the duke, "for we shall die if we stay here long."

"We are discouraged," the count spoke up, "but since we can't get across, we must take a chance. Let's build a raft without delay, one large and strong enough to carry us safely, for we must travel through the cave: there is no other way out. Whether we succeed or die is up to God." They set to work at once and quickly made a large, sturdy raft of mighty trees which they felled with their swords (having no other tool), carried to the bank, and bound firmly to strong crosspieces with willow twigs. As soon as it was finished, they stepped fearfully onto the raft and commended themselves earnestly to our Lord, his dear mother, and all his saints: they often fell on their knees with faces turned toward heaven before steering into the cave. We still hear of the wondrous adventure the knights had then. They entered with great alarm, often suffered violent jolts inside, and were badly frightened before they emerged. With many of the bumps and jars they thought death was at hand, but our Savior helped them to survive the peril unharmed.

Before coming out of the cave, they endured troubles and hardships enough with crashing back and forth in the darkness, which was somewhat relieved when the interior of the mountain began to gleam with all kinds of beautiful, colored stones: even the river bed below glistened. Among them Duke Ernst saw one which was very bright, broke it free from the rock, and brought it with him out of the frightful peril. The stone glitters with such radiance that it is called "the orphan" and is well known today, since one can see it in the imperial crown. That proves the story is true. However, if anyone still thinks this tale has been invented, let him come to Bamberg, and the master who set it into verse will put his doubts to rest without any falsehoods. Moreover, it has been written down in Latin and is therefore a true story with no lies.

As the knights came close enough to the end to see daylight, the cave widened, and in a short time they floated out into a broad land. Very happy at this, the duke and his men steered to the bank and left the raft there. They went on and entered a large forest where they came upon clearings tilled by people whose language they did not understand. They hurried toward the peasants—men, women, and children—who fled as soon as they caught sight of the strangers. The knights therefore soon found enough bread to still their hunger and revive themselves, for their strength was gone, and went on through the forest. God had brought them swiftly into a beautiful land—called Arimaspi, so we've heard—a kingdom in which they saw many lovely cities. The duke was highly pleased. He and his men had entered the fief of a count who had built with great expense a castle which, believe me, was large, mighty, and splendid. The people of the country were strange and awesome—one can't deny that—for they had only a single eye, which was in the middle of their forehead. They were called the One-Stars—in Latin, Cyclopes.

As the knights approached the fine castle, they were concerned about what it would be like inside, how they would be received, and what might happen to them. "We shall go there trusting in God," said the duke. Soon they met the count, who was taking a walk in front of the castle with his knights, and were greeted by him in a most respectful and friendly manner. Indeed, the lord of the castle was very nice to the duke and his companions and led them at once to a splendid palace, where he made signs, not knowing their language, that they should take off their armor. They then received all the help they needed. The count, who was a gracious man, gave orders that his guests be well cared for and dressed in fine silks. He also brought them himself what they needed most, all kinds of food and clothing, which pleased them greatly. As a wise man, he knew by their manner that they were noblemen, and their wretched state therefore called forth his pity. The knights received many kindnesses from him for a long time.

It then happened that, because of a festival, the king of the land sent out word for all of his vassals and kin to come to his court. All the lords came, great and small, from far and near—and also this count, who arrived with a large retinue. He went before the king with the duke and his companions, who were well armed in gleaming hauberks and shining greaves and looked splendid. The king was surprised to see them and, after greeting each one, asked the count where he had gotten the knights or where they had come from. "Lord, I don't know who they are or from where," was the reply. "They came into my castle wasted by hunger, and I ordered my people to feed them well, as one can easily see by looking at them. They do not understand our language, but their conduct is very manly." The king looked at their helmets, shields, and swords, and was pleased with their manner: he thought them noble and likable. So he asked the count to turn the knights over to him and was happy when this was done.

The monarch took charge of them and at once had a strong and beautiful Castilian horse led into the courtyard before them, since he hoped to find out by this means which of the knights was the leader. The valiant Ernst reached for the bridle, sprang on its back without using a stirrup, and rode it with skill. At this, the king gave orders that the duke and his companions were to be given such service as he himself required, and furnished well with all sorts of things. He also assigned them a chamberlain who was to get them whatever they needed, and commanded his people to serve them in any way they wished, which was done willingly. Thus did God come to their aid.

When the festival ended, the knights remained therefore with the king, who looked after them well for a long time. It was more than a year before they learned the language. Then the king sent for the duke and asked him to be so kind as to tell him his name and where he was from and also whose vassal he was and how he came to this land. The knight answered that he had been a duke at home and had been driven away without cause by one of the most powerful monarchs ever to rule that empire from its beginning. He also told him about the manners and habits of his own country and how he had gotten to this one. After the king had learned of the customs in many lands and had heard the whole story of how the duke happened to come there and what misfortunes he had suffered since leaving home, he ordered his people to make every effort to take care of the knights: he repeated this several times. Afterwards he was always very honest and friendly toward the duke, giving him silver, gold, and whatever else he wanted. In such a fashion did God care for the knights.

I'll say no more about that here, but go on with the story. One of the neighbors of the king of Arimaspi was a strange race of people, called the Flat Hoofs, which often caused him trouble and did much harm to his land. Their feet were very broad and shaped like a swan's, and they had a great deal of power in forest and swamp areas. They wore no shoes and when a storm came up, lay down and raised one foot over themselves—which was wondrous to see. If the storm lasted for some time, they lifted the other foot to rest the first and thus were always protected from bad weather.

The Flat Hoofs were arrogant people with frightful devices for hurling missiles. They resolved to send an army against the king of Arimaspi and in a day and a night gathered a large force for the invasion. They planned to attack the king by laying waste his land with fire and pillage. When word came to him that a host of Flat Hoofs had entered the country, he was sorely distressed. However, he soon raised a strong army of bold warriors and moved it onto a broad heath where the enemy was encamped: a battle to the death between the two armies would decide the outcome. The

Flat Hoofs had brought their missiles for nothing, since these did not help them after the duke entered the conflict. He took over the king's banner and led the foremost troops, while the adversary moved against him, platoon after platoon, with bold disdain. Many died in the struggle which followed.

The duke and his men faced them bravely, thrusting and slashing until they broke through the enemy's front and forced them to fall back. The Flat Hoofs were then slaughtered dreadfully on the battlefield, as many of the paths on the heath were strewn with dead men who had been cut down. The king of Arimaspi stood by the duke fearlessly with his army, and together they so crushed the invaders that few escaped. But it was Duke Ernst who had won the victory. Things had gone well for him: one can't imagine the number of warriors he and his men had slain and captured.

The battle was won, and those who got away fled to their strongholds or into the forest, wherever they could save themselves. The king, however, camped that night on the battlefield, which resounded with loud rejoicing until dawn. He then decided to present gifts. He summoned his faithful warriors to his tent and asked them to thank the duke for having helped him so faithfully to preserve his honor. Praising the bravery of his guest, he said, "Handsome youth, you have saved my honor and life with skill and bravery, and from now on shall govern whatever part of my land you wish. Out of gratitude I shall enfeoff you with so much that you may indeed enjoy both fame and esteem." With this the king invested Duke Ernst with a duchy, people, and land—thus rewarding him for his aid—and gave the duke's men such wealth that they went away heavy-laden and relieved of every want. The king and the duke agreed that Count Wetzel should be placed in charge of the duchy and given power over all its people, rich and poor. Afterwards the king rode to Lucerne, as his castle was named, while Duke Ernst and his knights were led to his fief. His affairs had greatly improved.

In taking over his land, the duke won the support and good will of its people with gifts of silver, gold, and fiefs: each accepted gladly, and no one was left out. His subjects were therefore pleased with him, and rightly so, and he continued to add to his esteem by being trustworthy and upright: he shared good fortune and bad with all of them. The count too neglected nothing and used his power with honor. Both therefore were thought to be the very best lords in any land, near or far. They lived without reproach.

It was not long, thus the story goes, until Duke Ernst heard of an unusual race of people who lived by the sea in a land next to his own, thought themselves very wise, and could raise a large army when they wanted. Like the Flat Hoofs, they looked strange, for their ears were so long they came down to their feet. We are told that the people covered themselves with their ears and wore no other clothing. They were big and strong, built like noble knights, and had the courage to fight well, although a lot of them were later defeated by the duke. They carried sharp javelins, shining and skillfully made, which killed whatever was struck. They had sworn enmity to the king, plagued him with warfare, and often done great harm to his land. The duke's people, who had endured all this in the past, now complained to him about it and begged him to put an end to it.

After hearing the account, Ernst at once sent for his fighting men and, collecting a fine army, traveled down to the sea and asked to be guided into the land of the enemy. Meanwhile the Ears had gathered a host of warriors who were eager to fight the duke, so there was little delay. They hurried toward him from afar, for which haste they paid dearly that day in the battle. His men cut them up with their swords, killing those who did not flee, until most of the enemy's army lay wounded or slain on the field. The struggle lasted into the darkness, but the duke won the victory: his people were happy at this and rejoiced. They camped on the battlefield that night. At dawn they saw many warriors lying in their blood, for there had been severe losses on both sides. No matter how long it should take, the duke did not want to leave before so crushing this race throughout its land with a stern hand that it would pay him tribute from then on and swear to serve him in battle anywhere along the sea. When this was done, he led his army home. The duke had lost some warriors, but it was his fortune to be victor wherever he appeared in battle.

Duke Ernst was very happy when he returned to his castle and therefore held a great banquet for his men, giving out gold and clothing. Now he was told of another land close by, called Prechami, in which dwelt the smallest people in the world. It was a kingdom which lived in constant fear, as I shall explain. It was always full of cranes, which had so taken over that the little people were afraid to venture onto the fields. They had to live in thick forests and could barely defend themselves from the birds even there. I'll tell you how they fed themselves: from the eggs they stole from the cranes—these and whatever could be raised in the forest were their only food. They killed the young they found and seized as many eggs as they could. They knew of no other way to hold out, for they were quite defenseless against the cranes, except when they gathered an army to do battle with them. The ones they killed or captured then were divided equally among all of them as food until good luck came again.

As soon as the duke heard the story, he summoned a hundred knights and journeyed by ship to the land to find out how the people were getting along. The warriors went into a large forest and found many of them in one place. The duke asked who their king was and promised they need have no fear, saying, "You have my word for it." They were all pleased at this and took him to their ruler, who kissed each one of the knights. This is no lie: there was none among them whom he did not receive in a most friendly manner. Duke Ernst at once asked the king—who hardly reached to his belt—to show him where the birds were. Before doing so, however, the monarch sent messengers to the other parts of his realm for warriors, who came and led the duke to the place he wanted to see. They found a huge flock of birds, more than one could count or imagine.

The cranes, a battle-hardened race which would flee from no one, did not fly away from the army, but defended themselves bravely. They were attacked fiercely by the forces of the king and the duke, which killed so many that nobody—I tell you truly—neither man or woman, could have any idea of their number. The little people were partly avenged. However, Duke Ernst remained there six weeks, at the king's request, to help him drive the cranes from his realm. By then they had killed all of the birds which had once filled the land, and its people had gained a great deal by the duke's campaign. The king sent for him and asked him to remain there always: he would turn over his power to the duke and gladly be subject to him. "I cannot do it, sir," answered the noble knight. "May God preserve your land for you, since I do not have the time and must return home. But, if you want to do me a favor, you can let me have a few of your men, and, believe me, sir, I shall be devoted to your service as long as I live."

"I'll gladly give you as many as you want," said the king. So the duke took two who had been proposed by his attendants and looked handsome and courtly. Before he departed, the king thanked him for the great victory he had given him. Then Duke Ernst said good-bye and set out at once for Arimaspi. He traveled joyfully and praised almighty God.

Not far from Arimaspi lived a savage race called the Canaanites. They were giants and fierce warriors who had conquered many lands and forced them to pay tribute. A host of bold men had died at their hands, for they killed everyone who refused payment. His men counseled the king of Canaan to send a messenger to the ruler of Arimaspi to tell him that, if he valued his life and wanted to remain in his land, he should send tribute and come at once himself to receive his land as a fief and become a vassal of the Canaanite king. The messenger was also to say that his lord would not discuss the matter and was only sorry that the king of Arimaspi had been free for so long. A mighty giant was therefore sent to Arimaspi and, going before its sovereign, politely spoke as he had been directed. The king feared there would be great suffering if the country were invaded and that he could neither defend it nor save his life. He thought he would either have to flee or gain a peaceful settlement by accepting the land as a fief. However, he sent for the best of his nobles—among them Duke Ernst—to come to a council and, when they arrived, told them of the giant's message. "I am greatly concerned," he added, "because they are so powerful that no one can withstand them."

The king's vassals could think of nothing better than to advise him to send the tribute which would allow them to remain at peace with the giants. But the duke spoke at once and said, "You lessen your own esteem by advising your lord to do what will shame him in his homeland. In my country a nobleman would rather die with honor than become the vassal of one of his peers. Sir, I have wiser counsel for you. Send back word to their monarch that he is too lowly to be your liege lord: that is idle fancy and he should not make such demands again if he cares for his honor and well-being; otherwise you will humble him. Say that, if he should attack you, you will so defend your land that his tribute will sour and he will never cease to be pained by the payment he will collect from us here."

Very pleased, the king sent for the messenger, gave him costly presents, and said, "You can now go back and tell your lord that he should think better of his plans for me and be more friendly, since his wanting to extort wealth from me is pure folly. He shouldn't count too much on my silver and gold. If he wishes to become my vassal, I shall be glad to treat him well, but if he insists on my paying tribute to him and wants to be my enemy, tell him that we are at war. It will cost him dearly, for I'll give him such tribute from my free land that he'll never cease to lament his loss and shame as long as he lives."

When he heard this, the messenger hurried home and told his king what had been said. The latter was enraged that the ruler of Arimaspi should be so insolent as to scorn his demand and was not at all inclined to pay tribute himself in order that this fellow might be gracious and spare his life. "Noble king," declared his counselors then, "don't lose your temper about it, for we shall indeed take care of him."

And the messenger said, "Since he has insulted you, I would advise you to invade his land and do battle with him. You should let him see you. The king would gladly have become your vassal if it had not been for a little man who advised him very boldly. He could not have spoken more proudly if all the empires in the world had been subject to him, and before the council was over, he talked the king out of submitting to you. He looks very stately, although I never saw anyone so small: he hardly reaches to my knee. I was and still am surprised at how fearless he appeared in the council and when he went before the monarch with advice. Let us set out at once," added the messenger. "If you capture him, the campaign will be worthwhile even though you should gain nothing else."

The giant king was annoyed that the little man had spoken so strongly against paying tribute, and swore fiercely to delay no longer, but to expel, capture, kill, or hang him: he was to suffer disgrace one way or another. The monarch then called up a thousand of his giants and left for Arimaspi. The warriors carried long and thick steel rods to fight with and made a great din which sounded over fields and heath. They suffered for this later.

As soon as the people of Arimaspi learned that the giants were coming in force to their land, they gathered and prepared to fight against the mighty army in the manner which the duke had advised. He had caused swords and spears to be made for them, and now he urged all the troops not to be afraid. "You must follow me. Weapons in hand, we shall go quickly to the forest through which they must pass, for we can defend ourselves from them there. We'll wait for them in the forest, where they can't use their rods: this will save our lives. However many of them attack us there, we can set upon them with swords and spears and make them regret that they undertook or even thought of this invasion."

When the giants entered the forest, they encountered the bold warriors and, seeing that they were being attacked, began to swing away with their dreadful rods. The duke moved his troops back under the trees to safety, and now, to the misfortune of the invaders, his shrewdness became clear. His men struck at the lower legs of their enemies with swords and spears and felled many of them. Because of their huge weight, they crashed down like trees, making the forest resound. The tribute they demanded was being paid with steel, but they could not carry it off. The giants struck their comrades while vainly trying to hit their foes and thus suffered great harm from each other as well as from the duke's men. A large number were badly wounded and had to be borne away. When at last three hundred mighty giants lay dead, the others fled, and the struggle was over. Since they couldn't use their rods because of the trees, they ran back to Canaan. As soon as the giants began their hasty retreat and the duke was master of the battlefield, he asked his men to help him capture one. They saw a strong giant who was too badly wounded to flee and, surrounding him, set upon him with their weapons and did not stop until he gave up his rod. Duke Ernst then let him live and turned him over to his men, who joyfully led him back to their country. A crushing defeat had been suffered by the giant monarch, and the victory had been won by the king of Arimaspi, who afterwards reigned in his land as no one's vassal and was never again attacked by the giants. He thus maintained his honor.

The king was pleased at the triumph and, when he set out for home, sent messengers ahead to tell the news of their splendid success against the giants. Everyone rejoiced that they had de-

fended themselves so well against such tall, strong men, and old
and young thanked Duke Ernst, whose cunning had given them
the victory. Because of his great liking for the duke, the king had
a banquet for him after they came home and gave him gold and
precious stones. All the people honored the nobleman who had
brought them esteem and renown, for all had profited from his
wisdom. The happy knight then went back to his duchy, where
the people received him warmly: he was as dear to them as life
itself.

So it was that the duke returned. He was very pleased at having
the injured giant and took good care of him, often treating and
binding up his wounds, until he fully recovered. The lord let the
giant know that he liked him and, as soon as he was well, gave
him good clothes and allowed him to go about freely wherever he
wished. The giant said he would never leave the duke and later
was a great deal of help to him. We are told that he was only
fifteen years old and by no means fully grown, and yet no fir in
the forest would have reached to his knee: he was indeed huge
and frightening. Besides the giant, there were now at the court the
two men of Prechami and many Ears and Flat Hoofs, all of whom
got whatever they wanted and more from their lord. He kept them
with him as wonders, and in afteryears these strange beings often
made long hours short and pleasant.

Duke Ernst had ruled his duchy with honor for six years when
one morning, as he was taking a stroll in front of his castle, he
saw a ship from Ethiopia enter the harbor. He asked those on
board to tell him the news and also whose ship it was. "We sailed
from Ethiopia as merchants," they answered, "and could not prevent the wind from driving us here. Indeed, we came to this land
quite against our will. Have mercy on us, noble warrior, for God's
sake, and help us to escape with our lives, and we'll give you as
much of our goods as you want: your kindness alone shall set the
limit. We only beg you to leave us just enough to keep us from
starving to death before we get home."

After he had heard the whole story, the duke knew what sort
of land they came from. Then he asked if it were at war, and they
told him all about that, saying, "The troops of the king of Egypt
are doing much harm to the king of Ethiopia in his country. They
have plagued him with bitter strife so he will turn from Christian-

ity and increase the number of heathen unbelievers. Large armies of knights often invade us, although it does them no good, for they have to flee from the country's forces and the knights of the king. He is not going to give up his faith."

When the duke learned this, he asked the merchants if they could assist him to leave the country secretly. "I have long wanted to go to Jerusalem," he said, and promised to pay them well if they helped him to get there. He added that, since there was a war in their country, he felt inclined to stay a while with its king before going on to Jerusalem. The merchants were very pleased with his words and promised faithfully to do whatever he proposed.

So late one evening Duke Ernst secretly had many things brought to the ship: the best of his gold, silver, and other costly treasures, the finest silk cloth and clothing he could find, pearls and precious stones, the manifold articles which might be useful and suitable to take along, and whatever else he really liked—all this came quickly and stealthily into the ship. With the same secrecy he brought the giant and his other wonders—Flat Hoofs, Prechamis, and Ears—to the vessel of the Ethiopians. Two men of Arimaspi of whom he was fond were with him while this was being done, and he asked them to go along. They were happy to do so because they liked having him as a lord. Everything went into the vessel with great stealth, and at last also the four knights who had come with the duke, as I have already told you.

They were in high spirits as they hoisted the sails and set out on their journey, aided by the best wind anyone ever had. Thus did the lord and his men escape from that country. The wind drove them to a harbor in Ethiopia, and the duke left the ship with his band. The merchants found lodgings for them, in which they stored their possessions, and then led them to a fine castle where they met the king. The merchants told the monarch who the lord was and also the rest of the story—where they had taken him on board and how they had returned home—all in detail. Afterwards the duke took his wondrous men and went before the king, who received him with honor, saying, "You and your retinue are welcome here." And the lord, standing beside his giant and other followers, thanked him. The king and all his men were greatly astonished at these creatures and had to admit they had never seen anything so strange or heard the like in the whole world. They were glad Duke Ernst had come.

The homeless wanderer then asked the king to let him remain there in order to pass the time in his service until he could find out how to get to Jerusalem. The knight told him about his travels and promised to serve the king well if the latter would help him continue his journey. "Believe me," answered the monarch, "if you want to settle down with your giant in my country, I'll keep you the rest of your life and give you enough land for you and your men to live here in high esteem. I'll do this at once if you wish."

The duke said that he was grateful for the honor which had been offered but added, "There is still no reason to do this, since I have earned nothing as yet. When I do something for you that seems to you to merit a reward, I can accept with honor whatever favor you grant me." From that time on the king cared for him as if he were his own son, and the duke later fully repaid this kindness.

Soon afterward news came to the monarch that his realm was being invaded by many warriors under the command of the king of Egypt. The latter intended to conquer and destroy the Christian lands and had led such a mighty army of knights out of the heathen countries that no one could defend himself against it. Hearing this report, the king became very angry and quickly raised an army from the Christians of the land. When the nobles came to his court, all declared they would be glad to protect their country and willingly took an oath to take part in the campaign against the heathen. They collected a large force of many thousands, which the king led out onto a broad heath. Duke Ernst was happy that he would be in this battle and promised God to fight for him there and also to give to His church and worship Him forever if he should return alive. He pledged all this, and many died because of it.

The heathen army appeared in great strength but was to suffer many losses in the battle which followed. The narrow paths were made wide with swords that day, and wondrous feats were seen. The duke entered the struggle early as a part of the king's army, and while the giant carried the banner powerfully against the enemy, he and his troops—who followed him closely—performed great deeds of valor. It would take a long time to tell of every spear he broke and how many knights he unhorsed, but I can say that the banner was so well defended that a host died before it. The battle lasted all day until the sun was low in the west, as blows fell on steel and bones and blood flowed freely. The heathen wore little armor, and therefore many of their companies were completely destroyed by the Christians. The latter wielded swords and spears until they broke through the troop in which the mighty king of Egypt himself was riding and fighting bravely. When the duke caught sight of him, he galloped toward him and struck him from his horse, wounding him badly. Thus did Duke Ernst valiantly capture the king in the fierce battle, but at the same time he lost one of the knights who had first sailed off with him and had later been saved from the griffins.

The Ethiopians defended their country well. The duke and his giant struck down their foes like cattle, and the Christian army began to triumph across the entire battlefield. The lines of the heathens had been broken in so many places that at last they had to turn and flee, carrying with them a lot of mortally wounded and leaving the field to their enemies. The king of the Ethiopians was overjoyed as he gathered his army and returned with it to the capital. He had the wounds of the heathen king treated without delay and, when they had healed, sent him back to his land with orders to urge his nobles to help him work out a friendly pact with the Christian king and thus lessen his own troubles. The ruler of Egypt gave hostages which were to be held until he had made amends for all the harm done, that there might be peace as long as the two kings lived. And both gave solemn promises to keep the agreements. Every prisoner, heathen and Christian, was set free. All wanted to forget war so completely that it would never be thought of again.

Duke Ernst then spoke to the king of Ethiopia about his journey to Jerusalem and bitterly lamented the many hindrances in the way. The monarch was sorry he did not want to stay there, but nevertheless commended him at once to the care of the king of Egypt with the urgent request that the duke be brought safely to Jerusalem. And in order to win the lasting thanks and good will of the Ethiopian ruler, the king promised to help Duke Ernst get there or any place else he wanted to go. When this was agreed upon, the knight prepared to depart. The Egyptian monarch also did not wait longer, but rode to the king's castle and took leave of him and his vassals. The duke left the court with great honor after receiving from the Ethiopian king two pack horses laden with gold, and a fine dromedary.

The homeless wanderer and his followers therefore traveled to Alexandria with the king of Egypt and remained at his court over a month. The duke then reminded the king of the duty to get him to Jerusalem, as had been promised, and the monarch ordered four of his noblemen to take him there and gave him so much gold and fine silk cloth because of his bravery that a camel was hardly able to carry it. After the king had shown him great respect and esteem, the knight said good-bye and left for Jerusalem with an escort of two thousand men, which pleased him very much. When he neared the city and the news spread that the lord was coming of whom such wonders were told, all the people rejoiced and went forth a league—some mounted, others on foot—to receive him with honor into the land. They led him straight to the Church of the Holy Sepulchre, where the knight made an offering to the glory of God over His grave. He gave half of his strange creatures and much wealth besides—gold, precious stones, and fine silks—from the rich treasure he brought with him. He also made large gifts to the temple and other holy places. Duke Ernst lived here more than a year and during this time caused a lot of trouble for the heathen. He fought them fiercely wherever they met, brought them much harm and shame, and led his own troops back from the battles with honor. For this he was highly esteemed.

The duke spent the year in constant conflict with the heathen. Indeed, hardly a day passed without his doing something to them, and they hated him bitterly for it. Meanwhile, pilgrims from Germany came across the sea and told him the news and also what was said of him at home. Many took back reports about him, so the emperor learned he was in good health and in Jerusalem. He heard this from a knight who had seen him there and who furthermore told the monarch everything that had happened to the duke and all about the wondrous creatures which were still with him. The knight had seen these himself and could thus vouch for the truth of the story.

It then pleased the emperor to let all the princes know that Duke Ernst was alive and in Jerusalem. When they heard this, they were glad that he was still living and said, "Let us forgive his crime and lend our help that he may be removed from the empire's ban and regain the favor of the emperor." In the meantime, answering Queen Adelheid's prayer, God in heaven had so ordained that the emperor was forced to believe Count Heinrich had lied about the

duke and that he himself had treated him unjustly. He therefore
sent word that Duke Ernst was to come secretly to the emperor,
who would forgive his crimes, give back what had been taken
from him, and make good his losses. These, it was said, were the
monarch's intentions.

I'll go on with the story. While the nobleman lived in Jerusalem,
he was well-liked for his bravery and for causing the heathen such
distress that they were always lamenting the injury done them. He
often heard it said that the emperor spoke very kindly of him and
prayed God to send him home so he could learn from him about
his many strange adventures. The duke also heard that all of the
princes were supporting his cause. He therefore took leave of the
people of Jerusalem and had someone show him the way to the
harbor of Acre, where he boarded a ship and sailed for more than
six weeks. The wind drove them about at will, and they suffered
so greatly that, to the duke's deep regret, his Flat Hoof died. At
last the ship entered the harbor at Bari, where he was greeted
warmly.

Before Duke Ernst left the city, he laid an offering on the grave
of Saint Nicholas, readily giving bright silk and broad gold bands.
He then departed and soon neared Rome. When its citizens learned
of his coming, he was received with honor, as a throng rode and
walked out to meet him. They escorted the famous man into the
great Church of Saint Peter, where there are so many holy relics.
He also gave an offering here: splendid silk cloth and a fabric of
silk interwoven with gold which could not have been finer. The
people kept him in Rome as a highly esteemed guest, served by
all, for more than a week and would not even think of letting him
depart until they had heard every little bit of his story. They were
amazed by his strange creatures.

At last the noble lord commended them to God, for he wanted
to take his leave. They were sad at this, but could not keep him
from going and therefore prayed God to watch over him.

The duke went on, entered Bavaria without anyone knowing
who he was, and sent for a vassal who, he knew, would not reveal
his presence. The man told him a meeting of the Imperial Diet had
been proclaimed for Bamberg at Christmas time and that the emperor would be at the Christmas mass there wearing his crown.
"You should go there stealthily, sir," he said, "you and Count

Wetzel. And in secret I'll care for those of your retinue whom you wish to leave with me, so you can travel without being afraid someone will notice them while you are on the way." The duke and the count thought it a good plan and set out for Bamberg at once.

They reached a forest near the city late on Christmas Eve and remained there until it was almost time for early mass. Then they went furtively into the city and to where they found the queen at prayer. When they fell down before her, she noticed them and asked who they were. The count said that it was the duke, her son, and that she should be kind to him and help him come to favor so that the emperor for God's sake would pardon his offense. The queen sprang to her feet at once and embraced her son, kissing him often as the tears flowed from her eyes. She told him to return secretly to his lodging and not to approach the emperor until he heard them singing the carol service. He should then come before the emperor and be prepared to fall at his feet as soon as the Gospel was read. "In the meantime," she added, "I must talk with the princes so they can help us." The lord therefore left her and went to a hiding place. With God's aid he was that day to see the end of all of his troubles.

As soon as she finished speaking with him, the lady sent for the princes and told them in confidence about her son: that he had come there in hope of forgiveness from everybody. She asked them in God's name to hear her plea and entreat the emperor to show him mercy and to turn the matter over to them. The lords promised her that for the sake of the worthy knight they would use all the influence they had and force the monarch to grant him his favor or at least give him an ill-humored pardon. Each assured the queen of his aid, and she was happy. When the princes entered the house of God, the emperor, dressed in imperial robes and wearing a crown, was standing beside the queen, as he did at festivals. A bishop chanted the mass before the great throng in the vast cathedral, went to the lectern while the Gospel was being read, and spoke the tender words of God.

The outlaws waited no longer, but came, in sackcloth and barefoot, and fell at the emperor's feet to ask him for pardon. The princes also stepped forward and, one after the other, urged him for the sake of God, the passion of Christ, and that holy day to be merciful to them. "Whatever he may have done to me," spoke the monarch, "even if he tried to take my life, is now forgiven for the sake of God, and I shall not hold it against him." With these words he raised up the knight, whom he did not recognize, and kissed him on the lips. The duke thanked him properly, and the emperor, looking closely into his eyes, knew who it was. Then, regretting his act, he bowed his head and would not speak to him. But the princes cried out, "Lord and mighty emperor, what you have done so publicly before the entire empire, you should rightly let stand. You have forgiven the offense for God's sake and ours and would make yourself a laughingstock if you did otherwise." "Well, since you lords think I should," he replied, "and want him pardoned, I will put away my anger forever and be friendly to him." The monarch gave him silver and gold and made good the losses he had suffered, while the princes waived their claims on the duke for damages and were happy that he had returned.

As soon as the mass was over, they all swarmed about him to welcome and receive him with honor: the queen's heart was full of joy. At last the emperor asked Duke Ernst where his strange retinue was and, when the knight answered, "In Bavaria," sent messengers who hurried day and night to bring it to the monarch's court. Everyone who saw the creatures thought them wondrous indeed and declared with a single voice that they would never see the like again. Then the emperor asked the knight to give him some of them. Duke Ernst resisted, for he didn't want to, but finally let him have the One-Star, the man with the long ears who sang so sweetly, and one of the little people. He wouldn't part with the others—especially the great giant, whom he would entrust to no one—and took them back to Bavaria when he left. The monarch kept the duke with him for twelve days so that he could learn all about the many wondrous adventures and where the strange creatures had been found. He was so taken by the account that he thought of nothing else and neither listened to lawsuits nor even left his chamber until he had heard the whole story. But that was not the end of it. He had a scribe write down why and by what means the duke was banished, how long he held out before leaving his land, and how he departed and returned. No one who heard this part of the duke's tale could keep from weeping.

The emperor then gave the duke back his lands, and from that time on the latter ruled the country he had inherited, caring for people and land in a splendid manner and presenting gifts and fiefs like a great warrior. The emperor remained fond of him till death and withheld nothing until he was as rich and powerful as before, indeed even more. Thus did Duke Ernst overcome all his troubles.

Translated by J. W. Thomas
and Carolyn Dussere

Reinhart the Fox

Heinrich der Glîchezaere

May God Lighten our Journey

L isten to strange, but true accounts of a wild beast, tales in which one can see likenesses to many things. It was always bent on deceit and trickery and therefore often got into trouble. It was called Reinhart the Fox and was very cunning.

Now I'll tell you what the story is about. A rich peasant had a comfortable place that looked out over a plain and was near a village. Here he had his own land and income, with plenty of rye and millet, and everything was going well for him. His name was Lanzelin and his wife's was Granny Runzela. He had one great cause for distress: since the farmyard and the garden were not enclosed tightly enough, he constantly had to guard his fowl from Reinhart and had to suffer losses that didn't please him at all.

"Lanzelin, you old fool," said Runzela, "I have now lost ten of my hens to Reinhart, and I'm angry." So Master Lanzelin got a scolding he still hasn't paid back. Nevertheless, he did as she said and built a good fence which he thought would protect Schantecler and his wives, whom Reinhart planned to kill.

Early one morning Reinhart went to the farm with the intention of playing an evil trick on Schantecler and did indeed cause him much grief. The fence seemed to him too thick and too high, but he pulled away a piece of brushwood with his teeth and stretched out: he was glad to see no one was there. Schantecler was sleeping

next to the fence close by when the hen Pinte saw his mortal enemy squirming through. "Husband!" she cried and fled with her
companions onto a roost. Schantecler came running and told her
to get back to the fence at once.

"In this enclosed garden you'll never need to worry about any
beast," he said, "but pray to God, dear wife, that he will protect
me. Truly I had a bad dream—that I was in a red fur whose neck
was of bone—and I am afraid it means trouble. Let it be told to
the holy angel! May he interpret it to my good, for my heart is
indeed heavy."

"My lord and my love," said Lady Pinte, "I saw a movement in
that brush. If my senses do not deceive me, there is something evil
in here. May Almighty God shield you! A cold chill goes over me
and I shudder with dread. I tell you, I am afraid we are in danger."

"By God," replied Schantecler, "a woman can get more frightened than four men. We have often heard that the meaning of
many dreams isn't revealed for seven years."

"Don't be angry," said Pinte, "and fly up on this thorn bush.
Remember that our children are still very small. If you died, husband, I would be sad and in need the rest of my life. I am so
worried about you that I am sick at heart. May our Lord protect
you!" When he did fly onto the thorn bush, his enemy was running right behind him, and Pinte quickly took flight. Schantecler
was now out of reach, but Reinhart tricked him into coming down.
To do this he put his guile to work.

"Who is that up there?" he asked. "Is it you, Sengelin?"

"No, I am not he," answered Schantecler. "That was my father's name."

"That may well be," said Reinhart. "I am sorry to hear of your
father's death, for he was polite to even the least of creatures.
Nothing is as fine as this except loyalty to kinfolk. However, to
tell the truth, you act unfriendly: your father didn't sit so high.
He liked my father and never saw him without flying up to welcome him. Moreover, he never failed, early or late, to beat his
wings, close both eyes, and sing to him as only a happy rooster
can."

"I'll do it," said Schantecler, "because my father taught me
how—you will have a great welcome," and he sprang down joy-

fully and began to beat his wings. The fool was too hasty and sorely regretted it for, while he was flapping and singing, Reinhart seized him by the head. Pinte cried out in grief, but Reinhart only ran, heading for the forest at top speed. Master Lanzelin heard the clamor and wailed, "Oh, my chickens!"

"Where are you running so fast?" asked Schantecler. "Are you going to let that peasant berate you? Can't you answer him?"

"I will, by God," said Reinhart (and shouted back), "You're wasting your time." Schantecler didn't like his position at all and was delighted to get his neck out of Reinhart's mouth. Then, to the latter's dismay, he quickly flew into a tree and was safe. Looking down at Reinhart, he said, "You will get no thanks for your trouble. Indeed the ride you gave me seemed much too long. I tell you truly that I won't return with you under any condition."

"By God," exclaimed Reinhart on hearing this mockery, "only a fool responds to an injury of mere words or chatters too much when he should be still."

"God knows that he who is always on his guard isn't stupid," answered Schantecler. With this the jeering and quarreling ceased.

Since Master Lanzelin was coming, Reinhart hurried off, blind with rage at having lost the meal he had counted on. He was getting very hungry when he heard a titmouse. "Good day, neighbor," said Reinhart. "I long to kiss you, but by Almighty God you act so strangely. You should have more faith. It is really a shame that I find so little of it in you. I swear by the loyalty I owe your child, my godchild, that I am fond of you and harbor no malice."

"Reinhart," replied the titmouse, "I have often heard many very wicked things about you and am afraid of your dreadful eyes. If you will close them, I'll kiss you three times on the mouth with all good will." The guile of the little creature caused Reinhart to be very pleased: indeed he was delighted. Since the titmouse was still standing on a high limb, he closed his eyes tightly, as he had been directed. Thereupon she picked up a piece of dung with her toes, hopped from branch to branch, and let it fall on Reinhart's mouth. She could see at once the deceitfulness of her neighbor, for his teeth were ready and quickly snapped up the dung.

The titmouse had eluded him, and Reinhart had gone to considerable pains for a poor snack. "Good Lord," he said unhappily, "how can it be that a little bird should fool me? It distresses me, and that's no lie." Reinhart used cunning, but this was a day when nothing could go right for him.

He then saw, perched high in a tree, a raven named Dizelin who had been clever enough to obtain a fresh cheese. Reinhart couldn't stand to have him eat it all by himself and tried to think of a way to cheat him out of it with a cunning lie. He sat down under the tree in which the raven was eating the cheese and asked, "Is it you, Dizelin? Cousin, I am glad to see you here with me: nothing could make me happier. I would like to hear you sing, if you would do your father's song. He had a fine voice."

"I won't find fault with my father," replied Dizelin, "but the truth is that none of my ancestors could sing better than I, which pleases me." Then he began to sing so loudly that the forest resounded. Reinhart urged the raven to let him hear the melody again, and Dizelin forgot about the cheese on the branch as he raised his voice in song. Reinhart didn't expect to eat at once, but the cheese fell right in front of him.

Now hear how the arrogant Reinhart tried to kill his cousin, and for no reason. "My dear Dizelin," he said, "listen and help me. You don't know my distress: I was injured this morning, and the cheese is lying too near me. It has a strong odor that, I'm afraid, will be harmful to my wounds. Dear cousin, befriend me now! Your father was kind, and I have heard that blood is thicker than water. I am suffering greatly from the stench, and you can easily keep your cousin from dying like this." He began to sob.

Deceived by Reinhart, the raven quickly flew down. Because of loyalty, he wanted to give help in need, and it almost cost his life. He was about to take away the cheese and earn, so he thought, his cousin's thanks, when Reinhart eagerly sprang up with no sign of injury. He thus showed his own loyalty to the raven, who didn't know why he was being attacked. Reinhart was too clever for him, but his cousin did barely manage to escape after losing many feathers. For just then a hunter with four good dogs came onto Reinhart's trail, and the latter regretfully took flight. He had to leave the cheese to its rightful owner, the raven, and hide.

The dogs soon found and attacked him, and his cousin, who was very angry, did all he could to harm him. "What one peasant does to another is often repaid," he cried loudly. "So I have heard, and that has happened to you." Reinhart ran away from the dogs, but the raven wasn't sleeping and put them on his track. Reinhart couldn't have had worse luck: the dogs began to tear at him and the hunter to stab fiercely at him. It was high time for cunning. Seeing a fallen tree, he ran and ducked under it, while the dogs leaped over it and away, with the hunter urging them on. Reinhart then headed for the forest.

He met Dieprecht, the cat, embraced him, and exclaimed, "A thousand welcomes, cousin! I am happy to see you looking so well. I have heard much about your speed. You must let me witness it and, if what they say is true, I will vouch for it."

"Cousin," replied Dieprecht, "I am glad you have had a good report of me and am ready to oblige you." The treacherous Reinhart then led him to a place where there was a narrow path on which lay a trap. It was an evil way to treat a kinsman.

"Now run, my dear cousin," he directed. "I want to see what you can do."

"May St. Gall protect me against Reinhart's schemes," said Dieprecht (to himself), for he knew about the trap. He ran very fast and sprang over it.

"No beast was ever swifter than you, dear cousin," declared Reinhart when he returned, "but let me teach you something. You shouldn't jump so high. It could cost you your life if a vicious dog attacked you. I know a lot about such fights."

"You still don't need to tell me to run behind you," answered Dieprecht. "I'll show you some fine jumps, and that's no lie." Each was trying to trick the other. Reinhart ran after his cousin, but the latter was in no hurry and stopped still when he had leaped over the trap. Reinhart bumped into him, and his foot landed in it. Truly, this served him right.

Dieprecht said goodbye, commended his cousin to Lucifer, and hurried off. Reinhart remained behind in great distress, for he was sure he would die. Then he saw the hunter who had set the trap: now indeed he had to be clever. He laid his head down on the trap. The peasant quickly ran up and, since Reinhart's throat was as white as snow, he thought he had gained at least five shillings. He raised his axe and swung as hard as he could. Reinhart was unable to flee, but just in time he jerked his head away and the axe broke the trap. Reinhart had never been more pleased—he had thought he would be killed and his neckfur sold for five shillings. He moved without delay, because these lodgings didn't seem to him at all comfortable. Sadly watching him go, the peasant began to scold himself: now he would have to pay his rent with other goods.

Right after Reinhart survived this desperate plight, he encountered the wolf, Isengrin. Now listen to what Reinhart said as soon as he saw him: "May God grant you a good day, sir. Both you and my lady may be sure that I shall do whatever you command and shall serve you in any way I can. I have come to give you a warning, for I have learned that many men hate you. Do you want me as a comrade? You can depend on me. You are strong and I am crafty: nothing could withstand your strength and my cunning. I could tear down a castle." Isengrin went to talk with his wife and two sons, and all agreed that he should accept Reinhart as a companion: he regretted it later. Since Reinhart's thoughts and service were directed toward winning Hersant's love, Sir Isengrin had taken on an evil vassal, which had to do him harm.

One day Sir Isengrin led his wife to Reinhart and entrusted her to the latter's loyalty and honor, then set out with his sons for the open country in search of gain. He had picked a poor chamberlain, for Reinhart was courting Hersant's favor. An unusual tale now begins.

"Dear friend," said Reinhart to the lady, "if you could only see my distress: I am sorely wounded by my love for you."

"Be quiet," replied Isengrin's wife. "My lord is so handsome that I can easily do without the laments of a lover. Even if this weren't so, you wouldn't be good enough for me."

"Lady," continued Reinhart, "If I were lucky, I would be dearer to you than a king whose thoughts were turned to love but found you unworthy." Her husband then returned, and the suitor acted as if nothing had been said. Isengrin brought no plunder and was dejected with hunger as he told his wife how difficult it was in the fields. "I never knew things to be so bad," he said. "Every shepherd has a dog."

Fortunately for them, Reinhart just then caught sight of a peasant carrying a large ham, which he laughed to see. "Listen, Sir Isengrin!" he exclaimed. "What do you say, my friend? Would you perhaps like to have that meat?"

"Yes!" answered Isengrin and his family with one voice. Reinhart hurried at once to a spot which the peasant was to pass and then began to hold up one foot, limp badly, and let his back sink down as if it were broken. The peasant shouted at him and threw the ham on the ground, for he was in a hurry to get Reinhart's neckfur: he had a frightful club. Reinhart looked around and led him off toward the forest. Meanwhile Isengrin wasted no time, and, before the peasant could return, the ham was seized and quickly devoured. Reinhart was forgotten. The peasant turned back to get the ham and saw Isengrin, who had done him this injury, at a distance. When he found neither meat nor bone—because everything had been eaten—he began to lament loudly. He fell on the grass and bewailed the loss of the ham.

"Lucky me, to have such a comrade," laughed Isengrin. "We couldn't have had a better meal, and I thank him for it." He didn't know how it would turn out. Reinhart came up, pleased and eager. "Where is my share?" he asked.

"Ask my wife if she saved some of what she got," replied Isengrin.

"No, I didn't," she said. "It tasted splendid. May God reward you, Reinhart, and don't be angry if I never do."

"I'm very thirsty," declared Isengrin.

"If you would like wine," said Reinhart, "I'll give you plenty."

"I'll be your servant as long as I live," answered Isengrin, "if you can get me enough of it."

With cunning designs, Reinhart led Isengrin, Hersant, and their sons to a monastery farm and then took them to where the wine barrels were. Isengrin got drunk and, not expecting any harm, sang one of his father's songs. The guardians of the wine exclaimed, "How did this happen? I think we heard a wolf," and six men came quickly, each with a staff. Reinhart fled at once, while Isengrin and Hersant paid for the wine by being beaten. Their hosts were most unfriendly. "If I get out," cried Sir Isengrin, "I'll never touch wine again." Things had gone amiss for them there. The gate was closed, but they leaped over a hedge and thus made a shameful escape. Sir Isengrin then lamented the injury and disgrace. Both he and his wife were black and blue, and his sons also had not been passed over. "To tell the truth, father," they said, "the song and the other foolishness was untimely."

Just then Reinhart came up. "What's all this about?" he asked.

"We four paid dearly for the wine, God knows," replied Isengrin. "Moreover, my own sons have belittled me. That makes me furious. The pains I have taken with them have gone for nothing."

"Restrain yourself, friend," said Reinhart soothingly. "I'll tell you the truth: it would be no wonder if my godson spoke foolishly, because he is still young."

With this he and Isengrin went off together. Soon they met Baldwin, the donkey, whom his master had sent ahead with a heavy load. Reinhart asked him to stop and said, "Tell me, Baldwin, why do you want to be a miserable wretch? I'm surprised that your burdens don't kill you. If you want to stay with me, I'll free you from this distress and give you enough

[lacuna]

He left his friend. Isengrin was faint from loss of blood. "I am filled with grief to lose my life," he mourned, "and even more because of my dear wife. She is noble and good and has kept free of any kind of folly. She always abhorred evil. I also feel sorry for my sons, who will be orphans, although their mother's hand will lead them safely home. It is also a comfort to know that she won't take another husband."

The lament was heard by Kunin, who called, "What is the matter, Sir Isengrin?"

"I am frightfully wounded," was the answer, "and I don't think I'll recover. My dear wife will die of grief."

"No she won't," declared Kunin. "She hasn't behaved as well as you said just now. A short time ago I saw Reinhart courting her while between her legs. Doesn't that sound like infidelity?" This was cruel news for Isengrin, and he fell into such a swoon that he didn't know whether it was night or day. Kunin laughed at this.

When Isengrin came to himself, he cried, "Oh what trouble I have! And you add to it by telling me a hateful lie. Were I so foolish as to believe it, I would tear your eyes out. If I had you down here, you would never leave the spot."

"You are a fool," answered Kunin. Isengrin let out a howl, which, to his great joy, at once brought Lady Hersant and his sons. Weeping, he said to them, "I was never so glad to see you, dear wife and sons, for I am mortally wounded. Kill Reinhart! He is the one who did this to me. Moreover, Kunin has almost driven me out of my mind just now. As badly injured as I am, he told me a dreadful story: that you had become Reinhart's wife. I almost died, for I never would have gotten over it. But one shouldn't believe a liar, and God knows I didn't think he was dependable."

"I haven't seen Reinhart for three days," said Lady Hersant. "Sir Isengrin, I must tell you to stop this senseless talk." Then all Isengrin's wounds were licked, and he soon recovered.

Reinhart set out for his lair, because he was afraid guests would be coming. He quickly built a house in front of a cave in the forest and carried food into it. One day Isengrin went by, suffering greatly from hunger. Another disgrace awaited him. Reinhart, who had plenty of supplies, had just broiled some eels, which Isengrin smelled. "Aha!" he thought, "this may well be some very good food." The odor led him to his kinsman's door, where he sat down and began to knock.

Reinhart, who could do wonders, called out, "Why don't you go away? No one will go out there today, you may be sure, or come in either. Where are your wits, you simpleton? Why don't you leave? It is afternoon: not for the Nibelung treasure would we monks say a word now."

"Kinsman," said Sir Isengrin, "are you going to spend the rest of your life here as a monk?"

"Yes," he answered, "for you denied me your favor without cause and wanted to kill me."

"I will forgive whatever you may have done to me," said Isengrin, "in order to have you as a comrade."

"It should be easy to pardon me," replied Reinhart. "May I drop dead right now if I was ever disloyal to you. If you will be grateful, I'll give you two eels that I have left over today." Isengrin was pleased at this and opened widely. Reinhart threw them into his mouth.

"I would be healthy forevermore," exclaimed the foolish Isengrin, "if I were cook here."

"You can have plenty," said Reinhart, "should you want to join this brotherhood. You will be in charge of the roasts." Isengrin made up his mind at once.

"I promise to do so," he declared.

"Well stick your head in," was the answer. Isengrin was eager to: his trouble was near. He pushed his large head in, and Brother Reinhart doused him with hot water that actually took off hair and hide.

"That hurts!" cried Isengrin.

"Do you think you can gain paradise in comfort? That comes from ignorance. You should be glad to suffer the pain, kinsman, for this brotherhood is such that, when you are dead, you will share a thousand masses daily. Those of Zitias will lead you to the blessed heavenly kingdom; be sure of that." Isengrin believed it and didn't regret the loss of his hair and hide.

"Brother," he said, "your eels in there are common property now that we have become God's children, and I will complain to Zitias if one is refused me."

"Nothing will be withheld from you," replied Reinhart. "In brotherly love we shall place at your disposal whatever we have. However there are no more fish here. Do you want to go with me to a pond in which so many fish are swimming that no one can count them? The brothers put them there."

"Let's go," said Sir Isengrin, and they set out in full accord. They saw at once that the pond was frozen over, but a hole had been cut in the ice so that one could get water. This and the hate of his brother brought Isengrin to grief. Reinhart had remembered a pail being there and, when—to his great satisfaction—he found it, he tied it to his brother's tail.

"In nomine patris!" exclaimed Isengrin. "What's this?"

"You must lower the pail in here and stand very quietly while I go to stir them up. We shall catch a lot of fish, for I see them through the ice."

"Tell me, brother in love," said Isengrin, who was not very wise, "are there really fish in here?"

"Yes there are, a thousand. I've seen them."

"That's good. We shall do well."

The night became cold, his brother didn't warn him, and Isengrin was stupid enough to let his tail freeze in the ice. Because of Reinhart's treachery, it froze more and more tightly.

"This pail is getting heavy," said Isengrin.

"I've counted thirty eels in it," answered Reinhart. "This will be a successful trip. If you can stand still now, a hundred will go into the pail."

When dawn came, Reinhart said, "I'll tell you something: I am

afraid that we shall have to pay dearly for our plenty. I am sorry
there are so many fish in the pail, but I don't know what to do
about it now. I don't believe you can lift them. Try to get them
out." Isengrin began to jerk, but his tail was fast in the ice and
wouldn't budge.

"I'll go and bring the brothers at once," said Reinhart. "We can
all profit from this prize." It was rapidly becoming light when
Reinhart left, and Isengrin the Fisher got some very bad news that
turned his sport to sorrow. He saw a knight following his trail
with dogs. It was Sir Birtin, a terror to all beasts, who was pur-
suing him, which turned out badly for Isengrin. When the hunter
caught sight of him, he called to his dogs, "At him!" and urged
them on. They began to tear at Isengrin, who, badly frightened,
started biting in all directions. Sir Birtin galloped up, drew his
sword, and quickly dismounted. Then he ran awkwardly onto the
ice and raised the sword.

This added to Isengrin's dismay. He had taken on too heavy a
load, which caused him grief. We hear wise people say that
whoever picks up more than he can carry must abandon it along
the way. Sir Isengrin now had to do this. He was attacked from
all sides. Sir Birtin took aim at Isengrin's back, but his feet slipped,
he fell, and the blow went astray. Undeterred, he quickly got to
his knees. However his swing had been so deflected that the blade
struck Isengrin's tail and cut it off. Both were deeply distressed.
Sir Birtin complained bitterly because he had missed, while Sir
Isengrin lamented the loss of his beloved tail, which he had to
leave behind as a forfeit as he ran away.

Reinhart, who had often deceived others, today was deceived
himself, but his cleverness helped him out of great trouble. His
path took him to a monastery farm where he knew many chickens
were, yet he gained nothing by this because there was a good wall
around it. He went along the wall until he came to a gate in front
of which was a well that was deep and wide. Reinhart looked in,
which he later regretted, and saw his own image. A surprising
thing now happened, for he whose guile had done such wonders
was fooled here. Reinhart thought he saw his wife—who was as
dear to him as his own self—and could not keep from going to
her, because love makes one brave. That's why it seemed good to
him. He laughed into the well, and the image bared its teeth. He

owed it no thanks since this led him to jump in for joy. Reinhart made the leap because of his great love, and got wet up to the ears.

He swam around for a long time before finding a stone on which he could rest his head. Who doesn't believe it, doesn't need to give [the storyteller] anything. Reinhart was thinking that the leap had indeed cost him his life when Isengrin, without his tail, came from the forest and hurried toward the farm. You must know that he had not yet eaten and wanted to catch a sheep. He didn't find one and now came past the deep well, where the fool was tricked. Listen to what happened to Isengrin when he looked in. He saw his image and thought it was his loved one, Lady Hersant. At once he put his head down and smiled, and the image smiled back. This misled him, and he began to tell her of the shame he had suffered and to bewail his injury. Isengrin howled loudly, and his voice answered him as it resounded in the well, which, as was soon clear, also contained much rascality.

"Who is that?" asked Reinhart. Isengrin was duped again.

"Is it you, friend Reinhart?" he replied. "Tell me, for God's sake, what you are doing in there."

"My body is dead," said Reinhart, "and my soul lives in peace. You may be sure of that. I am here in heaven where I am in charge of this school. I can teach the children well."

"I am sorry about your death," said Isengrin.

"I am glad. In the world you endure troubles every single day, while in paradise I have much greater joys than one can imagine."

"My brother and kinsman," asked Isengrin, "how did Lady Hersant get there? I have never taken any plunder without giving her part of it."

"It was her good fortune," answered Reinhart.

"Tell me, dear kinsman," said Isengrin then, "how did her head get so burned?"

"That happened to me also, dear comrade. She ducked into hell. You have often heard indeed that no one can enter paradise without getting a taste of hell. That is where she lost the hide and hair." Reinhart wanted to get out. Isengrin saw his eyes and asked, "Tell me, kinsman, what is shining there?"

"Those are jewels," answered Reinhart at once, "splendid carbuncles that shine here day and night. Out there you don't see any such things. Cattle, swine, and many fat kids are in here too, all running around unguarded. We have many kinds of food."

"Could I ever come in?" asked the foolish Isengrin.

"Yes, just do as I tell you. I shall win praise through you. Now use your wits: sit down in the pail." The well was so made that when one pail went down the other went up. Isengrin did as his kinsman said and, after facing toward the east, got in the pail. This showed a lack of sense. Reinhart did not forget to climb into the other one. Isengrin, who was the loser, passed his kinsman on the way down.

"Reinhart, where am I?" he cried.

"I tell you truly that I'll be glad to let you have my seat in heaven, because I want to go home. To the devil with you!" Reinhart set out for the forest, and Isengrin went to the bottom. He would have been in dire straits if the well had not been almost empty. Nevertheless he thought paradise disagreeable and would gladly have been far away.

Since the monks needed water, one of them went to the well. He quickly took a turn on the windlass and found the load much heavier than ever before. When he leaned over the well to learn what was wrong, he saw Isengrin at the bottom, sitting in the pail. The brother did not linger, but ran back to the monastery as fast as he could and hurriedly told his strange tale: that Isengrin was in the well. He knew, for he had seen him.

"This is the vengeance of God," declared the monks and set out for the well. The prior took a long, heavy pole, and another man had a candle stick: things looked bad for Isengrin. There was a lot of noise.

"Everyone be careful that he doesn't get away," they cried. They turned the windlass and quickly pulled up the stupid Isengrin. The prior almost killed him. Isengrin suffered this because Reinhart had deceived him. Truly Reinhart played many spiteful tricks on him. What was he thinking of to let himself be duped so often? The world then was just as it is now, and many men overcame their difficulties with deceit better than those who acted uprightly. It has been like this a long time. A lot of people today say dishonesty is quite new. God knows that some folks, both young and old, have such manifold hardships that they think these things never happened to anyone before. None of us suffer more from treachery than others of whom we have heard.

Isengrin was so severely beaten they thought he was dead. However, when the prior caught sight of the bare spot on his head, he said to the monks, "We have done wrong. I see a tonsure, and I can tell you something more: this wolf has been circumcised according to Old Testament law. Oh! If only we had spared him these blows, for indeed he was a penitent."

"We would have been happy if we had noticed sooner," replied the monks. Then they departed. Had Isengrin not lost his tail and the hair on his head this troop of God's men would have hung him. Whatever misfortune happened to Sir Walther von Horburg, he always used to say bravely, "It is as likely to turn out to my advantage as to cause me grief." So it was with Isengrin.

When the monks left him, he crept to the forest and at once began to howl. Lady Hersant and his sons came as soon as they heard him, and he told them of his distress. "Dear wife and sons," he lamented, "Reinhart's counsel has cost me my life. For God's sake, feel for me! For no reason at all Reinhart caused me to lose my tail and lured me to my death. His great treachery brought me many kicks and blows." His godson threatened vengeance on Reinhart, and their friendship was at an end. They all kept wailing loudly until Isengrin had had enough.

"Lady Hersant, my dear wife," he exclaimed, "why are you harming your beauty so? Your weeping pains me. For God's sake, don't do it any more!"

"Oh! Oh! I can't do without it. I am distressed that my husband has no tail. Poor me, how will I ever get over it?" A feud was begun, and Isengrin trotted forth to waylay Reinhart. The latter went to his lookout post, for whoever undertakes a feud with insufficient arms must depend on clever stratagems. This is how their hostility began.

A lynx soon heard of this enmity and was greatly troubled by it. He was the offspring of a fox and a wolf, which is why he was concerned.

"Dear kinsman," he said to Isengrin, "with what do you charge my cousin? You are both of my family, and I would be glad to act as arbiter. If you will tell me your grievance, a hearing will be arranged, and Reinhart will have to make amends for whatever he has done to you."

"Listen, my dear cousin," answered Sir Isengrin, "it would take a long time to tell, because I have many grievances for injuries I have suffered from him. It is his fault that I have no tail, and he tried to seduce my wife. If he were innocent of the latter, I would forget about the other. However I can't refuse you and will accept your invitation to a trial." It was announced that a hearing would be held in three weeks.

Sir Isengrin brought with him many of his relatives. I shall name some of them, whom you no doubt will know: the elephant and the bison, who seemed giants to Isengrin; the stag Randolt and the doe, both of whom liked him; and the bear Brun and the wild swine, who were also on his side. The large beasts there—I don't need to name them all—stood by Isengrin, but they would have been better off elsewhere. Reinhart was accompanied by Crimel, a badger, who helped him then and never forsook him in need as long as they lived. The hare and the wren came, as well as a great many little creatures I shall not name.

Following Sir Brun's advice, Isengrin had made a wise decision: he had brought along Sir Reize, a fierce dog, on whose teeth Reinhart was to deny his guilt. They had told Reize to lie as if dead and almost outwitted Reinhart, who himself used so many tricks. Crimel saw where Reize was lying and said, "Listen to me, Reinhart, for I am telling the truth and you won't be able to reproach me: Reize will kill you. If your foot comes in front of his mouth, you will never recover."

Then the lynx, who had summoned them there, said to Reinhart, "Now consider how you will convince Isengrin before us all that you did not try to seduce his wife."

"By God," he replied, "he will soon agree that I have cleared myself. If only the world were as free of treachery as I have always been." Reinhart went to confer with his kinsmen. He asked them to step aside with him and said, "Do you know what I saw? Reize is alive. May God preserve you all: I'm going to leave." And he set out for the open country.

"See, Reinhart is running away!" cried many wild beasts. Isengrin became very angry and started after him, but Lady Hersant was running far ahead of her husband, which was a bad mistake. She wanted to kill her lover in order to prove her innocence and gain Isengrin's favor. However Reinhart knew all sorts of knavish schemes. He shrewdly brushed his tail across the mouth of his ladylove as he headed for his castle, a fine badger hole in which his race still takes refuge. He escaped into it, and Lady Hersant dashed in right behind him, as far as her hips. Then she couldn't get in or out. She soon had to suffer disgrace, because Reinhart took note of his good fortune, ran out another opening, and sprang onto her. Isengrin was sorely grieved by what happened now, for he saw her raped.

"My very dear friend," said Reinhart, "you should stay all day with me. God willing, no one will know, and I'll gladly keep silent for the sake of your honor." Lady Hersant was greatly ashamed and bit the stone angrily, but her strength availed her little. When he saw Isengrin running up in a rage, Reinhart added, "I had better leave," and went back in. Isengrin was followed by his two sons and soon by many fierce beasts, who later could testify to the rape of his dear wife. Lady Hersant was pulled out by her hind legs, and Isengrin began to weep. "Reinhart has often deceived me," he lamented, "but I would let it all go if it were not for the evil deed I have just seen: this is too much."

Reinhart went to the entrance and said, "I have done nothing to you. My kinswoman wanted to come in, and I told her that she was welcome. I'll let my godson decide whether I have harmed you."

"Truly," replied the latter, "I can't mediate any longer, but must be your enemy. You will die if I get my hands on you."

"No, no, godson!" exclaimed Reinhart, "that would be an evil deed that would never be forgiven as long as you live. We must be chained together for all time."

"Lady Hersant," said Isengrin, "it has indeed now been seven years since our marriage. Many handsome beasts of our two families were there, and since then we have shared many joys. Now Reinhart has dishonored us. Oh, that he was ever godfather to our child. I can never be happy about it." Lady Hersant then wept and embraced Isengrin, so too did his sons. Theirs was the shame. They all then trotted off angrily.

"Good friend," called Reinhart, "my dear Sir Isengrin, you should remain the rest of the day. But if you must go, you might at least leave my lady friend. She rightly should be mistress here." Sir Isengrin did not answer.

This took place during a public peace that a lion, Frevel by name, had proclaimed under threat of execution. He ruled the land,

and no beast was so strong that it would not have had to come before his court of justice. Except for God, he was their complete master, whom they all obeyed. His own distress caused him to decree the peace, for he firmly believed he carried grim death in him. I'll tell you how it happened.

Frevel once went to an army of ants, ordered them to stand still, and told them something they did not know: that he was their lord. When they would not accept him, he became angry, leaped with rage onto their castle, and attacked the little creatures. He thought it his duty. More than a thousand died and many were seriously wounded, but there were also many who remained unharmed. He fiercely vented his wrath on them and leveled their castle. Then, after doing them untold harm, he went his way. The ants began to lament the great injury caused them in the loss of their kinfolk. There was no joy among them; it was a sorrowful day.

When the lord of the castle, a frightful ant, came out of the woods, he heard the sad story: that his citizens had suffered this terrible wrong.

"Who did this to you?" he demanded. Those who were still alive loudly bewailed their trouble. "It was because of our loyalty," they said. "Frevel told us we were to be subject to him, but we wanted no lord except you and therefore had to take the consequences. He tore down the castle and killed many of our kin. We shall be completely dishonored if that is not avenged."

"I would rather die," said the lord and at once started after the lion. He found him sleeping under a linden tree and ran up to him fiercely.

"Good God," thought the ant, "how shall I avenge my people? If I kill him, I won't be able to carry him away." He thought for a while and then leaped with all his force into Frevel's ear: this caused the king distress. Reinhart was hiding close by and watching.

It is said that one is not wise to disdain his enemy. The ant went straight to the brain, and the lion was in serious trouble. He sprang up startled. "Merciful God!" he cried. "What evil is this? Oh, that I have neglected the exercise of justice! That is why I am in this sad state. But it will never happen again." The lion roared loudly, and many beasts heard him. They hurried up and asked, "What has happened to you?"

"I must confess that I am in pain," he answered. "I am sure that God is punishing me for neglecting justice." He at once ordered a court session, and messengers were quickly despatched to all parts of the empire. It was to be held in a certain meadow in six weeks. No one objected. A strong and imposing throne was obtained that cost more than a thousand marks.

I'll tell you who came. The first, so I have heard, were the panther, the elephant, the ostrich, and the well-known bison. The court got quite large with the arrival of the sable and the marten, the fleet leopard (who was wearing a crest), the hart and the bear, the mouse and the mole, the lynx and the roe, the wren and the gray squirrel, the goat and the ram. The ibex hurried down from the mountains; the hare, the wild swine, the otter, and the marmot came from the forest; even the camel appeared. The beaver, a band of hedgehogs, the ermine, and the squirrel would not have wanted to miss the court—nor would the aurochs and Kunin, the stallion and Baldwin, Reize, and the seal, Crimel, and many beasts I know nothing about and cannot name. Hersant, Isengrin, and his sons also came. Reinhart was not there, but nevertheless was to bring distress to his enemies.

The king opened the session at once with an order for silence. Then Isengrin made a plea for justice and asked for an advocate. He was assigned one, Brun the Bear, who began, "My lord, in accordance with the law and by your grace, Isengrin requests he be permitted to change counselors if I do not represent him properly."

"That will be granted," said the king.

"Mighty lord and king, Sir Isengrin complains to you of pain and disgrace in that he now stands before you without a tail. He is greatly shamed by this, and it was Reinhart's doing. Moreover, his noble wife, Lady Hersant, was dishonored against her will by Reinhart during the public peace you decreed under threat of execution."

Crimel then sprang forward and said, "Mighty king, hear me also. This statement is not credible and may well be a deliberate falsehood. How could my cousin assault her since she is larger than he? However, if love caused him to lie with her, it would not be surprising, for such things happen all the time. Yet no one here knew of it. Now tell me, Lady Hersant, why is your husband spreading scandal about you? That must be painful for you. He is also bringing shame on his children, these handsome youths. The charges I have heard are frivolous. I tell you truly, lord and king, listen to his injuries being examined, and if Reinhart has harmed Sir Isengrin's wife by so much as a lentil, I will accept the punishment in my kinsman's stead."

Isengrin spoke again. "I tell you, my lords," he lamented, "the injuries do not trouble me half as much as the disgrace." The king then asked the hart to make a decision under oath as to what was just in the matter.

"Sir Isengrin has been wronged beyond measure," stated Randolt. "No one can deny it. And he should not have to suffer from Reinhart's guile. Sir, it must be offensive to you. Is he to dishonor a noble woman and live? For shame! I condemn him and swear that I do so only because that is my best judgment. You should besiege him and, if you can capture him, order that he be hanged without delay. You thus will have done what will honor you."

The king himself was angry. "Do you lords agree?" he asked. They all said, "Yes," one after the other and were eager to make the assault on Reinhart. No one objected but a camel from Thuschalan who was wise, upright, and gray with age. She bowed low and said, "Sir King, listen also to me. I hear many good men saying what to me seems wrong. Perhaps they don't understand the matter well enough. On my oath I am right in maintaining to you that, if a man is accused here at court in his absence, he should be told about it and summoned three times. Should he not appear, he has harmed himself and has forfeited his life. I declare this under oath." Isengrin was unhappy at this, but all the other beasts, large and small, quickly agreed with the camel. And so it was decided.

Just then Schantecler and Lady Pinte appeared. They were bewailing their daughter who lay dead on the bier they were carrying: the red Reinhart had killed her that very day. The bier was placed before the king, who was embarrassed. However Isengrin was pleased.

Schantecler began a loud complaint. "King," he cried, "hear what I have to say. You should know that Reinhart truly scorns your authority and has taken pains to show it. Oh! Oh! He has killed my lovely daughter." The lament sorely troubled the mighty king, and he spoke angrily, "By my beard, it is certain that Reinhart the Fox must leave this country or die by my hand."

The hare saw the king's wrath, and the timid fellow thought he was lost: fear caused him to be seized by a fever. Hares are still like that. The king ordered his chaplain, Sir Brun, to go with his pupils and sing a mass. Then the dead one was quickly buried. The hare lay down on the grave and went to sleep. He was very pleased at this, and I must tell you why: it made his fever go down. However, suddenly he started up, hurried straight to the king, and told him that the chicken was a saint before God's face. When the people were told of this, they all maintained it was a sign and began to sing a hymn.

No one was thankful to Reinhart. On the contrary, all of them asked the mighty king to avenge the crime at once. "God has performed a miracle in our midst," they said. "Reinhart should never have martyred this saint who had never done anything wrong."

The king told his chaplain to go after Reinhart, a task which Sir Brun would very much have liked to decline. However he did as the king commanded and set off into the forest. Reinhart was full of guile, and the whole country had to suffer for it. Brun found him in front of his castle, which was in a large rock and protected him well from his enemies. It is still called "the evil cave." Reinhart knew how to receive the chaplain of the mighty king.

"Welcome, noble cleric," he said. "Tell me how things are at court. I know that you are the king's counselor."

"Serious charges have been brought against you. If you are concerned about your honor, come forth and defend yourself. I have been sent to bring you."

"Sir Chaplain," replied Reinhart, "let us go eat first. Then we shall be better able to journey to the court. I know a tree that is full of honey." Reinhart was not very trustworthy.

"Fine, come on," was the answer, "I always liked that." Sir Brun then went with Reinhart, who led him to where a peasant had forced a log open with a wedge. The devil must have put it there.

"My dear friend," said Reinhart, "we shall share equally. However be careful, for there are many bees in it." Brun didn't hold back because of bees, but stuck his head right into the log. Reinhart jerked out the wedge, the log snapped together, and the chaplain was caught. The meal might have seemed to him too long.

"Ow! Ow!" cried Brun.

"Why are you acting like that?" asked Reinhart. "I warned you beforehand. Still the bees really don't hurt much. Eat all you want. The king is indeed rich enough to pay me for it." With this he hurried off.

The chaplain began to wail. Then he heard a wagon coming, became very frightened, and pulled away as hard as he could. When the driver caught sight of him, he didn't say a word until he got back to the village. Once there he ran to the church and seized the bell ropes. He rang the bells so loudly the sound filled the village and all of the peasants gathered. The driver told them a bear had been caught without the skill of a master huntsman.

"The power of God did it," he said, "and I can easily lead you there." Everyone started out, women as well as men, for this was a dangerous matter. Then a conceited dandy came at Brun with a pole. The chaplain heard the commotion and was terrified. He quickly braced his feet against the log and pulled himself free, but both ears and much skin were left behind. The messenger departed at once: he had not enjoyed the honey.

Listen to some strange mockery. Reinhart was sitting in front of his castle and had not forgotten how to be a rascal. Just hear what he said when he saw Brun's bare head: "Good evening, Sir Chaplain, where have you left your skin? Did you pawn it for wine? Oh, that would disgrace me! You would say at court that I was a poor host." Sir Brun could not talk for rage and only glared fiercely at him. He came to the court bald and lamenting loudly. All the beasts crowded around and looked at the broad tonsure while the chaplain bewailed his boundless grief to his king.

"Reinhart did this to me!" he exclaimed. "I summoned him for you, and see, dear lord, to what distress he has brought me. I would rather be dead." Troubled and angry at the fate of his chaplain, the king at once asked the beaver what should be done about it.

"Sir, I know this—and will take an oath that I am impartial and swear on my honor that there is nothing to oppose my view—I would deprive Reinhart of life and property and place under the ban anyone who gives him aid. These lords can all agree to this."

"That is right," said Randolt. "Many nobles will agree."

"I won't," the elephant spoke up vexed. "A decision has already been made, as you all heard, and no one can change it: he is to be summoned three times. May the devil enter the mouth of him who doesn't keep his oath, whether he intends to help or to harm someone." They all assented, for he was right. This was to cause trouble for Sir Dieprecht.

The king had him step forward and then told him to go after Reinhart.

"Sir, I don't know the law," protested Dieprecht quickly, "and he is a relative of mine."

"You cannot be excused for any reason," stated Randolt. "Moreover, you two aren't friends." At this the king ordered him to go on pain of death.

"Since I have to, I will," said Dieprecht and set out at once. He found his cousin (who had many evil traits) in the forest. Now listen to what Reinhart said when he saw him: "Welcome, kinsman! I am sorely grieved that you have neglected me. I was never so happy to receive a guest."

"Thank you," replied Dieprecht. "It also seems very long to me. The king sends me to you and swears you will have to leave the country if you do not appear before him. Everyone is bringing charges against you. You made a bad mistake when you sent his chaplain back without some of his skin."

"My good cousin," said Reinhart, "I haven't seen Brun this year except for when Sir Isengrin chased me. What do you say, cousin, won't you come with me? I'll be glad to give you what I have. I've got a large house here and keep many mice in it for my guests. You may select the best." However, Reinhart betrayed his kinsman.

The night was bright as he led Dieprecht—who was looking forward to the meal—to the house. In it lived a priest who had suffered much from Reinhart, and Dieprecht was to pay for it. The priest had set a snare in front of a hole, as people still do. He was after Reinhart but caught his cousin, who barely escaped with his life. Dieprecht hurried into the snare and was trapped. The peasant's housekeeper heard the noise and cried, "Get up! By God, we've caught the fox that has done us so much harm."

The holy clergyman leaped up startled, seized a linchpin, and ran to where he found Dieprecht, whom he thought was Reinhart. Dieprecht regretted having come and howled loudly, but, because of the darkness, the priest missed, cutting the snare in two. Dieprecht was ready to leave and ran at once. The housekeeper inside became very angry and struck the priest on the ear. Then she got a piece of firewood and beat him black and blue. Had it not been for Werenburg, his mistress, she would have killed him.

"God gave Reinhart into my hands," she cried, "and you took him away from me."

"Lady," replied the thrashed clergyman, "I had bad luck. Now be kind to me."

Dieprecht left the mice there and quickly departed. With great effort he ran all night and was back at the court by morning. He went to the king with the snare and bitterly accused Reinhart.

"King," he said, "I was in great danger. Reinhart tried to get me killed while I was acting as your messenger, but God protected me. Sir, your chaplain and I must not go to Reinhart again."

Troubled by the complaint and tormented by his illness, the king was furious. He asked the boar how he would decide the matter of his messengers, Brun and Dieprecht, being so unjustly treated.

"I would condemn him to proscription and loss of honor and property," he replied angrily, "his wife to being a widow, and his children to being orphans."

"I agree with that," said Isengrin. The king then asked all of them, the wise and the foolish, whether they concurred. Crimel did not hesitate.

"Kind and noble king," he said, "my cousin is not to blame for Sir Brun's losing his skin, and he has no right to be angry. It is quite possible that Sir Dieprecht too is wrong, for he hates Reinhart. Therefore no one should propose a sentence—not for any bribe—that would dishonor you and so degrade your court that people elsewhere would laugh at it, because my cousin should be summoned one more time."

"You yourself shall be the courier," declared the king. "I so order you on pain of death. If God wills, your cousin will give you a messenger's reward." All had to laugh, but Crimel was not worried. He quickly entered the forest and sought out his kinsman. Now listen to the strange and unusual things that the Dissembler tells us, for they are true. His name is Heinrich, and he is the one who composed the book about Isengrin's troubles. However, he will not force his account on anyone who thinks it false. Now let us return to our story.

Crimel arrived at Reinhart's castle, and its master was very pleased to see him.

"Welcome cousin," he said with a smile. "Tell me what complaints they are making about me at court."

"The mighty king has heard serious charges against you," answered Crimel, "and has threatened you fiercely. If you do not appear before him today, you must leave the country or die at once. But if you do come before the court in Isengrin's presence, all the people will condemn you."

"That won't keep me away," replied Reinhart. "I'll never be found guilty." With this they sat down and ate. As soon as they were finished, Reinhart hurried into his bedroom and got out his court apparel—a traveling coat of linen, the best he had—and slipped it on. He picked up a physician's bag and walked as if he were carrying boxes of cloves and cinnamon and were a doctor: no one could ever tell you how cunning he was. Indeed he did have many unfamiliar herbs with him. Then he took a staff in hand and, leaving the forest, set out for the court with his cousin.

"God protect me from evil liars," he said, crossing himself, "so that they may not trouble me."

When they approached the court, many a frightful beast cried out, "You can now see something strange. Here comes Reinhart, who has treated many beasts shamefully and is Lady Hersant's lover. No one should complain if both of them were hung from a limb. Why did she have anything to do with the villain?"

They had a right to denounce him angrily, although Sir Isengrin sorely regretted that his wife was subjected to this scorn.

"He caused me suffering, too," added the chaplain.

"Lord and king," exclaimed Dieprecht, "see how he stands there, the one who has insulted you so! Now don't let him get away from you. You should have him hanged, for he is indeed a traitor."

Schantecler grieved for his child. "King," he lamented, "we know indeed that you are our lawful ruler. We therefore find it painful that you should let this murderer stand there. He ought to be hanged at once."

"Lord," said Dizelin the Raven, "hang my cousin."

However Reinhart was very clever. "King," he said, "what is all this noise? I have been at many courts, but have never seen such bad manners. I truly feel sorry for you."

"You are right," replied the king, and further outcries were forbidden.

"Mighty king," continued Reinhart, "Master Pendin, a physician of Salerno, offers his service and says that he wishes he could see your majesty and also all those here, young and old. Lord you have a sickness which they cannot cure, and I therefore went to Salerno because I wanted to help you recover. I know that your trouble, whatever it might be, is in the head. Master Pendin sends word that you should take, every day without fail, this electuary he has sent you."

"I'll do it," answered the king at once and let his anger slip away.

"In these seven weeks," said Reinhart, "I have gotten many a thorn in my feet, which pain me sorely—the physician also says that, if you can find an old wolf, you should have him flayed, and that you must likewise have the skin of a bear."

"That will be the chaplain," stated the king.

"These will cure you, noble lord—but you must get a cat skin too, at any cost, or you will surely die."

The king then had Isengrin and his chaplain come forward and said, "You must give me your skins: I will reward your families for this at all times as long as I live. Master Reinhart has told me what to do about the illness that constantly troubles my head."

"Mercy, lord," begged the chaplain. "What strange deed are you going to commit? God knows that he whom you consider a doctor has killed many more than he has healed and, moreover, has been condemned before you."

"It would be a terrible thing," said Isengrin, "if I were to be thus compensated for the crime against my wife. See how your physician has disgraced me behind," he added, showing the stump of his tail. "The like could happen also to you."

Sir Brun and Sir Isengrin wished they were somewhere else, but that was not to be. They could not escape. The king ordered many of his strong servants to seize them, and they were flayed. Dieprecht too suffered this cruel fate. It was all because of Reinhart, who now said, "That's fine, but we also need a boiled hen and some good bacon from a boar."

"It must be Lady Pinte," said the king and ordered Schantecler to step forward.

"I need your wife for a remedy," he declared.

"No, no, lord!" cried Schantecler. "I love her as myself. Eat me and let her go!"

"That cannot be," said Reinhart. Schantecler hurried away as the king commanded that Pinte be seized. When this was done, they cut a large piece out of the thigh of the boar, who thought the remedy quite a burden.

"We still must have a thong from a deer," said Reinhart, and the king had the hart come before him.

"Randolt, you must give me a strip of your hide: I shall always be grateful to you."

"For God's sake, spare me, my lord. The whole world will find it laughable that you should listen to one here who has never been trustworthy. It was the devil who taught him to be a doctor."

"I was always very fond of you, Randolt. If I were to die through your fault, you would never get over it." The hart did not dare refuse the king and had to give up a strip of skin from his nose to his tail. Reinhart was a calamity for all of them.

"King," said the wonderworker, "if you were a poor man, I could not help you. As it is, through the grace of God, we have everything needed to make you well, provided that you take my advice."

"Master," replied the king, "I shall do whatever you say."

Reinhart knew many tunes. "My Master Pendin," he continued, "desires no reward from you except a beaver pelt."

"He shall have it," answered the mighty king. "I will surely send him one." He then commanded the beaver to come forward and give up his skin. Many beasts saw this and said to each other, "What are we doing here? We had better go before we lose our skins." They left at once, and the court melted away. Crimel remained there, as did the camel from Thuschalan and the elephant who had given the good advice: the doctor had them both stay. The others departed quickly, leaving the king alone with his retinue.

Reinhart now asked the king to order a bath brought to him. The king did so at once, and the leopard had to manage it somehow. I tell you truly that a tub of water soon appeared, and good servants warmed it to just the temperature that Master Reinhart wanted. They would have grieved at their lord's death. The doctor put a lot of herbs in the water, carefully wrapped the cat skin around the king's head, and had him sit down in the bath. Soon he felt a vein that led to his patient's heart and said, "King, you may well rejoice, for you will recover. You were close to death, but my skill is healing you. Now get out; you have bathed as much as you should. A long bath makes an invalid weak, and you have already gotten a little pale."

The king felt sick and answered like a man who was eager to get well, "I'll gladly follow your orders." So Reinhart bedded him down on the pelt of the chaplain who had been very dear to him and covered him warmly—God help us—with a skin that Isengrin had worn, and had lost through no fault of his own. Reinhart had been very clever. He had made the king's head so hot that the ant noticed it and crawled out, straight into the cat hair. Then the master took this hat to the light and let the sun shine in. It was a great success: he saw the ant.

"Ant, you shall die!" he exclaimed angrily. "You have caused my lord great distress, and that will cost you your life."

"I had to," replied the ant, "because the king destroyed a splendid castle of mine and caused me such great sorrow I can never cease to lament: many of my kinfolk were slain there. That is why I did it. If you will let me live, you shall be lord of a thousand castles here in my forest." This made sense to Reinhart, and he freed his prisoner at once. The ant set out happily for the forest, but he would have died had he not paid the ransom. Such things happen every day. Whoever can give a bribe can achieve more with it than the one who tries to fulfill his lord's command with service. God help us! Reinhart then went back to the invalid.

He felt the king's forehead and asked, "How is your brain now?"

"Fine, master. May God reward you! You have treated my case very well."

"We shall do still more. Does anyone know whether the hen was cooked with parsley?"

"Yes, it was," said a lord high steward who stood nearby.

"Then have it brought here to me." This was done and Reinhart ordered his lord to drink the broth. Lady Pinte was not forgotten, however, for the doctor ate her himself. The treacherous glutton thereupon gave the boar's bacon to Crimel and ordered the king to stand up and walk around a bit. Afterwards he urged the king to invest his friend the elephant with a land.

"That shall be done," replied the king. "He shall have Bohemia." This made the elephant very happy. The king commanded him to receive the fief formally, then the good knight departed. He had come there as a poor man and gained the office of a prince. However when the elephant rode into the land to which the king had sent him and announced that he was its lord, he was sorely beaten and left in sadness. If his skin had not been so thick, they would have killed him.

Reinhart was not satisfied with his malice in setting the elephant over a country, but began to petition the king urgently on behalf of his judge, the camel.

"I want to do something for her," he said. "Let her be the abbess at Erstein. Then your soul will be saved, because a lot of praying is done there." The king was very glad to do this. She found great favor with him, and he invested her with his right hand: she was certain that she would be a rich abbess. After taking leave of the king, she sprang merrily across the court, thanked Reinhart for her new-found wealth, and departed at once. Later this caused her trouble. As soon as she arrived at the cloister, all those who heard about her came quickly, looked her over with great interest, and asked who she was.

"Indeed I am to proclaim a message to you," she said. "The mighty king has invested me with this fief and made it mine. I am to be the abbess here."

The nuns took this as an insult, which almost cost the camel her life. They raised a loud clamor and beat her almost to death. They also caused her great distress with stylus's, as her hide revealed, and chased her into the Rhine. Thus did Reinhart reward his defender. It is true also today that whoever helps a dishonest man out of his troubles finds him still deceitful. This must happen many times, for we have seen it often enough. This was the way Reinhart served his judges.

The doctor had not yet exhausted his deceit—he knew many evil tricks—and soon betrayed the king.

"My lord," he said, "I shall give you a potion that will cure you at once."

"Do so," replied the king.

Then he brewed the king's death. Reinhart was wicked and treacherous, which was clear to see, for he poisoned his lord. No one should lament this too much: what did he expect from Reinhart? It is too bad, God knows, that many dissemblers are more highly regarded at court than is a man who has always been loyal.

If a lord chooses to follow their counsel and they cause his death, that is good news. Unfortunately evil liars constantly push themselves forward, while the faithful remain outside the door.

When the potion was given to the king, Reinhart explained that he wanted to go after some herbs and departed. He did nothing more in that place, but plied his arts elsewhere. Taking his dear kinsman, Crimel, by the hand, he said, "Let me tell you something: the king may not recover. We must not remain here any longer." At once they set out together for the forest. There Reinhart saw Sir Brun, the chaplain, without his skin. Listen to what he said.

"Tell me, noble cleric, how is it that you are not wearing your skin? Was it too heavy? I'll tell you the truth: it seems to me that anybody who wants you to act as his advocate in winter should lend you a pelt. He can't refuse you one, for you will need it. Oh, my! Who has taken your skin?

Sir Brun was not at all pleased to see Reinhart and could not speak for anger. Although his wrath was great, he only growled furiously to himself as Reinhart left him and went on to his castle.

Meanwhile the king was beginning to feel severe pain. "Where is Master Reinhart?" he asked. "Have him come quickly. I don't know what sort of illness is attacking me. It has struck right at my heart. He is an excellent doctor and can drive it away with the good herbs he has."

When they had searched for him, the king was distressed to hear the sad news that the master had departed. "I am sorry that I ever saw Reinhart," he exclaimed tearfully. "It will cost me my life, because he has poisoned me, and for no reason: I never harmed him. His advice led me to have my noble chaplain flayed. I must admit that he who relies on a traitor will suffer, for it has now happened also to me."

The king then turned to the wall and died: his head played him a three and his tongue curled to a nine. They could not keep from weeping at the death of the noble king, and all of them fiercely threatened the good Reinhart. Whether this story be true or not, may God give us a wonderful life!

Here the tale ends. Sir Heinrich the Dissembler composed it but did not rhyme it well. This was done later by another—who knows how to make good verses—and in such a manner that the story itself remained just as it was, although he said more in some lines than had appeared before and shortened others that had too many words. Let those who would now reward him pray that God may grant him happiness as long as he lives and then send his soul to where it will have joy without end. Amen.

Translated by J. W. Thomas

The Reward of the World

Konrad von Würzburg

You lovers of the world hear this tale how a knight who strove after the world's reward from morning until night achieved success! Often he thought about just what he could do in order to attain the reward of worldly honor and he knew well how to increase his praise in many places through deeds and words. He was so accomplished he was held to be among the best in all the German lands. He had kept himself from disgrace all the years of his life; he was courteous and well-bred, handsome and virtuous. Whatever a man should have in the world in order to pursue the highest praise, the wise nobleman knew how to get. This excellent man was often seen wearing the finest of garments. Further, he was greatly skilled and often engaged in the stalking of game, falconry, and the chase. The chessboard and the lyre were his recreation. If the path to chivalric combat were shown to him—even more than one hundred miles away!—the nobleman would have ridden there courageously and resolutely and would have fought there gladly in hope of precious love's reward. He was so devoted to the ladies—who were of good manner—and served them with such longlasting constancy throughout all his years that all blissful women commended and praised this delightful man. As the books instruct and I have found written of him, he was called Sir Wirnt of Gravenberg. He had performed worldly deeds all his life and his heart passionately desired love, both secret and open.

Thus the celebrated man sat in a chamber well provided with amusements and held a book in his hand, wherein he found a tale

114

written about love. With it he passed the day until vespers and his
delight with the sweet story he was reading was very great. As he
was sitting thus, there came to him a woman after his heart's desire and adorned to perfection according to his own ideal, so lovely
in appearance that never was seen a more beautiful woman. Her
beauty set her completely apart from all the ladies there are now.
Indeed, a more lovely child never glided from woman's breast. I
swear by my baptism that she was far more beautiful than Venus
or Pallas and all the goddesses who cultivated love before. Both
her countenance and her complexion were gleaming like a mirror.
Her beauty gave forth such a bright light and delightful glow that
the palace itself was illuminated by her. Perfection had spared none
of its craft and had used its best powers on her. Whatever one
says about beautiful women, she surpassed all; there was never a
lovelier woman beheld on earth. She also was attired in great
splendor. The clothes and the crown this same fine lady wore upon
and above her body was so glorious that truly no one could afford
them, even if one would find them for sale.

Sir Wirnt of Gravenberg drew back from her in awe—probably
twice!—as she came stealing in. His complexion grew very pale
upon her arrival. He wondered greatly why the lady had come.
Up jumped the amiable man frightened and pale and he received
the beautiful one very graciously, as he well knew how to do. He
spoke pleasantly, "Be most welcome, lady! As much as I have seen
of ladies, you surpass them all completely." The lady answered
courteously, "Dear friend, may God reward you! Be not so afraid
of me, for I am the very same lady whom you have served for a
long while and whom you still serve willingly. Even though you
stand before me terrified, I am yet the very same woman for whom
you have often risked body and soul. Because your heart has joy
on account of me, it does not grow weary. You have been courtly
and noble all your years; your worthy body, sweet and without
fault, has fought for me and has told and sung whatever good it
knows of me. You have always been my vassal, both morning and
night, and you always knew how to strive for the highest com-
mendation and worthy praise. You blossom like a sprig of May in
many and varied virtues. Since childhood you have borne the gar-
land of honor and you have always been constant and true in your
loyalty to me. Thus, most noble and worthy knight I have come

here so you may view to your heart's content my body of excellent
quality both front and back and see how beautiful I am, how perfect. You will see the high reward and rich prize you can receive
from me for your noble service and you will consider it. I have
been so well served by you that I will gladly let you ponder what
reward shall be your due." The noble lord wondered greatly about
the woman's words. For the youth had never before seen her with
his eyes and yet the lady had said he was her devoted vassal. He
said, "If you please, my lady. If I have served you, I am, upon my
oath, not aware of it. Indeed, I do not believe I have ever seen you
before. But since you wish, good woman, to declare me your vassal, my heart and body are ready to serve you with willing travail
as long as I live. You have such grace and virtue that your joy-
bringing youth can reward me very well. Lucky me that I have
lived this day! For that reason I rejoice that you, O lovely lady,
are of a mind to accept my service. Most virtuous lady, pray tell
me by the joyful fortune that is in you, O beautiful one, what your
name is or by what manner are you known. Let your name and
your land be revealed to me here so that I may then know with
certainty whether I have ever heard tell of you."

Speaking most courteously, the lady replied, "Dear friend, it shall
be done. I will gladly tell you my name so highly praised. You
need never be ashamed that you are subject to me. I am served by
whomever on earth is of wealth and property. I am of such exalted spirit that emperor and king's son are under my dominion.
Counts, freeborn, and dukes have knelt before me and followed
all my commands. I fear no one but God, for He has power over
me. I am called the World whom you have desired for so long.
Reward will be granted to you as I will now show you. Thus am
I come to you so that you may see."

Then she turned her back to him. On all sides it was completely
adorned and hung with worms and with snakes, with toads and
with vipers. Her body was full of blisters and horrible sores; flies
and ants dwelled therein in great numbers and the maggots ate
her flesh to the bone. She was so very foul and so abhorrent a
stench came forth from her frail body that no one could stand it.
Her glorious dress of silk looked very poor; it had become transformed into a shabby rag. Her merry, delightful complexion had
become piteous in color, as pale as ashes.

Thus she departed from there. May she be cursed by me and by all Christendom! When the noble and free knight considered this wonder, his heart told him at once that he who wished to render her service would be wholly damned. He parted forthwith from wife and children. He took up the cross on his garments, set out over the wild sea, and aided God's noble army in its struggle against the heathen. There the excellent knight was found in constant penance. He did this at all times until he died in body so his soul would find joy beyond.

Now all you children of this wild world, take heed of this true tale. For it is so true that one ought to listen to it gladly. The world's reward is full of sorrow—this you have all learned. I now come to the end: whoever is found in her service will be denied the joy which God—with full constancy—has prepared for the chosen.

I, Konrad of Würzburg, give this advice to all: Abandon the world, if you want to save your soul!

Translated by Ernst Hintz

The Tale of the Heart

Konrad von Würzburg

I am well aware that pure love has become scarce in the world. Therefore, knights and ladies should take an example from this tale, for it tells of absolute love. We have it on the good authority of Master Gottfried von Strassburg that whoever wants to set his foot straight upon the path of love must listen to the recounting and singing of things of the heart, which have previously happened to those who have gazed upon one another with loving eyes. It is undeniable: He who hears something of love sung or read always loves all the better. Therefore I intend to take pains that I render this beautiful tale faithfully so one will be able to find therein a model of love which will be pure and bright and free from all falsity.

A knight and lady had heart and spirit so interwoven in each other that both their spirits and their hearts had become as one. What was distressing for the lady was for the knight as well. As a result of that their end was bitter. Love had become so sovereign over both that it made their hearts ache intensely. Yes, sweet love caused their hearts great pain. It had inflamed them to the depths with its fire and so pierced them with its glow that words could never describe its power. No one could fully relate their devotion. Never was greater faithfulness borne by man or by woman as they bore for each other. Yet, according to proper convention, they could not come to one another so they might share in the duties of love. The most gracious, beautiful woman was married to a worthy man—which caused her much grief. Her beauty was so well guarded that her noble friend could never still the desire of his wounded heart which was torn out of love to her. This was the affliction endured by them; it was harsh and dreadful. He began to grieve so terribly for the sake of her wondrous love that he could not conceal his torment from her husband. He rode to the fair one whenever possible and, with woeful cries, made known to her his heart's lament. Because of this, misfortune befell him in the end and crushed him. The woman's husband observed both of them very carefully until he, unfortunately, realized from their behavior that love had completely entangled them in its snare and that both were withering away for want of each other. The good lord was filled with sorrow and thought, "If I do not take care with my wife, I see clearly that I shall regret it later since she is brewing up disgrace for me with this worthy nobleman. Indeed, if I can arrange it I will bring her out of his power. I shall journey with her over the wild sea so that in this way I can guard her until he turns his heart's desire away from her and she her mind from him. I have often heard it said that the beloved gradually becomes estranged from the lover if both are separated for a long time. Thus I am willing to go with her to Christ's Holy Sepulcher until she has forgotten entirely the great love which she bears the worthy knight."

Thus he decided to turn love into sorrow for the two lovers who would never have wanted to part of their own accord and he determined that he and his lady would visit Jerusalem in the Holy Land. When the knight, who burned for her gracious love, learned of this, he, in his melancholy, quickly resolved to follow her swiftly over the sea. For he would surely die at home should he decide to do without her. The heavy burden of love crushed him so forcefully he would have sought out grim death itself for her sake. Thus he delayed no longer in going to her. As the sweet virtuous one perceived his intention, she summoned him to her in secret. "My friend, my lord, my life," she spoke, "my husband, as you have heard, intends to take me from you in flight. Now mark what I say, dear friend: for the sake of your happiness prevent this journey which he is planning over the wide, wild ocean. Go there yourself before he does so he will remain here. For when he learns you have gone before him, he will stay and the suspicion he harbors will be averted and he will think, 'Were there anything to those tales which concern my good and beautiful wife, as I believe, then the proud and spirited knight would not have left the land.' In this manner he will be freed of the mistrust he bears me in his heart. You should also not regret being there for a while until the talk about us which is flying across the land has ceased. And, when the most pure Christ has sent you back here, you then may have your will with me, indeed on every occasion as soon as the rumors stop. Alas, that you cannot always be with me in accord with your will and I with you in accord with my desire! Now farewell, dear lord, and receive this ring from me. It will serve at all times as a reminder of the sorrow I suffer when my eyes see you not, for whatever happens to me, I will think of you. Your going sinks aching desire into the very depths of my heart. Give me a kiss of sweet friendship on my mouth and do, for my sake, that which I bid." With a troubled heart he said to her, "Gladly lady, regardless of what I may gain by it, I will do whatever you wish. I have so lost both heart and soul in my desire for you that I am bound to you like a vassal. Now grant me leave, dear lady, and know that my desire for you causes me great tribulation. Indeed, I am so completely bound up in you that I greatly fear I shall be borne a dead man to the grave before I have the good fortune ever to see you again."

With this the talk which they had about their hearts' sorrow was at an end. The two lovers parted in agony and bound themselves together in their hearts at that moment much more intensely than I could ever express to you. Both their hearts were dead to worldly joy and their bright, rosy mouths yielded sweet, gentle kisses after which they renounced all pleasure between them. The worthy knight departed at once with aching heart to the sea and set sail in the first ship he found there. He knew with certainty he would never be of joyful mind or truly happy again, unless God saw to it that he came home and heard news about his beloved. For that reason the pain in his heart was unrelenting and bitter. The virtuous knight began to pine away for her and wall up piteous regret in his heart. His old cares for the sake of her love became ever new. Indeed he displayed the manner of the turtle dove, for in longing for his beloved he avoided the green bough of happiness and dwelt constantly on the withered branch of care. He longed for her unceasingly and his sorrow became so great that the pain pierced him to his marrow, to the very depths of his soul; such were the deep sorrow and the inner burden which wounded him. Love's martyr spoke many an hour with a sigh on his lips, "Honored be the pure woman, whose life and sweet body requires such heartache of me. Truly, through her dominion, that dear lady of mine knows how to send bitter misery into my heart! How can she, perfect beyond measure, inflict such pain! If she does not ease this life of mine, I will surely die." Because of his heart's distress, grief was with him all the days and he lamented for so long until at last he fell into such a consuming sickness that he no longer wished to live. One saw clearly on him the grim misery and hidden sorrow which he bore within. And, when the noble knight saw with painful certainty that he was dying, he said to his squire, "Hear me, dear companion. I find that I must die out of love for my lady, for she has wounded me to death with longing sorrow. Thus, do as I tell you. When it is over and I lie dead, cut open my body and take from it my heart, bloody and etched with pain. Cover it entirely with balsam so it will long remain fresh. Heed now what else I have to tell you. Prepare a little coffin adorned with gold and jewels. Place my dead heart therein and put in the ring which my lady gave me so that both are together, closed and sealed and locked in this fashion. Bring them both to my lady that she may see what I have suffered for her and how my heart was wounded for the sake of her gentle love. She is so pure and faithful that her aching desire for me will ever remain in her heart, when she considers the pain I had to suffer for her. Thus do well and fulfill my command. May God, who never abandons a noble heart, through his intercession take pity on me, poor wretch. And may he grant to her for whose sake I must lie here dead much love, happiness, and a joyful life."

With this mournful sorrow the knight met his end. The squire wrung his hands in grief and ordered him to be cut open at once and fulfilled the knight's wish. What the noble man had earlier asked of him, he did then and left, a joyless man with the lifeless heart. He brought it, as ordered, to the same castle where he knew he would find her for whom his dear lord had suffered the pain of death.

When he came to the castle where the noble lady was at that time, her husband chanced upon him in an open field, where, as the story tells us, he intended to do some falconing. This caused the squire great misfortune. For when the knight saw him there, he thought at once, "Surely this one is sent here for no other reason than to bring my wife some word of his master who yearns for her love." He thereupon rode to the squire and intended to question him at once. Then he espied the box of beautiful design wherein the squire carried the heart and the lady's ring, for he had hung it upon his belt as if it were nothing special.

When the knight looked upon it, he greeted the squire and asked what he was carrying in it. The most clever and loyal youth then said, "Lord, it is only a little thing which has been sent with me from afar." "Let us see," the knight quickly spoke, "what lies hidden within." The squire spoke with great distress, "In truth, I shall not do it. No one may ever see it except the one who has a right to do so." "No, that is not the way it will be," the knight said. "For I shall take it from you by force and look at it against your will." After that it was not at all long until he had torn the little box from the squire's belt.

He opened it and saw the heart and with it found the lady's ring. By these two tokens he realized that the knight was dead and that both were to be a sign to his beloved of his distress. The knight said, "Squire, I will tell you what to do. Take any road you wish and I will keep this little gem for myself." He then rode home and ordered the cook to prepare a special dish from the heart with great care. The cook did this gladly. He took the heart and prepared it so well that no one will ever enjoy any other delicacy so excellently made with precious spices as the noble heart. When all was ready, there was no more waiting. The lord went to dine at the table and had the meal quickly brought to his wife. "Lady," he spoke most sweetly, "this is a little dish that you alone must eat and not share." Thus, the noble lady took and ate her friend's heart entirely without being aware of its origin. That sorrowful little morsel seemed so sweet in her mouth that she had never before at any time eaten a dish whose taste had pleased her better. When the faithful lady had eaten the heart, the knight quickly spoke, "Now tell me lady, how this food has pleased you. I suspect that in all your days you have never tasted a sweeter dish than this one." "Dear Lord," she said, "never shall I be as happy, even if I should partake of food that might seem as sugarsweet and as pure as this dainty morsel which I have just enjoyed. Truly, I consider it to be the best of all meals. Speak, my lord, was this noble food wild or tame?" "Lady," he spoke again, "hear well what I now reveal to you. This morsel was both tame and wild, so help me God! Wild, because it was free of all joy, and tame because it was oppressed by unceasing care. You have eaten the heart of the knight who has endured more than enough heartaches for your sake all of his days. Believe me when I tell you: he is dead from the longing of his suffering heart for your sweet love and has sent you his heart and the little ring as a sign into this land with his servant."

With this tale of woe the noble lady took on the appearance of a dead woman. Believe me, her heart grew cold within her body. Her white hands fell together in her lap and blood gushed forth from her mouth as the true debt demanded of her. "Yes," she spoke with great distress, "if I have eaten the heart of him who has borne faithfulness toward me never ceasing, I will now tell you truly that after this nourishment I shall never more partake of any other food. God, in his justice, will prevent me from eating any lesser food after such good and worthy sustenance. I will not partake of anything except of that ill fate called death. I shall sacrifice my poor life in grievous heart's torment for him who has given up his life for me. I would be an unfaithful woman, if I did not remember that he, most virtuous man, sent his dead heart to me. Alas, that after his bitter end I had even one more day of life! Truly, it will not be long now that I live alone without him, who never concealed his fidelity from me and who is held in the thrall of death." Her distress was very great and out of true sorrow she folded her beautiful white hands together and her heart broke from painful desire. The young one brought her sweet life to an end and thus balanced perfectly the heavy burden which her beloved had assumed for her. She repaid him with full constancy and great faithfulness.

May God grant that whatever I take, I may return it with less effort and better than her most pure heart did. I believe that at no time was love ever requited so completely, nor will it ever be. I can see this in the people who live today. For the separation which is caused by Lady Love does not burden them so harshly so that man and woman are bound together in such a way they would now suffer the pain of death for one another's sake. One must use more force to pluck a straw from the meadow by hand than to undo the band of love where two lovers lie. Those who would now bear burdensome suffering for the sake of each other are easily separated without the pain of death. Lady Love gives them a good buy these days. In times past she never stole off to unvirtuous folk for a lesser reward; formerly her sweetness seemed so good that many a noble mind was consumed unto death by her. Now her ways are changed and her order is so weak she can easily be bought for a mere pittance by the stingy. Thus hardly anyone suffers for her sake today. One no longer cares to heed and scarcely holds in esteem that which has made itself available to one and all, for by so doing it is of little value. So it is with love; if she could arrange things so she would become even dearer, there would be a burden of heartache placed on man and woman more firmly than now. There would be such contest on her account and such suffering for each other that one would see it gladly.

I, Konrad of Würzburg, can tell you nothing more. Whoever has pure feelings so that he does what is best, will happily place this tale in his heart in order to learn to bear love purely. No noble heart will ever fail!

Translated by Ernst Hintz

Helmbrecht

Wernher der Gartenaere

One person tells of what he has seen, another of that which has happened to him, the third of love, the fourth of gain, the fifth of great possessions, and the sixth of high spirits. Here I shall relate my own experience: what I have seen with my own eyes and can assure you is true. Once I saw a peasant's son who had blond, curly hair that fell far down over his shoulders and who wore a cap elegantly adorned with pictures. I don't believe anybody ever saw another cap with so many birds—parrots and doves—embroidered on it. Would you like to know what else was there?

There was a peasant called Helmbrecht, and it was his son of whom the story tells. They both had the same name, for the youth too was called Helmbrecht. I'll give you a short and simple account of the wonders depicted on the cap. (It can be trusted, for I am not guessing at anything.) From the hair at the back over the crown of his head to the lock in the middle of his forehead there was a border covered with birds that looked just as if they had flown there from the Spessart region. No peasant ever had a finer cap than that which Helmbrecht wore.

Do you want to hear what was embroidered by the right ear of this rustic fool? It was the story of how Troy was besieged after the bold Paris had stolen the Grecian king's wife (who was as dear to her husband as life itself), how towers and many stone walls fell when the city was conquered, and how Aeneas escaped to sea in his ships. It is too bad that a cap of which there is so much to tell should ever be worn by a peasant.

Now shall I tell you what was wrought in silk on the other side? On the left (this is no lie) appeared the mighty deeds performed by the four comrades in arms—Charlemagne, Roland, Turpin, and Oliver—in battle against the heathen. With bravery and cunning the king subdued Provence, Arles, and the land of Galicia, where formerly only heathen lived. And would you like to know what went from one ribbon to the other between his ears in back? I am telling you the truth: it was the story of how Lady Helche's sons and Diether of Verona were slain long ago by the fierce berserker Wittig in the fighting before Ravenna.

You surely want to learn about the other things the fool had on his cap, and I indeed know what was there. On the front border, from the right ear all around to the left—listen to this—was a dance scene such as one likes to see, embroidered in gleaming silk, with knights and ladies as well as youths and maidens. On one side each knight held two ladies by the hand (as is still done today) and on the other each youth danced between two maidens. Fiddlers were close by.

Listen to how the cap happened to be made for the forward and foolish Helmbrecht, for you haven't yet heard from where it came. It was sewn by a merry nun who had run away from her cell because she could think only about life at the court. Her fate was that of many today: I have often seen such whose bodies have betrayed them so their souls are disgraced. Helmbrecht's sister Gotelind had given a fine cow to the nun for her larder, and the latter, who was a skillful seamstress, repaid her by embroidering the cap and sewing clothing. Hear what Helmbrecht's mother did when Gotelind gave this cow. She supplied the nun with more cheese and eggs than she ever had during the entire time she had eaten at the cloister.

Besides the cap, Helmbrecht's sister provided him with lovely, white linen—no one ever wore better—so he would be admired. It was so finely spun that seven weavers had run away from the loom before the cloth was finished. His mother, moreover, gave him a mantle (of the best wool ever cut by a tailor) with the whitest sheepskin lining in the country. Then the good woman got her dear son a mail doublet and a sword, which he surely deserved, and two other things he doubtless needed: a dagger and a large pouch. He who is so attired is considered arrogant even today.

After she had dressed him thus, the youth said, "Mother, I must have a jerkin too, for I would be quite disgraced without one. And it should be so made that you can tell yourself when you see it that your son will do you honor whenever he goes." In her chest she had a skirt which, sad to say, she now had to give up and exchange for some blue cloth to outfit her son. I swear that no farmer, here or elsewhere, ever had a jerkin which was even a little better than his. The one who advised him about it knew what was suitable and could show him how to gain high praise.

If you would like to hear more about the jerkin, I'll be glad to please you by describing it. There was a row of golden buttons along the back, from the belt to the neck, and a row of silver-white buttons up to the clasp where the collar comes to the chin. There is no peasant between Hohenstein and Haldenberg who has taken such pains with a jacket or spent so much on one. How do you like this? In front were three crystal buttons, neither too large nor too small, with which the silly fool fastened the jerkin, and also many others strewn about—yellow, blue, green, brown, red, black, and white—that gleamed afar just as he had wanted. When he went dancing, they glittered so brightly he was regarded very fondly by both maidens and married women. I'll tell you the truth: beside this youth I would have made little impression on them. All around the seams where the sleeves were attached hung little bells that jingled loudly when he sprang about in the roundelay and resounded in the women's ears. If he were alive, Sir Neidhart could sing of it with his God-given talent better than I can tell it to you. At any rate you should know this: the mother sold many chickens and eggs before she could get him trousers and shoes.

After she had properly clothed his legs and feet, the vain youth said, "My dear father, I want to go to court and I need your help now. Mother and sister have given me so much that I shall be grateful to them as long as I live." His father was not pleased at this and replied sarcastically, "To go with your fine clothes I'll give you a fast horse that can leap hedges and ditches and run a long way without tiring. You need one at court, and I'll gladly buy it for you if I can find one cheap enough.

"Dear son, give up this journey. Courtly life is hard for those who have not grown up with it. You lead the team while I plow or I'll lead it while you plow, and together we'll cultivate the field. You will thus go to your grave with honor just as I shall do, or at least expect to. I am faithful and dependable—I never deceive anyone—and I pay my full tithe every year, as is right. I have lived without hate or envy."

"Say no more, dear father," answered the youth. "It cannot be otherwise, for I must indeed get a taste of court life. Moreover I shall never again carry your sacks on my shoulders or pitch manure on your wagon, and may God's anger strike me if I ever yoke your oxen again or sow your oats. Truly that would not be in keeping with my long, blond hair and curly locks, my fine clothing, and my elegant cap with the silk doves that ladies have embroidered on it. I'll never again help you till the fields."

"Do stay with me," said the father. "I know that Farmer Ruprecht will give you his daughter and with her many sheep and swine and ten head of cattle, old as well as young. At court you will be hungry, will have to sleep on the bare floor, and will have no one to help you. Now take my advice, for it will bring you profit and honor. No one succeeds who does not accept his station, and yours is that of the plow; there are enough courtiers as it is. I swear to you by God, my dear son, you will suffer disgrace and become the laughing stock of all those who really belong at court. You must listen to me and give up this plan."

"Father, I am certain that, with a horse to ride, I shall do as well with the manners of the court as those who have always been there. Whoever sees the beautiful cap on my head will swear a thousand oaths that I never led a team for you or guided a plow in a furrow. When I dress in the clothes that my mother and sister gave me yesterday, I surely shall not look at all as if I had once threshed grain on a barn floor or set posts. As soon as I have put on the trousers and the shoes of Cordovan leather, nobody will suspect I ever made a fence for you or anyone else. If you give me the horse, Farmer Ruprecht will never have me as a son-in-law, for I'll not relinquish my desires because of a woman."

"Be still a moment, my son, and listen to what I tell you. He who follows wise instruction gains wealth and respect, but the child who constantly ignores a father's counsel will finally come to shame and harm. If you really try to put yourself on the level of the wellborn courtier, you will fail, and he will become your enemy. And believe me, no peasant will complain about any injustice done you there. If a real courtier should seize all the property of a peasant, he would in the end do better in court than you. Listen to this, my son: if you take from the peasant just a little fodder for your horse and he gets the upper hand, then you are liable for everything others have stolen from him. You won't get a chance to defend yourself, but will pay at once, for God is on his side if he kills you during the robbery. Believe what I say, dear son. Stay here and take a wife."

"No matter what happens to me, father, I'll not give up my plan, for I must win a higher position. Have your other sons labor with the plow. Cows shall low before me as I seize and drive them off. I have remained here this long only because I have no horse. Indeed, I am sorry that I am not galloping away with other knights, pulling peasants through hedges by the hair. I can't bear poverty. When I can raise only one colt or calf in three years, the profit seems very small to me. I want to ride out for plunder every day so I can live well and be safe from winter's cold as long as people will buy cattle. Hurry, father, don't delay but give me the horse at once, for I'll not stay any longer with you."

I'll be brief. To get the horse the father gave up four good cows, two oxen, three bulls, four bushels of grain, and twenty yards of rough woolen cloth—the longest piece of such fabric ever woven, so we are told. All gone for nothing! He bought the horse for ten pounds and could not have sold it the same day for three. Seven pounds lost!

Listen to what the son said when he had dressed and was ready to leave. He shook his head, looked over one shoulder then the other, and exclaimed, "I am fierce enough to bite through stone. I could eat iron. The emperor himself should feel lucky if I don't lead him away captive and extort from him all he has, right down to his skin. And the same goes for the duke and several counts too. I'll trot across the fields and through the world with no fear for my life. Father, let me be my own master so that, from now on, I can grow as I will. You could raise a wild Saxon more easily than me."

"All right, son, I release you from my keeping. Go your own way. But since the training I gave you means less than your curls, take care that no one touches your cap and the silk doves or harms your long, blond hair. If you really want no more of my instruction, I am sorely afraid that in the end you will walk with a crutch and go where a child leads you.

"My dear boy," continued the father, "let me yet dissuade you. You should live from that on which I live and from what your mother gives you. Drink water rather than wine gotten through robbery. Over in Austria everyone, foolish and wise, considers stuffed rolls to be fit for a king. You should eat them, dear son, instead of trading a plundered cow to some householder for a hen. All week long your mother makes fine porridges. Stuff yourself with that and don't buy a goose with a plundered horse. Son, if you live as I have advised, you will be respected wherever you go; mix rye and oats rather than eat fish to your shame. This is your father's teaching, and you would be wise to follow it. If you will not, then go your own way. I want no part of whatever wealth or fame you may win, and you also need not share your misfortune."

"You drink water, father, while I drink wine. And you can eat oatmeal while I have boiled chicken: no one will ever stop me. Moreover I shall never again eat any bread but wheat rolls until I die. Oat bread is for people like you. A Roman law book says that a young child takes on a trait of its godfather. Mine was a noble knight. God bless him for giving me such a proud spirit and causing me to become so noble."

"Believe me," said the father, "I would much prefer a man who always did what was right. Even were he of low birth, he would please everyone better than a man of royal blood who was worthless and little regarded. If an upright man of humble parents and a nobleman who has neither decency nor honor come into a country where no one knows them, the son of the commoner will be considered better than the nobleman who has chosen shame rather than esteem. My son, if you want to be a true nobleman, I counsel you to act nobly, for good breeding is surely the highest nobility. You can accept this as the truth."

"Father, you are right," answered the son, "but my cap, hair, and fine clothing won't let me remain here. They are so splendid that they are more suited to a courtly dance than a harrow or plow."

"Oh that you were ever born! You would rather do evil than

good. Tell me this, handsome youth, if you have any sense left, who has the better life: the one who is reproached and cursed, who causes everybody suffering because he lives at others' expense and who disdains God's grace, or he from whom all people benefit and who doesn't mind striving night and day to be useful to others and thereby honor God? It seems to me that the latter would please God and man wherever he went, but whom would you like better? Tell me the truth, dear son."

"The man who helps people and doesn't harm anyone, father. His life is the better, of course."

"Dear son, you would be this man if you would take my advice. Till the land, and you will indeed be a blessing to many: rich and poor, wolf and eagle, and all other creatures on earth to which God has given life. Till the land: the produce makes many women beautiful and crowns many kings, for nobody ever became so great but that his splendor depended on farming alone."

"May God quickly spare me your sermon, father! If you had become a real preacher, your exhortations would have sent an entire army on a crusade. Listen to what I say: the more the peasants raise, the more they eat. Whatever happens to me, from now on I'll have nothing to do with a plow. By God, I would never get over the disgrace if I were to have dirty hands from plowing when I dance with the ladies."

"If you don't find it unpleasant," said the father, "ask such wise men as you encounter the meaning of a dream I had. You were holding two candles which burned so brightly they lit up everything around. My dear son, last year I dreamed this about a man who is now blind."

"You need not say more, Father, for I'll never change my mind because of a tale like that. I would be a coward to do so."

Since this warning did no good, the father continued: "I had another dream. You were walking with one foot on the ground and with the knee of the other leg resting on a piece of wood. What looked like the stump of a leg stuck out from under your coat. If the dream is to be useful to you, you must ask its meaning of those who know."

"It foretells health, good fortune, and joys of all kinds."

"Son, I had a third dream which I'll tell you. Just when you were about to fly high over the forest, one of your wings was cut off and there was no flight. Can this dream forbode anything good? Oh your poor hands and feet and eyes!"

"All your dreams predict good fortune for me," said young Helmbrecht. "Now get yourself another farm hand, for you will have to do without me no matter how much you dream."

"The dreams I have told you thus far are nothing compared to this last one. Listen to it. You were up in a tree (it was about one and a half fathoms from your feet to the ground) and a crow and a raven were sitting on a branch above your head. Your hair was unkempt. The raven was combing it on the right side, and the crow was parting it on the left. Oh son, what a dream! Oh the tree, the raven, and the crow! If the dream was no lie, I fear I shall suffer great sorrow for not having raised you better."

"Father, if you dreamed of everything in the world, evil and good, God knows I would not give up my plan until I died. I need to leave more than ever. May God protect you and my dear mother and bless your children. May God keep us all in his care." He thus took leave of his father, trotted past the gate, and rode away. I couldn't tell all about his experiences in three days, perhaps not even in a week.

At last he came to a castle, the lord of which was always feuding and was therefore glad to harbor those who were not afraid to ride and fight with his enemies. The youth joined his troop and became such a zealous robber that he would put in his sack even things others had let lie. He took everything: no booty was too small or too great. Whether it was rough or smooth, crooked or straight, Farmer Helmbrecht's son seized it. He took the horse and cow and left nothing behind that was worth as much as a spoon. He took jerkin and sword, coat and mantle, nanny goat and billy goat, ewe and ram—but later he paid for them with his own skin. He pulled blouses and skirts off the women, as well as their cloaks and fur coats. Afterwards, when the sheriff seized him, he wished he had not robbed women. You can be sure of this.

In the first year favorable winds murmured in his sails and his ships fared well. Since he always got the best part of the booty, he became arrogant. Then it occurred to him to go home to visit his family, as people have always done, so he took leave of his lord and his comrades, commending them to God's care.

Now comes an episode that one must by no means overlook. I only wish I could tell you how he was received at home.

Did they go to meet him? They ran, all together, with one crowding ahead of the other. His father and mother dashed toward him faster than they had ever run to save a calf from death. Who would get the reward for the news? They gladly gave the man who brought it a shirt and trousers. Did the milkmaid and the farm hand cry, "Welcome, Helmbrecht"? No, for they were advised not to. They spoke thus: "We bid you a hearty welcome, sir," to which he answered, "Dear *soete kindekin* [sweet children], God *lat* [grant] you eternal happiness." And when his sister ran up and hugged him, he said, *"Gracia vester* [God's grace be with you]." The young people reached the youth first, but the older ones were not far behind. All of them greeted him joyfully. To his father he said, *"Deu sal* [God keep you]," and to his mother, in Bohemian, *"Dobra ytra* [Good morning]." The man and his wife looked at each other.

"Husband," she said, "we have made a mistake. This is not our child. It is a Bohemian or a Wend."

"It's a Frenchman," replied the father, "certainly not the son whom I commended to God. Yet they are very much alike." Then the youth's sister Gotelind spoke, "It isn't your child, for he answered me in Latin. He must be a priest."

"Indeed," said the farm hand, "judging from what I heard, he is from North Germany or Brabant. He said, 'Dear *soete kindekin.*' I think he is a North German."

The farmer asked simply, "Are you my son Helmbrecht? I shall believe it if you will speak a single word as we do and as our fathers have done so that I can understand it. You say only, *'Deu sal,'* and I don't know what to make of that. Honor your mother and me by saying something in German and we shall be forever grateful. I'll curry your horse for you, my dear son—I, myself, not the farm hand—and do it so you will be really pleased."

"Oh, what *snacket ir geburekin* [are you babbling about, little peasant], and that vulgar *wif* [woman]? Indeed, no peasant shall ever *gegripen an* [touch] my *parit* [horse] or my handsome *lif* [self]."

This startled the farmer, but he spoke again, "If you are my son Helmbrecht, I'll boil you a chicken for this evening and roast you a second one. I mean it. However, should you be a Bohemian or a Wend and not my son, then go back to the Wends. God knows I have enough to do with my own children, and I don't give even a priest any more than just what is due him. If you aren't my son, you will never wash your hands to eat at my table, even though I might have all the fish in the world. Should you be North German, Flemish, or French you will need to have something in your pouch, because you will certainly touch nothing of mine even though the night lasts a year. Eat with the noblemen, sir, for I have neither mead nor wine."

Since it was already quite late, the youth thought to himself, "Good God, I'd better tell them who I am, because there is no innkeeper near here to take me in. It wasn't very clever of me to alter my speech. I won't do it anymore." Then he said, "I am he."

"Now tell me who," said the father.

"He whose name is the same as yours."

"And what is it?"

"Helmbrecht. A year ago I was your son and farm hand. That is the truth."

"No!" exclaimed the father.

"But it's true."

"Then tell me the names of my four oxen."

"I can do it quickly, because I once swung my goad over them and took care of them. One is called Uwer, and he is good enough for the fields of any peasant, no matter how able or rich he might be. The name of the second is Raeme: no gentler ox ever wore a yoke. I'll tell you also what the third was called—Erge. It is because I am clever that I can still name them. And if you want to test me further, the fourth was called Sun. If I named them rightly, then reward me by having someone open the gate."

"You don't need to wait longer in front of either the gate or the door," replied the father, "and both rooms and cupboards will be open to you."

I myself have never had such good treatment as the youth got there: curse the luck! While his mother and sister prepared a soft bed for him, his father took the saddle and bridle from the horse and gave it plenty of fodder. As much as I have roamed about, I have never been in a place where I was cared for as he was.

"Run into the bedroom," the mother called to her daughter, "and get a pad and a soft pillow." The latter was placed under his shoulder on a warm bench by the stove, where he waited in great comfort while the meal was prepared.

When the youth awoke and washed his hands, the food was ready. Now hear what was set before him. I'll begin with the first course, which I would be glad to get even if I were a great nobleman. It was made of finely chopped cabbage with a good piece of meat that was neither too fat nor too lean. Next came a fat, well-aged cheese. Then—listen, for I know all about it—they set a goose in front of the youth. No fatter one was ever broiled on a spit over the fire: no one was annoyed at this, they were glad to do it. The goose was as large and heavy as a bustard. Two chickens followed: one roasted and one boiled, just as the father had promised. A nobleman who was lying on a stand during a hunt would surely like to get such food. Many other kinds of fine dishes, fare about which most peasants know nothing, were placed before the youth.

"If I had wine," said the father, "we would drink it this evening. In its place, dear son, drink the best spring water that ever flowed out of the ground. I don't know of a spring like ours except the one at Wanghausen, and no one can bring it to us here."

When they had finished this most enjoyable meal, the farmer could wait no longer to ask about the court where his son had been. "Tell me what the customs are there," he said, "and then I'll describe to you the courtly behavior I once observed when I was young."

"Tell me about it, father. Afterwards I'll answer all your questions, for I know the new mode of life very well."

"Long ago when I was young, your grandfather Helmbrecht, my father, used to send me to the court with cheese and eggs, as tenant farmers still do. I saw knights there and took note of all their conduct. They were light-hearted and refined, and knew nothing of the meanness so common among men and women today. The knights had certain customs with which they endeared themselves to the ladies. One was called the bohort, so a courtier told me when I asked about it. They galloped about as if they were mad, but later I heard them praised for it. One troop charged the other and each man rode as though he wanted to knock somebody down. Among us peasants nothing ever happened like the things I saw at court.

"After the bohort was over, they passed the time by dancing to a merry song, but soon a minstrel came and began to play a fiddle.

Then the ladies stood (they were a delight to see), and the knights went to them and took them by the hand. It was a wondrous sight as the splendid knights and ladies, squires and maidens, rich and poor danced joyfully. When this ended, a man came and recited the adventures of a certain Ernst. There were many pleasant things to do, and each found the pastime that he liked. Some shot arrows at a target, others took part in a drive for game, still others hunted alone with hounds.

"He who was the least then would be the best today. Yes indeed, how well I once knew what manner of living causes honor and loyalty to flourish, before it was corrupted by evil. At that time the lords would not keep at their courts those deceitful shameless men who knew how to pervert justice with their cunning. Nowadays the one who can dissemble and deceive is thought wise, and is a respected man at court; sad to say, he has much greater wealth and esteem than the man who lives uprightly and strives for God's favor. I know this much of the old customs. Now, son, be so kind as to tell me about the new ones."

"I'll be glad to. The courtly thing now is 'Drink, sir, drink! You empty your cup and I'll drain mine. How could life be better?' Let me make this clear: in former times the highly respected men were to be found in the company of beautiful ladies, but now one sees them only where wine is sold. Morning and evening their greatest concern is how they can see to it that the tavern keeper, when the wine runs out, gets more which is just as good, so they can stay in high spirits. Their love letters go like this: 'My sweet barmaid, keep our cups full. Whoever has felt greater longing for a woman than for good wine is a monkey and a fool.' Today a liar is esteemed, deceit is courtly, and the one who can use cunning words to cheat another is considered well-bred. The slanderer is regarded as virtuous. Believe me, the old people who live like you are now cut off from society. Men and women avoid them as they would a hangman and scorn authority of both emperor and pope."

"God be merciful!" said the old man. "We should never cease to lament to him that evil has become so widespread."

"The old tournaments have disappeared and new ones have been introduced. Formerly the battle cry was 'Hey, knights, be merry!' Now they shout from dawn till dark, 'Let's hunt for cattle! Away! Away! Stab and slash! Put out his eyes! Cut off this man's foot and that man's hand for me. Hang him! Catch me a rich man who'll pay us a good hundred pounds.' Father, I could tell you all about the new customs if I wanted to, for I know them well, but I must sleep now. I have ridden far and need to rest tonight." They followed his wishes. There were no sheets in the house, but his sister Gotelind spread a newly washed shift over his bed. He slept until late in the morning.

I'll tell you what the young Helmbrecht did then. Now was the time for him to get out the delightful things he had brought his father, mother, and sister from the court. You will truly be pleased to learn what they were. He had brought his father as fine a whetstone as any mower ever tied in its case, the best scythe that was ever swung through the grass (what a gift that was for a peasant!), an axe such as no smith has forged for a long time, and also a hoe. The youth gave his mother a splendid coat of fox fur he had taken off a priest. (I'll be glad to tell you what was stolen or seized by force if I know.) He gave Gotelind a silk hair-ribbon he had taken from a merchant and a gold-studded belt that would have been more suitable for a nobleman's daughter than for his sister. For the hired man he had brought peasant shoes that he would not have carried so far or even touched for anyone else, since he was so refined. However, if Helmbrecht had still been his father's farm hand, the other wouldn't have gotten the shoes at all. He gave the maid a kerchief and a red ribbon, both of which she certainly needed!

Now guess how long the youth stayed at his father's house?

It was really only seven days, but, since he wasn't out plundering, it seemed to him like a year. Then he abruptly took leave of his parents.

"Don't go, dear, good son," said the father. "If you are willing to live on what I can give you until I die, stay here and eat at our table. Give up this courtly life, my son, for it is evil and bitter. I would rather be a peasant than a poor courtier with no income from land who has to ride about early and late at the risk of his life, always with the fear that his enemies will maim or hang him if they capture him."

"Father," replied the youth, "I thank you very much for your hospitality, but it has been more than a week since I have had any wine, and I am therefore fastening my belt at three holes less. The buckle won't be back where it was until I round up some cattle. Some plows will be stopped and their oxen driven away before I rest up and put on weight again. There is a rich man who has offended me more than anyone ever did before: I once saw him ride across my godfather's grain field. If he lives long enough, he will pay dearly for the insult to me. I am greatly provoked that he should thus cause my dear godfather's work to go for nothing, and his cattle, sheep, and swine will run because of it. I know another rich man who has also wronged me—he ate bread on top of fritters—and I'll avenge it or die. There is still a third rich man who has offended me, indeed more than anyone else. Not even a bishop could get me to overlook the pain he caused me."

"What did he do?" asked the father.

"He loosened his belt at the table. Why, I'll take everything of his that I can capture. The oxen that pull his plow and his wagon will help me to get Christmas clothing. No matter how I look at the matter, I really can't see what this stupid fool is thinking of, nor some others either who have caused me great distress. I'd be a coward not to get revenge. Then there is the man who blew the foam from his beer into the mug of another. If I don't make him suffer for it at once, I truly will not be worthy of the esteem of ladies and not deserve to gird a sword at my side. It will soon be told of Helmbrecht that he emptied a large farm, for, if I don't find the man, I'll at least drive away his cattle."

"I would be very grateful," said the father, "if you would tell me the names of your young companions who have taught you to seize a rich man's property because he ate bread after fritters. I'd like to know their names."

"My two comrades, Lemberslint [Lamb-Devourer] and Slickenwider [Swallow-the-Ram], taught me this," answered the youth. "I'll also name you others who are my teachers: Hellesac, Rütelschrin, Küefraz, and Müschenkelch [Hell-Sack, Shake-Open-the-Coffer, Cow-Eater, and Chalice-Crusher]. That makes six. You can see now, Father, what sort of young men belong to our troop. There is also my friend Wolvesguome [Wolf-Jaws]: he treats acquaintances and strangers alike. However dear to him his aunts, uncles, and cousins might be, he doesn't leave them, man or woman, a thread of clothing to cover their nakedness, even in freezing weather. My friend Wolvesdrüzzel [Wolf-Throat] can open any lock or iron chest without a key. In one year I counted a hundred large chests whose locks flew open as soon as he came near, and he drove horses, oxen, and cows without number from farmyards, the bars of which moved from their places when he arrived. I have another comrade who has a more distinguished name than any other youth. It is Wolvesdarm [Wolf-Gut] and was given to him by a mighty duchess, the noble and freeborn Narie von Nonarre. He likes robbing and stealing so much that he never tires of them, winter or summer. He never took a single step from evil toward goodness: evil deeds draw him like a grain field draws crows."

"Tell me, what name do your friends use when they call you?"

"I'll never be ashamed of my name, Father. It is Slintezgeu [Swallow-the-Land] and I am no joy to the peasants who live near me. Their children have to eat water porridge, but that's not all the distress I cause them. I gouge this one's eye out, tie another on an anthill, pull the hair out of that one's beard with tongs, and smoke a fourth in the smokehouse. I tear the scalp off of some, crush the limbs of some, and hang others by their heels. Whatever the peasants have belongs to me. When the ten of us ride out together, we can defeat twenty men who are waiting for us, even more."

"My dear son, you know those men whom you have named much better than I. Yet, when God himself wants to take charge, a single sheriff can make them go where he commands, however fierce they may be and though there were three times as many of them."

"Even if all kings were to command it, Father, I'll never again act as I have done in the past. I have protected you and mother from my companions and have saved you many chickens and geese as well as cattle, cheese, and fodder. I shall not do this any more. You are attacking the honor of fine young men, none of whom ever does anything that he shouldn't. They have a right to rob and steal. If you hadn't spoiled matters with your foolish chatter and hadn't spoken so scornfully of us, I would have given your daughter Gotelind to my friend Lemberslint as his wife. Then she would have had the best life that any woman in the world ever had with her husband. Had you not said such bitter things about us, he would have given her a wealth of furs, cloaks, and linen, as good as the clergy's best, and she could have eaten fresh beef every week if she had wanted it." [The father and mother go off, and the youth is alone with his sister.]

"Now listen, sister Gotelind. When my friend Lemberslint first asked me for your hand, I said at once, 'Believe me, if you and she are destined to marry, you will never regret it. I know her to be very loyal, and you need have no fear that you may perhaps hang a long time on the gallows. She will cut you down with her own hands and take you to your grave at the crossroads. Then she will carry incense and myrrh around the grave every night for a whole year. You can count on it; the fine and noble lady will fumigate your bones. And if you have the good fortune to be blinded [instead of hanged], she will take you by the hand and lead you through all the lands. Should they cut off one of your feet, she will bring your crutches to your bed every morning; and you need not worry if you also lose a hand as punishment, for she will cut your meat and bread for you the rest of your life.'

"To this Lemberslint replied, 'Should your sister Gotelind accept me, I will give her a wedding present that will enable her to live very well. I have three full sacks that are as heavy as lead. One is filled with fine, uncut linen of a quality that would be worth fifteen kreutzers a yard if one wanted to buy it. She will praise this gift. In the second sack are many veils, skirts, and shifts. She will not be poor if she becomes my wife, for I shall give her all this on the day after the wedding and also whatever booty I take from then on. The third sack is stuffed full of costly cloth and many-colored furs, two of which are lined with fine wool. One fur is sable. I have hidden the sacks in a ravine nearby and will give them to her that morning.'

"May God preserve you Gotelind, for your father has spoiled this. Your life will be bitter. No woman ever suffered more grief than you will feel now when you marry a peasant. With him you will have to crush, beat, and scape the flax and trench the turnips, from all of which the faithful Lemberslint could have saved you. Oh, sister Gotelind, it will pain me if you should have to sleep night after night with a rude peasant whose caresses repel you. One should cry out against your father—he is not my father indeed! I tell you truly that a well-bred courtier came secretly to mother when she had carried me fifteen weeks. I have inherited his traits and those of my godfather. God bless them! Because of them I have always had a noble spirit."

"I don't think I am really his child either," said Gotelind, "for a stately knight lay with mother while she bore me in her womb. He seized her late one evening when she was in the woods looking for the calves. That is why I am so refined. Dear brother Slintezgeu," she continued, "God will reward you if you see to it that Lemberslint becomes my husband. Then my frying pan will sizzle, my cupboards be filled, my beer be brewed, my grain finely ground, and grapes be gathered for my wine. Once I get the three sacks, I shall be free of want and have plenty to eat and to wear. Look, what could displease me then? I'll have everything a woman wants from her husband.

"I also expect to give him all a man would like to get from a strong woman like me. I have everything he wants. Father has been making me wait even though I am three times as strong as my sister was when she got married. She could walk without a crutch the next morning and didn't die from the pain. I don't think I shall die of it either unless some calamity occurs. Dear brother, please don't repeat what I am about to say: I'll go with you along the narrow road to the pine forest—I want to lie by his side. For know this: I am willing to give up Father, Mother, and all my kinfolk."

Neither of the parents learned of this decision, and her brother quickly agreed that she should follow him. "I will marry you to this man," he said, "no matter how much it displeases your father. You will become Lemberslint's wife and gain both esteem and wealth thereby. If your mind is made up, I will send a messenger who will lead you to us. Since you two love each other, everything will go well with you. I shall arrange your wedding and see to it that many doublets and robes are given away in your honor: you may depend on it. Get ready sister, and Lemberslint will do the same. I must go now, goodbye. I feel toward Father as he does toward me. Farewell, Mother."

The youth went back the way he had come and told his friend of Gotelind's assent. Overjoyed, Lemberslint kissed his hand and his clothing all around, then bowed toward the wind that was blowing from the direction of Gotelind.

Now hear what crimes were committed. Many widows and orphans were robbed of their possessions and left in distress before the valiant Lemberslint and his wife sat down on the bridal seat, for plunder was gathered from all around to supply them with food and drink. The young men were by no means idle at this time. Early and late, in wagons and on the backs of horses, they brought everything to the house of Lemberslint's father. When King Arthur married Lady Guinevere, the wedding celebration was nothing compared to that of Lemberslint: these people didn't live on air. As soon as all was ready, Helmbrecht sent the messenger, who soon brought his sister to him. On hearing that Gotelind had arrived, Lemberslint hurried to meet her. Just listen to how he received her!

"Welcome, Lady Gotelind," he said.

"I thank you, Sir Lemberslint," she replied, and many loving glances passed back and forth between them. With refined and courtly words Lemberslint shot his arrow at Gotelind, and she paid him back with woman's speech as well as she could.

Now let us give Gotelind to Lemberslint to be his wife and Lemberslint to Gotelind to be her husband. An old man who could talk well and knew the ceremony stood up, placed them both in a ring, and said to Lemberslint, "If you will take Gotelind as your lawful wife, say 'yes.'"

"Yes," said the youth at once. The man asked him again, and he again replied, "Yes." Then he spoke a third time, "Do you take her willingly?" and the youth declared, "By my soul and body, I shall be glad to have this woman." Thereupon the man asked Gotelind, "Do you willingly take Lemberslint to be your husband?"

"Yes, sir, if God will let me have him."

"Do you take him willingly?" he repeated.

"Willingly, sir, give him to me."

"Will you take him?" he asked a third time.

"Gladly, sir, now give him to me." Then Gotelind was given to Lemberslint as his wife, and Lemberslint to Gotelind as her husband. At once all began to sing, and the groom stepped on his bride's foot [a marriage rite].

Since the meal is now ready, we must not forget to supply the bridal couple with court officials. Slintezgeu was the marshal and saw to it that the horses had plenty to eat; Slickenwider was the cupbearer; and Hellesac served as the lord high steward who directed local guests and strangers to their places. The unreliable Rütelschrin was chamberlain; Küefraz was chef and dispensed everything boiled and baked that came from the kitchen; Müschenkelch gave out the bread. It was no modest wedding feast. Wolvesguome, Wolvesdarm, and Wolvesdrüzzel emptied many dishes and large beakers there. The food vanished from in front of these young men as if a wind had suddenly swept it away from the table. I know each of them devoured all the food the lord high steward brought him from the kitchen. Could a dog have gnawed anything from the bones they discarded? I doubt it, for, as a wise man has said, "everyone is ravenous when his end approaches." The reason they ate so greedily is that they were never again to sit down happily together to eat.

Then the bride spoke, "Oh! Dear Lemberslint, I am frightened. I am afraid there are strangers near who intend to harm us. Oh! Father and Mother, why am I so far away from you! I greatly fear that Lemberslint's three sacks will bring me pain and disgrace. My heart is so heavy. If only I were at home! I would much rather endure my father's poverty than this anxiety. I have always heard people say that he who wants too much gets nothing at all. Greed hurls us into the depths of hell, for it is a sin, and I have come to my senses too late. Oh, why was I in such haste to follow my brother here? I shall have to suffer for it." Indeed it was soon clear to Gotelind that she would have been better off eating cabbage at her father's table than eating fish with Lemberslint.

They had sat for a while after the meal, and the bride and groom had paid the minstrels, when suddenly they saw five men coming, one a sheriff who defeated the ten robbers without a struggle. Each crowded ahead of the other as they tried to escape by hiding in the oven or slipping under benches. He who formerly would not have run from four enemies was now pulled forth by the hair by the sheriff's helper alone. I tell you truly that a real thief, however bold he may be and even if he has killed three men at one time, can never defend himself against a sheriff. This one therefore bound the robbers at once with strong ropes. Gotelind lost her wedding dress. Later she was found behind a hedge in a wretched state, holding her hands over her breasts. She had been badly frightened: let him who was there say if anything else had happened to her.

God works miracles, as you can see in this story. A thief who could defeat an army by himself cannot resist a sheriff. When he sees one, even far off, his sight becomes dim and his color pale. He may have been brave and strong before, but a lame sheriff can capture him now. His boldness and cunning vanished as soon as God decides to punish him.

Now listen to the account of the sentencing, of how the thieves, carrying heavy burdens, crept before the court of justice and were hanged. Gotelind was grief-stricken when two cowhides were quickly tied about Lemberslint's neck, but his load was the lightest because he was the bridegroom. The others had to carry more. His brother-in-law Helmbrecht Slintezgeu walked before the sheriff bearing three rawhides, and this was just. Each carried his burden, which became the portion of the judge. They were given no lawyer. May God shorten the life of anyone who wants to lengthen theirs! That is my wish. I know a judge whose nature is such that for pay he would spare a fierce wolf even if it attacked everyone's cattle. This is really true, although it should never be done.

The sheriff then hanged nine of the prisoners and let one live— he had the right to do as he wished with the tenth—and this was Helmbrecht Slintezgeu: what is destined will be. God never overlooks the man whose deeds are evil, as can be seen in the case of Helmbrecht. He was punished for the offense to his father when the sheriff put out his eyes, but that was not the whole penalty: the offense to his mother cost him a hand and a foot. He suffered this shame and distress because he had not greeted them with respect. He had said to the one, "What are you babbling about, little peasant?" and had called the other a "vulgar woman." For this sin he had to endure such torment that he would a thousand times rather have died than to live on so miserably.

With grief and remorse the blind thief Helmbrecht parted from Gotelind at a crossroad, as a boy and a crutch brought him home to his father's house. However the father did not give him shelter and help him in his great trouble, but drove him away. Listen to what he said:

"*Deu sal,* Sir Blind Man, I learned this greeting long ago at the court. Just go on, little Sir Blind Man. I am sure that you have all that a young nobleman wants: you will be esteemed even in France. I say this because I greet all blind young men thus, but why should

I speak further? By God, you will leave my house at once, Sir Blind Youth, and if you don't hurry, I'll have my farm hand give you a beating such as no blind person ever got before. Any bread that I wasted on you this evening would be cursed. Get out."

"Oh no, sir! Let me spend the night here," replied the blind man. "I want to tell you who I am. For God's sake, recognize me!"

"Well speak quickly," said the father, "and hurry off, for it is late. Find yourself another host, because you will get nothing from me."

"Sir," he answered with grief and shame, "I am your son."

"Has the youth who called himself Slintezgeu become blind? Why he wasn't afraid of the threats of the sheriff or of all the judges, however many there might be. You were going to eat iron when you were mounted on the horse for which I gave up my cattle. It doesn't trouble me that you are now creeping along as a blind man. What I regret is the loss of the wool cloth and the grain, since I don't have enough bread myself. I wouldn't give you a crumb if you were at the point of death, so be on your way at once and don't ever come back."

"Since you will no longer accept me as your child," said the blind man, "for God's sake overcome the devil and let me enter your house as a beggar. In Christian charity grant me what you would give another who was sick and destitute. The people of the region hate me, just as you do now, and I shall die if you are not merciful."

The farmer laughed scornfully, but he was sick at heart, for the other was still his own flesh and blood even though he stood blinded before him. "You rode willfully through the world: your horse never ambled, but always went at a trot or a gallop. You were so inhuman that many peasant men and women lost everything because of you. Now tell me if the three dreams haven't come true. But there is more to be told, and things will go still worse for you. Just leave my door quickly before the fourth dream is fulfilled. I would sooner care for a complete stranger the rest of my life than give you half a loaf of bread. Farm hand, bar the door. I want to get some rest tonight."

He thus reproached the blind man for all he had done. The sight of him was a nightmare to the farmer. "Boy," he cried, "lead this hideous creature away from me. This is for you," and he struck the boy. "I would do the same to your master, but I am ashamed to strike a blind man. I am well-bred enough to keep from it, still that can change. Be off at once, you treacherous Russian. I care nothing for your distress." The youth's mother, however, put some bread in his hand, as if he were a child.

The blind thief went on his way. Whenever he passed a field, the peasants would shout at him and the boy, "Hey there, Thief Helmbrecht! If you had tilled the soil as I do, you wouldn't be led around as a blind man." He lived a year thus in misery before he was hanged.

I'll tell you how it happened. Early one morning he was going through a forest seeking food when Helmbrecht was seen by a peasant (who was chopping wood, as peasants do) from whom he once had taken a cow that had calved seven times. As soon as the peasant recognized the blind man, he asked his friends if they would help him.

"Truly," said one, "if no one stops me, I'll tear him to bits. He pulled the clothes right off my wife and me. I have a just claim to him."

"If there were three of him," exclaimed another, "I would kill them by myself. The rogue broke open my storeroom and took everything I had there."

The fourth of the woodcutters trembled like a leaf with desire. "I'll wring his neck as if he were a chicken," he cried, "and I have a right to. While my child was asleep, he rolled it up with the bedding and shoved it into a sack. This was at night. When it woke and cried, he shook it out into the snow. It would have died if I had not come to rescue it."

"How pleased I am that he has come," the fifth spoke up, "for today he shall provide me with a sight to delight my heart. He raped my daughter, and I would hang him from a limb even though he were three times as blind. I myself lost everything, even my clothes, and barely escaped from him with my life. Now that he has crept into this deep forest, I would get vengeance if he were as large as a house."

"At him!" they shouted then, and all of them rushed at Helmbrecht. While they avenged themselves with blows, they cried, "Watch out for your cap, Helmbrecht!" The part of it that the sheriff's helper had left unharmed was now ripped to bits. It was horrible: there wasn't a piece left the size of a penny. The parrots and larks, falcons and turtledoves which were embroidered on the cap were strewn on the road. Here lay a lock of hair, there a shred of cloth. If I ever told you the truth, you must believe what I say about the cap and the tiny scraps into which they tore it. You never saw a head so bald, since all of Helmbrecht's curly, blond hair lay in the dirt. However, this was the least of his troubles.

After they had heard the wretch make his confession, one of the peasants picked up a fragment of soil and placed it in the mouth of the sinner as a wafer to help him against hellfire. Then they hanged him from a tree, and the prophecy of the father's dream thus proved to be true. Here the story ends.

Let this be a warning to other children who will not listen to their father and mother. If they act like Helmbrecht, I can safely predict they will end as he did. He is still hanging by a willow withe, and the wagon traffic that had disappeared from the roads and highways is moving peacefully again. Now give heed and follow good advice whether it comes from an unlettered man or a sage. I wonder if there are still some young admirers of Helmbrecht about? Should there be, they will become little Helmbrechts, and I know you will have no peace until they, too, have been brought to the gallows.

Pray that God may be merciful to him who reads you this story and to the poet, Wernher the Gardener.

Translated by J. W. Thomas

Historia & Tale of Doctor Johannes Faustus

The sorcerer, wherein is described specifically and veraciously:
His entire life and death,
How he did oblige himself for a certain time unto the Devil,
And what happened to him,
And how he at last got his well-deserved reward.

Rare revelations are also included, for these examples are most useful and efficacious as a highly essential Christian warning and admonition, that the laity, in order to protect themselves from similar maculations of the most shameful sort, have especial cause to heed and to avoid such a desperate fate.

Here Beginneth Doctor Faustus: His *Vita* & *Historia*

I

Of His Parentage and Youth

Doctor Faustus, the son of a husbandman, was born in Roda in the Province of Weimar. His parents were godfearing and Christian people with many connections in Wittemberg. A kinsman who dwelt there was a citizen and possessed of considerable wealth. He reared Faustus for the parents and kept him as his own child, for, being himself without issue, he adopted this Faustus, made him his heir, and sent him to school to study theology. Faustus, however, strayed from this godly purpose and used God's Word vainly.

Therefore we shall blame neither his parents nor his patrons, who desired only the best (as do all pious parents), nor shall we mix them into this *Historia*. For they neither witnessed nor experienced the abominations of their godless child. One thing is certain: these parents, as was generally known in Wittemberg, were quite heartily delighted that their kinsman adopted him. When they later perceived in Faustus his excellent *ingenium* and *memoria*, it did most assuredly trouble them, just as Job in the first chapter of that Book was concerned for his children, lest they sin against the Lord. Therefore pious parents do sometimes have godless, naughty children, and I point this out because there have been many who imputed great guilt and calumny to these parents whom I would herewith pardon. Such distortions are not merely abusive. If they imply Faustus had been taught such things by his parents, they are also slanderous. Indeed, certain charges are alleged—to wit: that his parents had permitted wantonness in his youth, and that they had not diligently held him to his studies. It is charged that, so soon as his cleverness—together with his lack of inclination to theology—was perceived, it being further public hue and cry that he was practicing magic, his family should have prevented it betimes. All such rumors are *somnia*, for the parents, being without guilt, should not be slandered. But now *ad propositum*.

Faustus was a most percipient and adroit fellow, qualified and inclined toward study, and he performed so well at his examination that the rectors also examined him for the *Magister* Degree. There were sixteen other candidates, to whom he proved in address, composition, and competence so superior that it was immediately concluded he had studied sufficiently, and he became *Doctor Theologiae*. For the rest, he was also a stupid, unreasonable and vain fellow, whom, after all, his companions always called the *speculator*. He came into the worst company, for a time laid the Holy Scriptures behindst the door and under the bench, did not revere God's Word but lived crassly and godlessly in gluttony and lust (as the progress of this *Historia* will sufficiently manifest). Surely the proverb is true: what is inclined to the devil will go to the devil.

Furthermore, Doctor Faustus found his ilk, who dealt in Chaldean, Persian, Arabian and Greek words, *figurae, characteres, coniurationes, incantationes;* and these things recounted were pure *Dardaniae artes, Nigromantiae, carmina, veneficii, vaticini, incantationes;* and whatever you care to call such books, words, and names for conjuring and sorcery. They well pleased Doctor Faustus; he speculated and studied night and day in them. Soon he refused to be called a *Theologus,* but waxed a worldly man, called himself a *Doctor Medicinae,* became an *Astrologus* and *Mathematicus*—and, for respectability, a physician. At first he helped many people with medicaments, herbs, roots, waters, receipts, and clisters. He became learned besides, well versed in the Holy Scriptures, and he knew quite accurately the Laws of Christ: he who knoweth the will of the Lord and doeth it not, he is doubly smitten. Likewise, thou shalt not tempt the Lord thy God. All this he threw in the wind and put his soul away for a time above the door sill, wherefore there shall for him be no pardon.

II

How Doctor Faustus
Did Achieve and Acquire Sorcery

As was reported above, Doctor Faustus's complexion was such that he loved what ought not be loved, to which his spirit did devote itself day and night, taking on eagle's wings and seeking out the very foundations of Heaven and Earth. For his prurience, insolence, and folly so pricked and incited him that he at last resolved to utilize and to prove certain magical *vocabula, figurae, characteres,* and *coniurationes* in the hope of compelling the devil to appear before him. Hence (as others also report and as indeed Doctor Faustus himself later made known) he went into a great dense forest which is called the *Spesser Wald* and is situated near Wittemberg. Toward evening, at a crossroad in these woods, he described certain circles with his staff, so that, beside twain, the two which stood above intersected a large circle. Thus in the night between nine and ten o'clock he did conjure the devil.

Now the devil feigned he would not willingly appear at the spot designated, and he caused such a tumult in the forest that everything seemed to be destroyed. He blew up such a wind that the trees were bent to the very ground. Then it seemed as were the wood with devils filled, who rode along past Doctor Faustus's circle; now only their coaches were to be seen; then from the four corners of the forest something like lightning bolts converged on Doctor Faustus's circle, and a loud explosion ensued. When all this was past, it became light in the midst of the forest, and many sweet instruments, music, and song could be heard. There were various dances, too, and tourneys with spears and swords. Faustus, who thought he might have tarried long enough now, considered fleeing from his circle, but finally he regained his godless and reckless resolve and persisted in his former intention, come whatever God might send.

He continued to conjure the devil as before, and the devil did mystify him with the following hoax. He appeared like a griffen or a dragon hovering and flattering above the circle, and when Doctor Faustus then applied his spell the beast shrieked piteously. Soon thereafter a fiery star fell right down from three or four fathoms above his head and was transformed into a glowing ball. This greatly alarmed Faustus, too. But his purpose liked him so well, and he so admired having the devil subservient to him that he took courage and did conjure the star once, twice, and a third time, whereupon a gush of fire from the sphere shot up as high as a man, settled again, and six little lights became visible upon it. Now one little light would leap upward, now a second downward until the form of a burning man finally emerged. He walked round about the circle for a full seven or eight minutes. The entire spectacle, however, had lasted until twelve o'clock in the night. Now a devil, or a spirit, appeared in the figure of a gray friar, greeted Doctor Faustus, and asked what his desire and intent might be. Hereupon Doctor Faustus commanded that he should appear at his house and lodging at a certain hour the next morning, the which the devil for a while refused to do. Doctor Faustus conjured him by his master, however, compelling him to fulfill his desire, so the spirit at last consented and agreed.

III

Here Followeth the Disputatio Held by Faustus and the Spirit

Doctor Faustus returned home and later the same morning commanded the spirit, who indeed appeared to hear what Doctor Faustus might desire of him (and it is most astounding that a spirit, when God withdraws his hand, can so deceive mankind) into his chamber. Doctor Faustus again commenced his machinations, conjured him anew, and laid before the spirit these several articles, to wit:

Firstly, the spirit should be subservient and obedient to him in all that he might request, inquire, or expect of him, throughout Faustus's life and death.

Secondly, the spirit would withhold no information which Faustus, in his studies, might require.

Thirdly, the spirit would respond nothing untruthful to any of his *interrogationes*.

The spirit immediately rejected the articles, refused Faustus, and explained his reason: he had not complete authority except in so far as he could obtain it from his lord who ruled over him. He spake, "Sweet Fauste, it standeth neither within my election nor authority to fulfill thy desires, but is left to the Hellish god."

Faustus replied, "What? How am I to understand thee? Art thou not thine own master?"

The spirit answered, "Nay."

Faustus then said to him, "Sweet spirit, explain it to me then."

"Now thou shalt know, Fauste," said the spirit, "that among us there is a government and sovereignty, just as on earth, for we have our rulers and governors and servants—of whom I am one—and we call our kingdom Legion. For although the banished devil Lucifer brought about his own fall through vanity and insolence, he raised up a Legion, nevertheless, and a government of devils, and we call him the Oriental Prince, for he had his sovereignty in Ascension. It is thus a sovereignty *in Meridie, Septentrione,* and *Occidente* as well. Well, inasmuch as Lucifer the fallen angel now hath his sovereignty and principality beneath the Heavens, we must, on account of this transformation, betake ourselves unto mankind and serve them. But with all his power and arts man could not make Lucifer subservient, except that a spirit be sent, as I am sent. Certainly we have never revealed to men the real fundament of our dwelling place, nor our rule and sovereignty. No one knoweth what doth occur after the death of the damned human—who learneth and experienceth it."

Doctor Faustus became alarmed at this and said, "Then I will not be damned for thy sake."

The spirit answered, "Wilt not agree? For thee no plea. If there be no plea, thou must come with me. Thou wost it not when we hold thee. Yet come thou must with me, nor helpeth any plea: an insolent heart hath damned thee."

Then Doctor Faustus said, "A pox take thee! Hence! Begone!"

Even in the moment when the spirit was about to withdraw, Doctor Faustus did change his vacillating mind. He conjured the spirit to appear at the same place at vespers to hear what else he would require. The spirit granted this and disappeared from before him.

IV

The Second Disputatio with the Spirit

At vespers, or at four o'clock in the evening, the flying spirit again appeared unto Faustus and proffered his obedience and subservience in all things, if so be that Faustus would tender certain articles to him in return. Would he do that, then his desires would know no want. These following were the several articles required by the spirit:

Firstly, that he, Faustus, would agree to a certain number of years, at the expiration of which he would promise and swear to be his, the spirit's, own property.

Secondly, that he would, to the further confirmation thereof, give himself over with a writ to this effect authenticated in his own blood.

Thirdly, that he would renounce the Christian Faith and defy all believers.

Should he observe all such points, every lust of his heart would be fulfilled. "And," spake the spirit, "thou shalt immediately be possessed of a spirit's form and powers." Puffed up with pride and arrogance, Doctor Faustus (although he did consider for a space) had got so proud and reckless that he did not want to give thought to the weal of his soul, but came to terms with the evil spirit, promised to observe all his articles, and to obey them. He supposed that the devil might not be so black as they use to paint him, nor Hell so hot as the people say.

V

Doctor Faustus's Third Colloquium *with the Spirit, Which Was Called* Mephostophiles—*Concerning Also the Pact Which These Two Made*

Now as for the Pact, it came about in this wise. Doctor Faustus required the spirit to come before him on the next morning, commanding him to appear, so often as he might be called, in the figure, form, and raiment of a Franciscan monk, and always with a little bell to give certain signals withal, in order that by the sound it might be known when he was approaching. Then he asked the spirit his name, and the spirit answered, "Mephostophiles."—Even in this hour did the godless man cut himself off from his God and Creator to become a liege of the abominable devil, whereto pride, arrogance, and transgression did bring and seduce him.

Afterwards, in audacity and transgression, Doctor Faustus executed a written instrument and document to the evil spirit. This was a blasphemous and horrible thing, which was found in his lodging after he had lost his life. I will include it as a warning to all pious Christians, lest they yield to the devil and be cheated of body and soul (as afterward his poor famulus was by Doctor Faustus to this devilish work seduced).

When these two wicked parties contracted with one another, Doctor Faustus took a penknife, pricked open a vein in his left hand (and it is the veritable truth that upon this hand were seen graven and bloody the words *o homo fuge—id est:* o mortal fly from him and do what is right), drained his blood into a crucible, set it on some hot coals and wrote as here followeth.

VI

Doctor Faustus's Instrumentum, or *Devilish and Godless Writ*

Obligatio

I, JOHANN FAUSTUS, Dr.,

Do publicly declare with mine own hand in covenant & by power of these presents:

Whereas, mine own spiritual faculties having been exhaustively explored (including the gifts dispensed from above and graciously imparted to me), I still cannot comprehend;

And whereas, it being my wish to probe further into the matter, I do propose to speculate upon the *Elementa;*

And whereas mankind doth not teach such things;

Now therefore have I summoned the spirit who calleth himself Mephostophiles, a servant of the Hellish Prince in Orient, charged with informing and instructing me, and agreeing against a promissory instrument hereby transferred unto him to be subservient and obedient to me in all things.

I do promise him in return that, when I be fully sated of that which I desire of him, twenty-four years also being past, ended, and expired, he may at such a time and in whatever manner or wise pleaseth him order, ordain, reign, rule, and possess all that may be mine: body, property, flesh, blood, etc., herewith duly bound over in eternity and surrendered by covenant in mine own hand by authority and power of these presents, as well as of my mind, brain, intent, blood, and will.

I do now defy all living beings, all the Heavenly Host and all mankind, and this must be.

In confirmation and contract whereof I have drawn out mine own blood for certification in lieu of a seal.

> Doctor Faustus, the Adept in the
> *Elementa* and in Church Doctrine

VII

Concerning the Service that Mephostophiles Used Toward Faustus

Doctor Faustus having with his own blood and in his own hand committed such an abomination unto the spirit, it is certainly to be assumed that God and the whole Heavenly Host did turn away from him. He dwelt in the house of his good Wittemberg kinsman, who had died and in his testament bequeathed it to Doctor Faustus. With him he had a young schoolboy as famulus, a reckless lout named Christoph Wagner. Doctor Faustus's game well pleased Wagner, and his lord also flattered him by saying he would make a learned and worthy man of him. A tune like that appealed to him (youth being always more inclined toward wickedness than toward goodness).

Now Doctor Faustus, as I said, had no one in his house save his famulus and his spirit Mephostophiles, who, in his presence, always went about in the form of a friar, and whom Doctor Faustus conjured in his study, a room which he kept locked at all times. Faustus had a superfluity of victuals and provisions, for when he desired a good wine the spirit brought it to him from whatever cellars he liked (the Doctor himself was once heard to remark that he made great inroads on the cellar of his Lord the Elector of Saxony as well as those of the Duke of Bavaria and of the Bishop of Saltzburg). He likewise enjoyed cooked fare every day, for he was so cunning in sorcery that when he opened a window and named some fowl he desired, it came flying right in through the window. His spirit also brought him cooked meat of a most princely sort from the courts of the nobility in all the territories round about. The fabrics for his apparel and that of his boy (he went sumptuously clothed) the spirit also had to buy or steal by night in Nuremberg, Augsburg, or Frankfurt. A similar injury was done the tanners and cobblers. In sum, it was all stolen, wickedly borrowed goods, so that Doctor Faustus's meat and clothing was very respectable, but godless. Indeed Christ our Lord doth through John call the devil a thief and a murderer, and that is what he is.

The devil also promised to give Faustus twenty-five crowns a week, which amounts to 1,300 crowns a year, and that was his year's emolument.

VIII

Concerning Doctor Faustus's Intended Marriage

While he lived thus day in and day out like an Epicure—or like a sow—with faith neither in God, Hell, nor the devil, Doctor Faustus's *aphrodisia* did day and night so prick him that he desired to enter matrimony and take a wife. He questioned his spirit in this regard, who was to be sure an enemy of the matrimonial estate as created and ordained by God.

The spirit answered, "Well, what is thy purpose with thyself?" *Viz.,* had Faustus forgot his commitment, and would he not hold to the promise wherein he had vowed enmity to God and mankind? If so, then neither by chance nor by intent dare he enter matrimony.

"For a man cannot serve two masters, spake the devil, God and us, too. Matrimony is a work of the Lord God. We, who take our profit from all that pertains to and derives from adultery and fornication, are opposed to it. Wherefore, Fauste, look thou to it: shouldst thou promise to wed, thou shalt then most assuredly be torn into little pieces by us. Sweet Fauste, judge for thyself what unquiet, antipathy, anger, and strife result from matrimony."

Doctor Faustus considered various sides of the matter, his monk constantly presenting objections. At last he said, "Well, I will wed, let come of it what may!"

When Faustus had uttered this resolve, a wind did fall upon his house and seemed about to destroy it. All the doors leapt from their hooks, and at the same instant his house was quite filled with heat, just as if it were about to burn away into pure ashes. Doctor Faustus took to his heels down the stair, but a man caught him up and cast him back into the parlor with such a force that he could move neither hand nor foot. Round about him everywhere sprang up fire. He thought he would be burned alive, and he screamed to his spirit for help, promising to live in accordance with every wish, counsel, and precept. Then the devil himself appeared unto him, so horrible and malformed that Faustus could not look upon him.

Satan said, "Now tell me, of what purpose art thou?"

Doctor Faustus gave him short answer, admitting he had not fulfilled his promise in that he had not deemed it to extend so far, and he did request Grace.

Satan answered him equally curtly, "Then be henceforth steadfast. I tell thee, be steadfast."

After this, the spirit Mephostophiles came to him and said unto him, "If thou are henceforth steadfast in thy commitment, lo, then will I tickle thy lust otherwise, so that in thy days thou wilt wish naught else than this—namely: if thou canst not live chastely, then will I lead to thy bed any day or night whatever woman thou seest in this city or elsewhere. Whoever might please thy lust, and whomever thou might desire in lechery, she shall abide with thee in such a figure and form."

Doctor Faustus was so intrigued by this that his heart trembled with joys and his original proposal rued him. And he did then come into such libidinousness and dissipation that he yearned day and night after the figure of the beautiful women in such excellent forms, dissipating today with one devil and having another on his mind tomorrow.

IX

Doctor Faustus's Quaestio *of His Spirit Mephostophiles*

Now after Doctor Faustus had for a time carried on such a very fine matrimony with the devil (as was reported above), his spirit committed unto him a great book containing all manner of sorcery and *nigromantia,* wherein he indulged himself in addition to his devilish wedlock (these *dardaniae artes* later being found with his famulus and son Christoph Wagner). Soon his curiosity did prick him and he summoned his spirit Mephostophiles, with whom he desired to converse and to whom he said, "Tell me, my servant, what manner of spirit art thou?"

The spirit answered and spake, "This *disputatio* and question, if I am to elucidate it for thee, my Lord Fauste, will move thee somewhat to discontent and to contemplation. Moreover, thou ought not have asked such of me, for it toucheth on our arcana.— But I must obey thee.

"Thou shalt know therefore that the Banished Angel at the time of his fall was still graciously and kindly disposed toward man, who had just been created. But soon the leaf did turn and Lucifer, become the enemy of God and all mankind, did presume to work all manner of tyranny upon men—as is every day manifest when one falleth to his death; another hangeth, drowneth, or stabbeth himself; a third is stabbed, driven mad, and the like other cases which thou might have observed. Because the first man was created so perfect by God, the devil did begrudge him such. He beset Adam and Eve and brought them with all their seed into sin and out of the Grace of God. Such, sweet Fauste, is the onslaught and tyranny of Satan. Likewise did he unto Cain. He caused the people of Israel to worship him, to sacrifice unto strange gods and to go lustfully in unto the heathen women. It was one of our spirits who pursued Saul and drove him into madness, pricking him on till he took his own life. Another spirit is amongst us, Asmodeus, who slew seven men in lechery. Then there is the spirit Dagon, who caused thirty thousand men to fall way from God, so that they were slain and the Ark of God was captured. And Belial, who did prick David's heart that he began to number the people, and sixty thousand perished. It was one of us who did send Solomon awhoring after false gods. Without number are our spirits that do insinuate themselves among men and cause them to fall. To this very day we still distribute ourselves over all the world, using every sort of guile and rascality, driving men away from the Faith and urging them on to sin and wickedness, that we may strengthen ourselves as best we can against Jesus by plaguing his followers unto death. We possess, to be sure, the hearts of the kings and rulers of this world, hardening them against the teachings of Jesus and of his apostles and followers."

Doctor Faustus answered and spake, "So hast thou possessed me also? Sweet fellow, tell me the truth."

The spirit answered, "Well why not? As soon as we looked upon thy heart and saw with what manner of thoughts thou didst consort, how thou couldst neither use nor get another than the devil for such an intent and purpose, lo, we then made those thoughts and strivings yet more impious and bold, and so prurient that thou hadst no rest by day nor by night, all thine aspirations and endeavors being directed toward the accomplishment of sorcery. Even while thou didst conjure us, we were making thee so wicked and so audacious that thou hadst let the very devil fetch thee before thou hadst forsaken thy purpose. Afterward, we encouraged thee yet further until we had planted it into thy heart not to falter in thy cause until thou hadst a spirit subservient unto thee. In the end, we persuaded thee to yield thyself to us finally and with body and soul. All this, Lord Fauste, canst thou learn from thyself."

"It is true," quoth Doctor Faustus, "there is no turning from my way now. I have ensnared myself. Had I kept god-fearing thoughts, and held to God in prayer, not allowing the devil so to strike root within me, then had I not suffered such injury in body and soul. Ay, what have I done, etc."

The spirit made answer, "Look thou to it."

Thus did Doctor Faustus take his despondent leave.

X

A Disputatio *Concerning the Prior State of the Banished Angels*

Doctor Faustus again undertook a discourse with his spirit, asking, "How, then, did thy master, Lucifer, come to fall?"

This time, Mephostophiles asked of him a three-day prorogation, but on the third day the spirit gave him this answer, "My Lord Lucifer (who is so called on account of his banishment from the clear light of Heaven) was in Heaven an angel of God and a cherub. He beheld all works and creations of God in Heaven and was himself with such honor, title, pomp, dignity, and prominence as to be the exemplary creature before God, in great perfection of wisdom, yea in such brilliance that he outshone all other creatures and was an ornament beyond all other works of God, gold and precious stones, even the sun and stars. For so soon as God created him He placed him upon the Mount of God as a sovereign prince, and he was perfect in all his ways.

"But so soon as he rose up in insolence and vanity and would exalt himself above Orient he was driven out from the House of Heaven, thrust down into fiery brimstone which is eternally unextinguished and tormenteth him forever. He had been honored with the crown of all heavenly pomp. But since he sat in spiteful council against God, God sat upon His Throne of Judgement and condemned him to Hell, whence he can never more rise up."

Doctor Faustus, having heard the spirit concerning these things, did now speculate upon many different tenets and justifications. He went in silence from the spirit into his chamber, laid himself upon his bed and began bitterly to weep and to sigh, and to cry out in his heart. For the account by the spirit caused him this time to consider how the devil and Banished Angel had been so excellently honored of God, and how, if he had not been so rebellious and arrogant against God, he would have had an eternal heavenly essence and residence, but was now by God eternally banished.

Faustus spake, "O woe is me and ever woe! Even so will it come to pass with me also, nor will my fate be the more bearable, for I am likewise God's creature, and my insolent flesh and blood have set me body and soul into perdition, enticed me with my reason and mind so that I as a creature of God am strayed from Him and have let the devil seduce me to bind myself unto him with body and soul, wherefore I can hope no more for Grace, but must needs be, like Lucifer, banished into perpetual damnation and lamentation. Ah woe and ever woe! To what perils I am exposing myself! What is my purpose with myself? O, that I were never born!"

Thus did Doctor Faustus complain, but he would not take faith, nor hope that he might be through penitence brought back to the Grace of God. For if he had thought, "The devil doth now take on such a color that I must look up to Heaven. Lo, I will turn about again and call upon God for Grace and Forgiveness, for to sin no more is a great penance." Then Faustus would have betaken himself to church and followed Holy Doctrine, thereby offering the devil resistance. Even if he had been compelled to yield up his body here, his soul would nevertheless have been saved. But he became doubtful in all his tenets and opinions, having no faith and little hope.

XI

A Disputatio *Concerning Hell,*
How It Was Created and Fashioned;
Concerning Also the Torments in Hell

Doctor Faustus had, no doubt, contrition in his heart at all times. It was a concern for how he had endangered his own salvation when he plighted himself to the devil for the sake of temporal things. But his contrition was the contrition and penance of Cain and Judas. Indeed there was contrition in his heart, but he despaired of the Grace of God, it seeming to him an impossibility to gain God's favor: like unto Cain, who also despaired, saying his sins were greater than could be forgiven him. It was the same with Judas.

And it was the same with Doctor Faustus. I suppose he looked up to Heaven, but his eyes discerned naught therein. They say that he dreamt of the devil and of hell. That means that when he recalled his transgressions he could not help thinking that frequent and much disputation, inquiry, and discourse with the spirit would bring him to such a fear of the consequences of sin that he would be able to mend his ways, repent his sins, and sin no more.

Thus Doctor Faustus again decided to hold discourse and a colloquium with the spirit, asking him, "What is hell; further, how hell was created and constituted; thirdly, about the manner of wailing and lamentation of the damned in hell; and fourthly, whether the damned could come again into the favor of God and be released from hell."

The spirit gave answer to none of these questions or articles, but spake, "As concerns thy purpose, Lord Fauste, thy *disputatio* on hell and hell's effects on man, thy desire for elucidation—I say to thee: what is thy purpose with thyself?

If thou couldst ascend directly into heaven, yet would I fling thee down into hell again, for thou art mine, walking my path toward hell even in thy many questions about hell. Sweet Fauste, desist. Inquire of other matters. Believe me, my account will bring thee into such remorse, despondency, pensiveness, and anxiety that thou wilt wish thou hadst never posed this question. My judgement and advice remains: desist from this purpose."

Doctor Faustus spake, "And I will know it or I will not live, and thou must tell it me."

"Very well," quoth the spirit, "I will tell thee. It costeth me little grief.

"Thou wouldst know what hell is, but the mortal soul is such that all thy speculations can never comprehend hell, nor canst thou conceive the manner of place where the Wrath of God is stored. The origin and structure is God's Wrath, and it hath many titles and designations, as House of Shame, Abyss, Gullet, Pit, also *Dissensio*. For the souls of the damned are also shamed, scorned, and mocked by God and His Blessed Ones, that they are thus confined in the House of the Abyss and Gullet. For hell is an insatiate pit and gullet which ever gapeth after the souls which shall not be damned, desiring that they, too, might be seduced and damned. This is what thou must understand, good Doctor.

"So soon as my master has fallen, and even at that moment, hell was ready for him and received him. It is a darkness where Lucifer is all banished and bound with chains of darkness, here committed that he may be held for judgment. Naught may be found there but fumes, fire, and the stench of sulphur. But we devils really cannot know in what form and wise hell is created, either, nor how it be founded and constructed by God, for it hath neither end nor bottom.

"That is my first and second report, which thou hast required of me. For the third, thou didst conjure me and demand of me a report as to what manner of wailing and lamentation the damned will find in hell. Perchance, my Lord Fauste, thou shouldst consult the Scriptures (they being withheld from me). But now even as the aspect and description of hell is terrible, so to be in it is an unbearable, acute agony. Inasmuch as I have already given account of the former, thy hellish speculations on the latter will I also satisfy with a report. The damned will encounter all the circumstances which I recounted afore, for what I say is true:

"The pit of hell, like womb of woman, and earth's belly, is never sated. Nevermore will an end or cessation occur. They will cry out and lament their sin and wickedness, the damned and hellish hideousness of the stench of their own afflictions. There will then be at last a calling out, a screaming and a wailing out unto God, with woe, trembling, whimpering, yelping, screaming and pain and affliction, with howling and weeping. Well, should they not scream woe and tremble and whimper, being outcast, with all Creation and all the children of God against them, bearing perpetual ignominy while the blessed enjoy eternal honor? And the woe and trembling of some will be greater than that of others, for, as sins are not equal, neither are the torments and agonies the same.

"We spirits shall be freed. We have hope of being saved. But the damned will lament the insufferable cold, the unquenchable fire, the unbearable darkness, stench, the aspect of the devils, and the eternal loss of anything good. Oh, they will lament with weeping of eyes, gnashing of teeth, stench in their noses, moaning in their throats, terror in their ears, trembling in their hands and feet. They will devour their tongues for great pain. They will wish for death, would gladly die, but cannot, for death will flee from them. Their torment and agony will wax hourly greater and acuter.

"There, my Lord Fauste, thou hast thy third answer, which is consonant with the first and second. Thy fourth question pertaineth to God: whether He will receive the damned into His Grace again. Thanks to thine other, related inquiries, and mine own views concerning hell and its nature, how it was created of God's wrath, we have been able to clarify certain fundamentals in advance. Thou shalt now receive one further, specific account (in spite of the fact that it will be in direct violation of thy contract and vow).

"Thy last question is whether the damned in hell can ever come again into the favor and Grace of God, and mine answer is No. For all who are in hell are there because God banished them there, and they must therefore burn perpetually in God's Wrath and severity, must remain and abide in a place where no hope can be believed. Yea, if they could eventually gain the Grace of God (as we spirits, who always have hope and are in constant expectancy) they would take cheer, and sigh in anticipation. But the damned have even as little hope as have the devils in hell of transcending their banishment and disgrace. They can have no more hope of salvation than can they hope for a twinkling of light in hell's darkness, for refreshment with a drink of water in hellfire's heat and anguish, or for warmth in hell's cold. Neither their pleading, nor their prayer, their crying, nor their sighing will be heard, and their conscience will not let them forget.

Emperors, kings, princes, counts, and other such regents will lament: had they but not lived in violence and lust, then they might come into the favor of God. A rich man: had he but not been a miser. A frivolous man: had he but not been vainglorious. An adulterer and philanderer: had he but not indulged in lechery, adultery, and fornication. A drunkard, glutton, gambler, blasphemer, perjurer, thief, highwayman, murderer, and their ilk: had I but not filled my belly daily with sumptuousness, pleasure and superfluity of drink and victual, had I but not cheated, blasphemed God in my heart, had I but not scolded wickedly and wantonly against God at every opportunity, had I but not borne false witness, stolen, sacked, murdered, robbed, then perhaps I could still hope for Grace. But my sins are too great and cannot be forgiven me, wherefore I must suffer this hellish torment. Hence may I, damned man, be sure that there is no Grace for me.

"Let it be understood then, my Lord Fauste, that the damned man—or the soul, if you will—can no more attain Grace than can he hope for an end to his sufferings or a tide wherein he might perchance be removed from such anguish. Why, if they could be given the hope of dipping water day by day from the sea at the sea shore until the sea were dry, then that would be a redemption. Or if there were a sandheap as high as Heaven from which a bird coming every other year might bear away but one little grain at a time, and they would be saved after the whole heap were consumed, then that would be a hope. But God will never take any thought of them. They will lie in hell like unto the bones of the dead. Death and their conscience will gnaw on them. Their firm belief and faith in God—oh they will at last acquire it—will go unheeded, and no thought will be taken of them. Thou thinkest perhaps that the damned soul might cover itself over and conceal itself in hell until God's Wrath might at last subside, and thou hast the hope that there might come a release if thou but persist in the aim of hope that God might still take thought of thee—even then there will be no salvation. There will come a time when the mountains collapse, and when all the stones at the bottom of the sea are dry, and all the raindrops have washed the earth away. It is possible to conceive of an elephant or a camel entering into a needle's eye, or of counting all the raindrops. But there is no conceiving of a time of hope in hell.

"Thus, in short, my Lord Fauste, hast thou my fourth and last report. And thou shalt know that if thou ask me more of such things another time thou shalt get no audience from me, for I am not obligated to tell thee such things. Therefore leave me in peace with further such probings and *disputationes*."

Again Doctor Faustus departed from the spirit all melancholy, confused and full of doubt, thinking now this way now that, and pondering on these things day and night. But there was no constancy in him, for the devil had hardened his heart and blinded him. And indeed when he did succeed in being alone to contemplate the Word of God, the devil would dizen himself in the form of a beautiful woman, embrace him, dissipating with him, so that he soon forgot the Divine Word and threw it to the wind.

Doctor Faustus: His *Historia*.
Here Followeth the Second Part:
Adventures & Sundry Questions

XII

His Almanacs and Horoscopes

Doctor Faustus, being no longer able to obtain answers from his spirit concerning godly matters, now had to rest content and desist from this purpose. It was in those days that he set about making almanacs and became a good *astronomus* and *astrologus*. He gained so much learning and experience from the spirit concerning horoscopes that all which he did contrive and write won the highest praise among all the *mathematici* of that day (as is, after all, common knowledge now). His horoscopes, which he sent to great lords and princes, always were correct, for he contrived them according to the advice of his spirit as to what would come to pass in the future, all such matters falling duly out even as he had presaged them.

His tables and almanacs were praised above others because he set down naught in them but what did indeed come to pass. When he presaged fogs, wind, snow, precipitation, etc., these things were all quite certain. His almanacs were not as those of some unskilled *astrologi* who know of course that it gets cold in the winter, and hence forecast freezes, or that it will be hot in the summer, and predict thunderstorms. Doctor Faustus always calculated his tables in the manner described above, setting what should come to pass, specifying the day and the hour and especially warning the particular districts—this one with famine, that one with war, another with pestilence, and so forth.

XIII

A Disputatio, *or Inquiry Concerning the Art of* Astronomia, *or* Astrologia

One time after Doctor Faustus had been contriving and producing such horoscopes and almanacs for about two years he did ask his spirit about the nature of *astronomia* or *astrologia* as practiced by the *mathematici*.

The spirit gave answer, saying, "My Lord Fauste, it is so ordained that the ancient haruspices and modern stargazers are unable to forecast anything particularly certain, for these are deep mysteries of God which mortals cannot plumb as we spirits can, who hover in the air beneath Heaven where we can see and mark what God hath predestined. Yes, we are ancient spirits, experienced in the heavenly movements. Why, Lord Fauste, I could make thee a perpetual calendar for the setting of horoscopes and almanacs or for nativity investigations one year after the other.—Thou hast seen that I have never lied to thee. Now it is true that the Patriarchs, who lived for five and six hundred years, did comprehend the fundamentals of this art and became very adept. For when such a great number of years elapse a luni-solar period is completed, and the older generation can apprise the younger of it. Except for that, all green inexperienced *astrologi* have to set up their horoscopes arbitrarily according to conjecture.

XIV

A Disputatio *and False Answer Which the Spirit Gave to Doctor Faustus*

The spirit, finding Doctor Faustus all sorrowful and melancholy, did ask him what his grievance might be, and what was on his mind. When he saw that Doctor Faustus would give him no answer, he became importunate and pressing, demanding to know the exact nature of Faustus's thoughts, so that he might be of some aid to him if at all possible.

Doctor Faustus answered, saying, "Well, I have taken thee unto me as a servant, and thy service doth cost me dear enough. Yet I cannot have my will of thee, as would be proper of a servant."

The spirit spoke, "My Lord, thou knowest that I have never opposed thee, but have ever humored thee. Except on one occasion, when I withheld information on one specific subject and under certain express terms, I have ever been submissive unto thee. Now why wilt thou not reveal thy desires? What is in thy mind?"

With such talk the spirit stole away the heart of Faustus, and he confessed he had been wondering how God created the world, and about the original birth of mankind. The spirit now gave Faustus a godless, un-Christian, and childish account and report on this subject, saying,

"The world, my Lord Fauste, hath never experienced birth and will never know death, and the human race has always existed. There is not any origin or beginning of things. The earth subsists, as always, of itself. The sea arose from the earth, and the two got along so very well that one would think they had carried on a conversation in which the land had required his realm from the sea, the fields, meadows, woods, grass, and trees; and that the sea had likewise demanded his own realm of water with the fish and all else therein. Now they did concede to God the creation of mankind and of heaven, and this is the way they finally became subservient to God. Thou wilt observe that I have explained how from one realm there finally arose four: air, fire, water, and earth. I know none other, nor briefer, way of instructing thee."

Doctor Faustus speculated on these things but could not comprehend them, for in the first chapter of Genesis he had read how Moses had told it otherwise. For this reason, he made no further comment.

XV

How Doctor Faustus Traveled Down to Hell

With each passing day, Doctor Faustus's end drew closer, and he was now come into his eighth year, having been for the most part of the time engaged in inquiry, study, questioning, and *disputationes*. In these days he again did dream of hell, and it caused him again to summon his servant, the spirit Mephostophiles, demanding that he call his own lord, Belial, unto him. The spirit agreed to do this, but instead of Belial a devil was sent who called himself Beelzebub, a flying spirit reigning beneath heaven. When he asked what Doctor Faustus desired of him, Faustus asked whether it could not be arranged for a spirit to conduct him into hell and out again, so that he might see and mark the nature, fundament, quality, and substance of hell.

"Yes," answered Beelzebub, "I will come at midnight and fetch thee."

Well, when it got pitch dark Beelzebub appeared unto him, bearing upon his back a bone chair which was quite enclosed round about. Here Doctor Faustus took a seat, and they flew away. Now hear how the devil did mystify and gull him, so that he had no other notion than that he really had been in hell.

He bare him into the air, where Doctor Faustus fell asleep just as if he were lying in a bath of warm water. Soon afterward he came upon a mountain of a great island, high above which sulphur, pitch, and flashes of fire blew and crashed with such a tumult that Doctor Faustus awoke when his devilish dragon swooped down into the abyss. Although all was violently burning round about him, he sensed neither heat nor fire, but rather little spring breezes as in May. Then he heard many different instruments whose music was exceeding sweet, but, as bright as shone the fire, he could see no one playing, nor dared he ask, questions having been strictly forbidden him.

Meanwhile, three more devilish dragons had flown up alongside Beelzebub. They were just like him and they went flying along ahead of him as he penetrated further into the abyss. Now a great flying stag with mighty antlers and many points came at Doctor Faustus and would have dashed him off his chair and down into the abyss. It frightened him greatly, but the three dragons flying ahead repulsed the hart. When he was better come down into the *spelunca,* he could see hovering about him a great multitude of serpents and snakes, the latter being unspeakably big. Flying lions came to his aid this time. They wrestled and struggled with the great snakes until they conquered them, so that he passed through safely and well.

When Doctor Faustus had attained a greater depth, he saw a huge, flying, angry bull come forth out of a hole which might have been an old gate. Bellowing and raging, he charged Faustus, goring his seat with such a force as to overturn pavilion, dragon, and Faustus, who now did fall off from his chair into the abyss, down and down, screaming woefully, wailing, and thinking, "All is over now." He could no longer see his spirit, but at last an old wrinkled ape caught him up as he fell, held him, and saved him. But then a thick dark fog fell upon hell, so that he could not see anything at all until presently a cloud opened from which climbed two big dragons pulling a coach along after them. The old ape was setting Faustus upon it when there arose such a windstorm with terrible thunder clasp and stench of sulphur and quaking of the mountain or abyss that Faustus thought he must faint away and die.

He was indeed enveloped in a deep darkness for about a quarter of an hour, during which time he had nó perception of the dragons or of the coach, but he did have a sensation of movement. Again the thick dark fog disappeared, and he could see his steeds and coach. Down the abyss shot such a multitude of lightning and flames upon his head that the boldest man—not to mention Faustus—would have trembled for fear. The next thing he perceived was a great turbid body of water. His dragons entered it and submerged. Yet Faustus felt no water at all, but great heat and radiance instead. The current and waves beat upon him until he again lost both steeds and coach and went falling deeper and deeper into the terror of the water. At last he found himself upon a high, pointed crag and here he sat, feeling half dead.

He looked about, but as he was able to see and hear no one, he began gazing on down into the abyss. A little breeze arose. All around him there was naught but water. He thought to himself, "What shalt thou do now, being forsaken even by the spirits of hell? Why thou must hurl thyself either into the water or into the abyss." At this thought he fell into a rage, and in a mad, crazy despair he leapt into the fiery hole, calling out as he cast himself in, "Now, spirits, accept my offering. I have earned it. My soul hath caused it."

Well, just at the moment when he hurled himself head over heels and went tumbling down, such a frightful loud tumult and banging assailed his ears, and the mountainpeak shook so furiously that he thought many big cannons must have been set off, but he had only come to the bottom of hell. Here were many worthy personages in a fire: emperors, kings, princes, and lords, many thousand knights, and men-at-arms. A cool stream ran along at the edge of the fire, and here some were drinking, refreshing themselves, and bathing, but some were fleeing from its cold, back into the fire. Doctor Faustus stepped up, thinking he might seize one of the damned souls, but even when he thought he had one in his hand it would vanish. On account of the intense heat, he knew he could not stay in this vicinity, and he was seeking some way out when his spirit Beelzebub came with the pavilion. Doctor Faustus took a seat and away they soared, for he could not long have endured the thunderclaps, fog, fumes, sulphur, water, cold, and heat, particularly since it was compounded with wailing, weeping, and moaning of woe, anguish, and pain.

Now Doctor Faustus had not been at home for a long while. His famulus felt sure that, if he had achieved his desire of seeing hell, he must have seen more than he had bargained for and would never come back. But even while he was thinking thus, Doctor Faustus, asleep in his pavilion, came flying home in the night and was cast, still asleep, into his bed. When he awoke early the next morning and beheld the light of dawn, he felt exactly as if he had been imprisoned for some time in a dark tower. At a somewhat later date, he became acquainted only with the fire of hell, and with the effects of those flames, but now he lay in bed trying to recollect what he had seen in hell. At first he was firmly convinced that he had been there and had seen it, but then he began to doubt himself, and assumed that the devil had charmed a vision before his eyes—and this is true, for he had not seen hell, else he would not have spent the rest of his life trying to get there. This history and account of what he saw in hell—or in a vision—was written down by Doctor Faustus himself and afterwards found in his own handwriting upon a piece of paper in a locked book.

XVI

How Doctor Faustus Journeyed Up into the Stars

This record was also found among his possessions, having been composed and written in his own hand and addressed to one of his close companions, a physic in Leipzig named Jonas Victor. The contents were as followeth:

Most dear Lord, and Brother,

I yet remember, as ye no doubt do, too, our school days in Wittemberg, where ye at first devoted yourself to *medicina, astronomia, astrologia, geometria,* so that ye are now a *mathematicus* and *physicus.* But I was not like unto you. I, as well ye know, did study *theologia*—although I nevertheless became your equal in the arts ye studied, too.

Now, as to your request that I report some few matters unto you and give you my advice: I, neither being accustomed to denying you aught, nor having ever refused to report aught to you, am still your servant, whom ye shall ever find and know to be such. I do express my gratitude for the honor and praise which ye accord me. In your epistle ye make mention of mine ascension into heaven, among the stars, for ye have heard about it, and ye write requesting that I might inform you whether it be so or not, since such a thing doth seem to you quite impossible. Ye remark in addition that it must have occurred with the aid of the devil or of sorcery. "Ay, how wilt thou bet, Fritz!" quoth the clown to the Emperor when asked if he had sullied his breeches.—Well, whatever means might have been used, it hath finally been accomplished, and of this *figura, actus,* and event I can make you the following report:

One night I could not go to sleep, but lay thinking about my almanacs and horoscopes and about the properties and arrangements in the heavens, how man—or some of the physics—hath measured those ornaments and would interpret them, even though he cannot really visualize such things and must hence base his interpretations and calculations quite arbitrarily on books and the tenets in them. While in such thoughts, I heard a loud blast of wind go against my house. It threw open my shutters, my chamber door, and all else, so that I was not a little astonished. Right afterward I heard a roaring voice saying, "Get thee up! Thy heart's desire, intent, and lust shalt thou see."

I made answer, "If it be possible for me to see that which hath just been the object of my thoughts and wishes, then I am well content."

He did answer again, saying, "Then look out at thy window where thou canst see our carriage."

That I did, and I saw a coach with two dragons come flying down. The coach was illuminated with the flames of hell, and inasmuch as the moon shone in the sky that night I could see my steeds as well. These creatures had mottled brown and white wings and the same color back; their bellies, however, were of a greenish hue with yellow and white flecks.

The voice spake again, "Well get thee in and be off!"

I answered, "I will follow thee, but only on condition that I may ask any question I like."

"Good," he answered, "be it then in this instance permitted thee."

So I climbed up onto my casement, jumped down into my carriage, and off I went, the flying dragons drawing me ever upward; and it did seem a miracle that the coach really had four wheels that crunched right along as if I were journeying over land.—To be sure, the wheels did gush forth streams of fire as they whirled around.

The higher I ascended, the darker did the world become, and when I would look down into the world from the heavens above, it was exactly as if I were gazing into a dark hole from bright daylight. In the midst of such upward shooting and soaring, my servant and spirit came whirring along and took a seat beside me in the coach.

I said to him, My Mephostophiles, what is to become of me now?"

"Let such thoughts neither confuse thee nor impede thee," spoke he and drove on higher upward.

XVII

Now Will I Tell You What I Did See

Departing on a Tuesday, and returning on a Tuesday, I was out one week, during which time I neither slept nor did feel any sleep in me. Incidentally, I remained quite invisible throughout the journey. On the first morning, at break of day, I said to my Mephostophiles, "I suppose thou dost know how far we are come" (now as long as I was up there I knew neither hunger nor thirst, but I could well observe only by looking back at the world that I was come a good piece this night).

Mephostophiles said, "In faith, my Fauste, thou art now come forty-seven mile up into the sky."

During the remainder of the day I discovered that I could look down upon the world and make out many kingdoms, principalities, and seas. I could discern the worlds of Asia, Africa, and Europe, and while at this altitude I said unto my servant, "Now point out to me and instruct me as to the names of these various lands and realms."

This he did, saying, "This over here on the left is Hungary. Lo, there is Prussia. Across there is Sicily—Poland—Denmark—Italy —Germany. Now tomorrow shalt thou inspect Asia and Africa and canst see Persia, Tartary, India, and Arabia.—But just look, right now the wind is changing and we can observe Pommerania, Muscovy, and Prussia. See, there is Poland—and Germany again— Hungary—and Austria."

On the third day I did look down into Major and Minor Turkey, Persia, India, and Africa. I saw Constantinople before me and, in the Persian and Constantinopolitan Seas, many ships with war troops shuttling busily back and forth. Constantinople looked so small there appeared to be no more than three houses there, with people not a span long.

Now I departed in July when it was very hot, and, as I looked now this way and now that, toward the East, South, and North, I observed how it was raining at one place, thundering at another, how the hail did fall here while at another place the weather was fair. In fine, I saw all things in the world as they do usually come to pass.

After I had been up there for a week, I began to observe what was above me, watching from a distance how the heavens did move and roll around so fast that they seemed about to fly asunder into many thousand pieces, the cloud sphere cracking so violently as if it were about to burst and break the world open. The heavens were so bright that I could not perceive anything any higher up, and it was so hot that I should have burned to a crisp had my servant not charmed a breeze up for me. The cloud sphere which we see down there in the world is as solid and thick as a masonry wall, but it is of one piece and as clear as crystal. The rain, which originates there and then falls upon the earth, is so clear that we could see ourselves reflected in it.

Now this cloud sphere moveth in the heavens with such a force that it runneth from East to West despite the fact that sun, moon, and stars strive against it, so that the momentum of the cloud sphere doth indeed drive sun, moon, and stars along with it. Thus we see how and why these bodies must proceed from East to West. Down in our world it doth appear—and I thought so, too—that the sun is no bigger than the head of a barrel. But it is in fact much bigger than the whole world: for I could discover no end to it at all. At night, when the sun goeth down, the moon must take on the sun's light, this being why the moon shineth so bright at night. And directly beneath heaven there is so much light that even at night it is daytime in heaven—this even though the earth remaineth quite dark. Thus I saw more than I had desired. One of the stars, for example, was larger than half the world. A planet is as large as the world. And, in the aery sphere, there I beheld the spirits which dwell beneath heaven.

While descending, I did look down upon the world again, and it was no bigger than the yolk of an egg. Why, to me the world seemed scarcely a span long, but the oceans looked to be twice that size. Thus, on the evening of the seventh day did I arrive home again, and I slept for three days in a row. I have disposed my almanacs and horoscopes in accordance with my observations, and I did not wish to withhold this fact from you. Now inspect your books and see whether the matter is not in accordance with my vision.

And accept my cordial greetings,

Dr. Faustus
The astroseer.

XVIII

Doctor Faustus's Third Journey

It was in his sixteenth year that Doctor Faustus undertook a tour or a pilgrimage, instructing his servant that he should conduct and convey him whithersoever he would go. He journeyed invisible down to Rome, where he went unseen into the Pope's palace and beheld all the servants and courtiers and the many sorts of dishes and fine foods that were being served.

"For shame!" he remarked to his spirit. "Why did not the devil make a Pope of me?"

Yes, Doctor Faustus found all there to be his ilk in arrogance, pride, much insolence, transgression, gluttony, drunkenness, whoring, adultery, and other fine blessings of the Pope and his rabble. This caused Doctor Faustus to observe, "Methought I were the devil's own swine, but he will let me fatten for a long while yet. These swine in Rome are already fatted and ready to roast and boil."

Since he had heard much of Rome, he remained for three days and nights in the Pope's palace, using his sorcery to make himself invisible. Now hear ye the adventures and the art which he used in the Pope's palace.

The good Lord Faustus, having had little good meat and drink for some time, came and stood invisible before the Pope's board, even as he was about to eat. The Pope crossed himself before taking meat, and at that moment Doctor Faustus did blow hard into his face. Every time the Pope crossed himself, Faustus would blow into his face again. Once he laughed aloud, so that it was audible in the whole hall; again, he did weep most convincingly. The servants knew not what this might be, but the Pope told his people it was a damned soul of which he had exacted penance and which was now begging for absolution. Doctor Faustus enjoyed this very much, for such mystifications well pleased him, too.

When the last course finally arrived and was set before the Pope, Doctor Faustus, feeling his own hunger, raised up his hands, and instantly all the courses and fine dishes together with their platters flew right into them. Together with his spirit he then rushed away to a mountain in Rome called the Capitolium, there to dine with great relish. Later he sent his spirit back with an order to fetch the daintiest wines from the Pope's table together with the finest goblets and flaggons.

When the Pope found out how many things had been stolen from him, he caused all the bells to be rung throughout the entire night and had mass and petition held for the departed souls. In anger toward one departed soul, however, he formally condemned it to purgatory with bell, book, and candle. As for Doctor Faustus, he accepted the Pope's meat and drink as an especial dispensation. The silver was found in his house after his death.

At midnight, when he was sated with the victuals, he bestrode a horse and flew to Constantinople. Here Doctor Faustus viewed the Turkish Emperor's might, power, brilliance, and court entourage for a few days. One evening when the Emperor sat at table Doctor Faustus performed for him an apish play and spectacle. Great tongues of fire burst up in the hall, and when everyone was hastening to quench them, it commenced to thunder and lightning. Such a spell was cast upon the Turkish Emperor that he could not rise, nor could he be carried out of there. The hall became as bright as the very homeland of the sun, and Faustus's spirit, in the figure, ornaments, and trappings of a Pope, stepped before the Emperor, saying, "Hail Emperor, so full of grace that I, thy Mahomet do appear unto thee!" Saying nothing more, he disappeared.

This hoax caused the Emperor to fall down upon his knees, calling unto Mahomet and praising him that he had been so gracious as to appear before him.

The next morning, Doctor Faustus went into the Emperor's castle, where the Turk has his wives or whores, and where no one is permitted except gelded boys who wait upon the women. He charmed this castle with such a thick fog that naught could be seen. Now Doctor Faustus transformed himself as had his spirit before, but posed as Mahomet himself, and he did reside for a while in this castle, the mist remaining throughout his stay, and the Turk during this same period admonishing his people to perform many rites. But Doctor Faustus drank and was full of good cheer, taking his pleasure and dalliance there. When he was through he used the same art as before and ascended into the sky in papish raiment and ornament.

Now when Faustus was gone and the fog disappeared, the Turk came to his castle, summoned his wives and asked who had been there while the castle was for so long surrounded with fog. They informed him how it was the god Mahomet who at night had called this one and that one to him, lain with them, and said that from his seed would rise up a great nation and valiant heroes. The Turk accepted it as a great benefit that Mahomet had lain with his wives, but he wondered if it had been accomplished according to the manner of mortals. "Oh yes," they answered, "that was the way it had been done." He had called them, embraced them, and was well fitted out—they would fain be served in such sort every day. He had lain with them naked and was certainly a man in all parts, except that they had not been able to understand his tongue. The priests instructed the Turk that he ought not believe it were Mahomet, but rather a phantom. The wives on the other hand said, be it ghost or man, he had been very kind to them and had served them masterfully, once or six times—nay, even more often—in a night; all of which caused the Turk much contemplation, and he remained doubtful in the matter.

XIX

Concerning the Stars

A prominent scholar in Halberstadt, Doctor N. V. W., invited Doctor Faustus to his table. Before supper was ready, Faustus stood for a while gazing out the window at the heavens, it being harvest time and the sky filled with stars. Now his host, being also a Doctor of Physic and a good *astrologus,* had brought Doctor Faustus here for the purpose of learning from him divers transformations in the planets and stars. Therefore he now leaned upon the window beside Doctor Faustus and looked also upon the brilliance of the heavens, the multitude of stars, some of which were shooting through the sky and falling to the earth. In all humility he made request that Doctor Faustus might tell him the condition and quality of this thing.

Doctor Faustus began in this wise, "My most dear Lord and Brother, this condition doth presuppose certain other matters which ye must understand first. The smallest star in Heaven, although when beheld from below it seems to our thinking scarcely so big as our large wax candles, is really larger than a principality. Oh yes, this is certain. I have seen that the length and breadth of the heavens is many times greater than the surface of the earth. From heaven, ye cannot even see earth. Many a star is broader than this land, and most are at least as large as this city.—See, over there is one fully as large as the dominion of the Roman Empire. This one right up here is as large as Turkey. And up higher there, where the planets are, ye may find one as big as the world."

XX

A Question on This Topic

"I know that to be true," saith this doctor. "But my Lord Faustus, how is it with the spirits who vex men and thwart their works (as some people say) by day and by night as well?"

Doctor Faustus answered, "We ought not to begin with this topic, but with the ordinances and creation of God, it being in accordance with these that the sun doth at break of day turn again toward the world with his radiance (it being also nearer in summer than in winter), and that the spirits then move beneath the cloud sphere where God hath committed them that they may discover all his portents. As the day progresses, they rise upward beneath the cloud sphere, for they are granted no affinity with the sun: the brighter it shines, the higher they do seek to dwell. In this context we might speak of forbidden days, for God hath not granted them light nor allowed them such a property.

"But by night, when it is pitch dark, then they are among us, for the brightness of the sun—even though it is not shining here—is in the first heaven so intense that it is as daylight there (this being why, in the blackness of night, even when the stars do not shine, men still perceive heaven). It followeth therefore that the spirits, not being able to endure or to suffer the aspect of the sun, which hath now ascended upwards, must come near to us on earth and dwell with men, frightening them with nightmares, howling, and spooks. Now what will ye wager and bet: when ye go abroad in the dark without a light—if ye dare do such a thing—a great fear will seize you. Furthermore, if ye are alone by night ye are possessed by strange phantasies, although the day bringeth no such things. At night some will start up in their sleep, another thinks there be a spirit near him, or that he be groping out for him, or that he walks round in the house, or in his sleep, etc. There are many such trials, all because the spirits are near to vex and plague men with multitudinous delusions."

XXI
The Second Question

"I thank you very much," spake the doctor, "my dear Lord Faustus, for your brief account. I shall remember it and ponder upon it my life long. But, if I may trouble you further, would ye not instruct me once more as concerns the brilliance of the stars and their appearance by night?"

"Yea, very briefly," answered Doctor Faustus. "Now it is certain that, so soon as the sun doth ascend into the third heaven (if it should move down into the first heaven, it would ignite the earth—but the time for that is not come yet, and the earth must still proceed along her God-ordained course), when the sun doth so far withdraw itself, I say, then doth it become the right of the stars to shine for as long as God hath ordained. The first and second heavens, which contain these stars, are then brighter than two of our summer days, and offer an excellent refuge for the birds by night.

"Night, therefore, observed from heaven, is nothing else than day, or, as one might also aver, the day is half the night. For ye must understand that when the sun ascends, leaving us here in night, the day is just beginning in such places as India and Africa. And when our sun shineth, their day waneth, and they have night."

XXII

The Third Question

"But I still do not understand," said the Doctor from Halberstadt, "the action of the stars, how they glitter, and how they fall down to earth."

Doctor Faustus answered, "This is nothing out of the ordinary, but an every-day happening. It is indeed true that the stars, like the firmament and other *Elementa,* were created and disposed in the heavens in such a fashion that they are immutable. But they do have their changes in color and in other external circumstances. The stars are undergoing superficial changes of this sort when they give off sparks or little flames, for these are bits of match falling from the stars—or, as we call them, shooting stars. They are hard, black, and greenish.

"But that a star itself might fall—why this is nothing more than a fancy of mankind. When by night a great streak of fire is seen to shoot downward, these are not falling stars, although we do call them that, but only slaggy pieces from the stars. They are big things, to be sure, and, as is true of the stars themselves, some are much bigger than others. But it is my opinion that no star itself falleth except as a scourge of God. Then such falling stars bring a murkiness of the heavens with them and cause great floods and devastation of lives and land."

Here Followeth the Third Part:
Doctor Faustus, His Adventures, the Things He Performed and Worked with His *Nigromantia* at the Courts of Great Potentates

XXIII
A History of the Emperor Charles V and Doctor Faustus

Our Emperor Charles, the fifth of that name, was come with his court entourage to Innsbruck, whither Doctor Faustus had also resorted. Well acquainted with his arts and skill were divers knights and counts, particularly those whom he had relieved of sundry pains and diseases, so that he was invited, summonsed, and accompanied to meat at court. Here the Emperor espied him and wondered who he might be. When someone remarked that it was Doctor Faustus, the Emperor noted it well, but held his peace until after meat (this being in the summer and after St. Philip and St. James). Then the Emperor summoned Faustus into his Privy Chamber and, disclosing to him that he deemed him adept in *nigromantia,* did therefore desire to be shown a proof in something which he would like to know. He vowed unto Faustus by his Imperial Crown that no ill should befall him, and Doctor Faustus did obediently acquiesce to oblige his Imperial Majesty.

"Now hear me then," quoth the Emperor. "In my camp I once did stand athinking, how my ancestors before me did rise to such high degree and sovereignty as would scarcely be attainable for me and my successors, especially how Alexander the Great, of all monarchs the most mighty, was a light and an ornament among all Emperors. Ah, it is well known what great riches, how many kingdoms and territories he did possess and acquire, the which to conquer and to organize again will fall most difficult for me and my succession, such territories being now divided into many separate kingdoms. It is my constant wish that I had been acquainted with this man and had been able to behold him and his spouse in the person, figure, form, mien, and bearing of life. I understand that thou be an adept master in thine art, able to realize all things according to matter and complexion, and my most gracious desire is that thou give me some answer now in this regard."

"Most gracious Lord," said Faustus, "I will, in so far as I with my spirit am able, comply with Your Imperial Majesty's desire as concerns the personages of Alexander and his spouse, their aspect and figure, and cause them to appear here. But Your Majesty shall know that their mortal bodies cannot be present, risen up from the dead, for such is impossible. Rather, it will be after this wise: the spirits are experienced, most wise and ancient spirits, able to assume the bodies of such people, so transforming themselves that Your Imperial Majesty will in this manner behold the veritable Alexander."

Faustus then left the Emperor's chamber to take counsel with his spirit. Being afterward come in again to the Emperor's chamber, he indicated to him that he was about to be obliged, but upon the one condition that he would pose no questions, nor speak at all, to which the Emperor agreed. Doctor Faustus opened the door. Presently Emperor Alexander entered in the very form which he had borne in life—namely, a well-proportioned, stout little man with a red or red-blond thick beard, ruddy cheeks, and a countenance as austere as had he the eyes of the Basilisk. He stepped forward in full harness and, going up to Emperor Charles, made a low and reverent curtesy before him. Doctor Faustus restrained the Emperor of Christendom from rising up to receive him. Shortly thereafter, Alexander having again bowed and being gone out at the door, his spouse now approached the Emperor, she, too, making a curtesy. She was clothed all in blue velvet, embroidered with gold pieces and pearls. She, too, was excellent fair and rosy-cheeked, like unto milk and blood mixed, tall and slender, and with a round face.

Emperor Charles was thinking the while, "Now I have seen two personages whom I have long desired to know, and certainly it cannot be otherwise but that the spirit hath indeed changed himself into these forms, and he doth not deceive me, it being even as with the woman who raised the prophet Samuel for Saul."

But desiring to be the more certain of the matter, the Emperor thought to himself, "I have often heard tell that she had a great wen on her back. If it is to be found upon this image also, then I would believe it all the better."

So, stepping up to her, he did lift her skirt, and he found the wen. For she stood stock still for him, disappearing again afterwards. Thus, the Emperor's desire was granted withal, and he was sufficiently content.

XXIV
Concerning the Antlers of a Hart

Upon a time soon after Doctor Faustus had accomplished the Emperor's will as was reported above he, hearing the signal for meat in the evening, did lean over the battlements to watch the domestics go out and in. There he espied one who was fallen asleep while lying in the window of the great Knights' Hall across the court (it being very hot). I would not name the person, for it was a knight and a gentleman by birth.

Now with the aid of his spirit Mephostophiles, Faustus did charm a pair of hart's horns upon the knight's head. This good lord's head nodded upon the window sill, he awoke, and perceived the prank. Who could have been more distressed! For, the windows being closed, he could go neither forward nor backward with his antlers, nor could he force the horns from off his head. The Emperor, observing his plight, laughed and was well pleased withal until Doctor Faustus at last released the poor knight from the spell again.

XXV
Concerning Three Lords Who Were Rapidly Transported to the Royal Wedding in Munich

Three sons of noble lords (whom I dare not call by name) were students in Wittemberg. They met together on a time and, talking of the magnificent pomp which would attend the wedding of the son of the Duke of Bavaria in Munich, did heartily wish they might go there, if only for a half an hour.

Such talk caused the one of them to take thought of Doctor Faustus, and he said to the other two lords, "Cousins, if ye will follow me, hush, and keep it to yourselves, then will I give you good counsel, how we can see the wedding and then be back to Wittemberg again in the self-same night. Here is what I have in mind: if we send for Doctor Faustus, tell him what we desire, and explain our plans to him, giving him a bit of money besides, then he surely will not deny us his aid."

Having deliberated and agreed upon the matter, they called on Doctor Faustus, who, touched by their present and also being well pleased with a banquet which they were clever enough to give in his honor, did consent to grant them his services.

The day arrived when the wedding of the Bavarian Duke's son was to be celebrated, and Doctor Faustus sent word to the young lords that they should come to his house arrayed in the very finest clothing they possessed. He then took a broad cloak, spread it out in his garden (which lay right beside his house), seated the lords upon it, himself in their midst, and at last gave strict command that none should speak a word so long as they be abroad—even though they be in the Bavarian Duke's Palace and someone should speak to them, they should give no answer—the which they all did pledge to obey. This matter being settled, Doctor Faustus sat down and commenced his *coniurationes*. Presently there arose a great wind which lifted the cloak and transported them through the air with such speed that they arrived betimes at the Duke's court in Munich.

They had traveled invisible, so that no one noticed them until they entered the Bavarian Palace and came into the hall, where the Marshall, espying them, indicated to the Duke of Bavaria how, although the princes, lords, and gentlemen were already seated at table, there were still standing three more gentlemen without who had just arrived with a servant, and who also ought to be received. The old Duke of Bavaria arose to do this, but when he approached and spoke to them, none would utter a word.

This occurred in the evening just before meat, they having hitherto observed all day the pomp of the wedding without any hindrance, for Faustus's art had kept them invisible. As was reported above, Doctor Faustus had sternly forbidden them to speak this day. He had further instructed them that so soon as he should call out, "Up and away!" all were to seize upon the cloak at once, and they would fly away again in the twinkling of an eye.

Now when the Duke of Bavaria spoke to them and they gave no answer, handwater was proffered them anyhow. It was then that Doctor Faustus, hearing one of the lords forget himself and violate his command, did cry aloud, "Up and away!" Faustus and the two lords who held to the cloak were instantly flown away, but the third, who had been negligent, was taken captive and cast into a cell. The other two lords did upon arrival at midnight in Wittemberg behave so glumly on account of their kinsman that Doctor Faustus sought to console them, and he promised that the young man would be released by morning.

The captive lord, being thus forsaken, in locked custody besides, and constrained by guards, was sore afraid. To make matters worse, he was questioned as to what manner of vision he had been a part of, and as to the other three who were now vanished away.

He thought, "If I betray them, then the ending will be bad."

He therefore gave answer to none who were sent to him, and when they saw that nothing was to be got out of him this day they finally informed him that on the morrow he would be brought down to the dungeon, tortured, and compelled to speak. The lord thought to himself, "So my ordeal is appointed for the morrow. If Doctor Faustus should not release me today, should I be tortured and racked, well then I needs must speak."

But he still had the consolation that his friends would entreat Doctor Faustus for his release, and that is indeed the way it fell out. Before daybreak Doctor Faustus was in the cell, having cast such a spell on the watch that they fell into a heavy sleep. Faustus used his art to open all doors and locks, and he brought the lord punctually to Wittemberg, where a sumptuous honorarium was presented him as a reward.

XXVI

Concerning an Adventure with a Jew

It is said that the fiend and the sorcerer will not wax three penny richer in a year, and even so did it come to pass with Doctor Faustus. Much had been promised by his spirit, but much had been lies, for the devil is the spirit of lies.

Mephostophiles had once reproached Doctor Faustus, saying, "With the skill wherewith I have endowed thee thou shouldst acquire thine own wealth. Such arts as mine and thine can scarcely lose thee money. Thy years are not yet over. Only four years are past since my promise to thee that thou wouldst want neither for gold nor for goods. Why, thy meat and drink hath been brought thee from the courts of all the great potentates, all by mine art." (What the spirit here states, we did already report above.)

Doctor Faustus, who did not know how to disagree with these things, began to take thought and to wonder just how apt he might be in obtaining money. Not long after the spirit had told him those things, Faustus went banqueting with some good fellows and, finding himself without money, went and raised some in the Jewish quarter, accepting sixty talers for a month's time.

The money-lender, when the loan fell due, was ready to take his capital together with the usury, but Doctor Faustus was not at all of the opinion that he ought to pay anything. The fellow appeared at Faustus's house with his demand and received this answer: "Jew, I have no money. I can raise no money. But this I will do. From my body I will amputate a member, be it arm or leg, and give it thee in pawn—but it must be returned so soon as I am in money again."

The Jew (for Jews are enemies to us Christians, anyhow) pondered the matter and concluded that it must be a right reckless man who would place his limbs in pawn. But still he accepted it. Doctor Faustus took a saw and, cutting off his leg withal, committed it unto the Jew (but it was only a hoax) upon the condition that it must be returned so soon as he be in money again and would pay his debt, for he would fain put the member back on. The Jew went away with the leg, well satisfied at first with his contract and agreement. But very soon he became vexed and tired of the leg, for he thought, "What good to me is a knave's leg? If I carry it home it will begin to stink. I doubt that he will be able to put it on again whole, and, besides, this pledge is a parlous thing for me, for no higher pawn can a man give than his own limb. But what profit will I have of it?"

Thinking these and such like things as he crossed over a bridge, the Jew did cast the leg into the water. Doctor Faustus knew all about this of course, and three days later he summoned the Jew in order to pay and settle his account. The Jew appeared and explained his considerations, saying he had thrown the leg away because it was of no use to anyone. Doctor Faustus immediately demanded that his pledge be returned or that some other settlement be made. The Jew was eager to be free of Faustus, and he finally had to pay him sixty guilders more (Doctor Faustus still having his leg as before).

XXVII

An Adventure at the Court of the Count of Anhalt

Doctor Faustus came upon a time to the Count of Anhalt, where he was received with all kindness and graciousness. Now this was in January, and at table he perceived that the Countess was great with child. When the evening meat had been carried away and the collation of sweets was being served, Doctor Faustus said to the Countess, "Gracious Lady, I have always heard that the greatbellied women long for diverse things to eat. I beg your Grace not to conceal from me what you would please to have."

She answered him, "Truly my Lord, I will not conceal from you my present wish that it were harvest time, and I were able to eat my fill of fresh grapes and of other fruit."

Hereupon Doctor Faustus said, "Gracious Lady, this is easy for me to provide. In an hour your Grace's will shall be accomplished."

Doctor Faustus now took two silver bowls and set them out before the window. When the hour was expired he reached out the window and drew in one bowl with white and red grapes which were fresh from the vine, and the other bowl full of green apples and pears, but all of a strange and exotic sort. Placing them before the Countess, he said to her, "Your Grace need have no fear to eat, for I tell you truly that they are from a foreign nation where summer is about to end, although our year is, to be sure, just beginning here."

While the Countess did eat of all the fruit with pleasure and great wonderment, the Count of Anhalt could not withhold to ask for particulars concerning the grapes and other fruit.

Doctor Faustus answered, "Gracious Lord, may it please your Grace to know that the year is divided into two circles in the world, so that it is summer in Orient and Occident when it is winter here, for the heavens are round. Now, from where we dwell the sun hath now withdrawn to the highest point, so that we are having short days and winter here, but at the same time it is descending upon Orient and Occident—as in Sheba, India, and in the East proper. The meaning of this is that they are having summer now. They enjoy vegetables and fruit twice a year there. Furthermore, gracious Lord, when it is night here, day is just dawning there. The sun hath even now betaken himself beneath the earth, and it is night; but in this same instant the sun doth run above the earth there, and they shall have day (in likeness thereof, the sea runneth higher than the world, and if it were not obedient to God, it could inundate the world in a moment). In consideration of such knowledge, gracious Lord, I sent my spirit to that nation upon the circumference of the sea where the sun now riseth, although it setteth here. He is a flying spirit and swift, able to transform himself in the twinkling of an eye. He hath procured these grapes and fruit for us."

The Count did attend these revelations with great wonderment.

XXVIII

The Manner in Which Doctor Faustus as Bacchus Kept Shrovetide

The greatest effort, skill, and art produced by Doctor Faustus was that which he demonstrated to the Count of Anhalt, for with the aid of his spirit he accomplished not merely the things I have told about, but he created all sorts of four-footed beasts as well as winged and feathered fowl, too. Now after he had taken leave of the Count and returned back to Wittemberg, Shrovetide approached. Doctor Faustus himself played the role of *Bacchus,* entertaining several learned students, whom he persuaded (after they had been well fed and sated by Faustus, had crowned him *Bacchus,* and were in the act of celebrating him) to go into a cellar with him and to try the magnificent drinks which he would there offer and provide them, a thing to which they readily assented. Doctor Faustus then laid out a ladder in his garden, seated a man on each rung, and away he whisked, coming by night into the cellar of the Bishop of Salzburg.

Here they tasted all sorts of wine, for this bishop hath a glorious grape culture, but when the good gentlemen were just in a fine temper, the Bishop's butler by chance did come downstairs and, seeing them (for Doctor Faustus had brought along a flint so that they might better inspect all the casks), did charge them as thieves who had broken in. This offended Doctor Faustus, who, warning his fellows to prepare to leave, seized the butler by the hair and rode away with him until he saw a great high fir tree, in the top of which he deposited the frightened man. Being returned home again, he and his Shrovetide guests celebrated a *valete* with the wine which he had brought along in a big bottle from the Bishop's cellar.

The poor butler had to hold fast all night to the tree, lest he fall out, and he almost froze to death. When day brake and he perceived the great height of the fir as well as the impossibility of climbing down (for it had no branches except in the very top), he had to call out to some peasants whom he saw drive by, and tell them what had happened to him. The peasants did marvel at all this and, coming into Salzburg, reported it at court. This brought out a great crowd, who with much exertion and effort with ropes did bring the butler down. But he never knew who those were whom he had found in the cellar, nor who he was who had put him into the tree top.

XXIX

Concerning Helen, Charmed Out of Greece

On Whitsunday the students came unannounced to Doctor Faustus's residence for dinner, but, as they brought ample meat and drink along, they were welcome guests. The wine was soon going round at table, and they fell to talking of beautiful women, one of the students asserting that there were no woman whom he would rather see than fair Helen from Greece, for whose sake the worthy city of Troy had perished. She must have been beautiful, he said, for she had been stolen away from her husband, and a great deal of strife had arisen on her account.

Doctor Faustus said, "Inasmuch as ye are so eager to behold the beautiful figure of Queen Helen, I have provided for her awakening and will now conduct her hither so that ye may see her spirit for yourselves, just as she appeared in life (in the same way, after all, that I granted Emperor Charles V his wish to see the person of Emperor Alexander the Great and his spouse)."

Forbidding that any should speak or arise from table to receive her, Faustus went out of the parlor and, coming in again, was followed at the heel by Queen Helen, who was so wondrously beautiful that the students did not know whether they were still in their right minds, so confused and impassioned were they become. For she appeared in a precious deep purple robe, her hair, which shone golden and quite beautifully glorious, hanging down to her knees. She had coal black eyes, a sweet countenance on a round little head. Her lips were red as the red cherries, her mouth small, and her neck like a white swan's. She had cheeks pink like a rose, an exceeding fair and smooth complexion and a rather slim, tall, and erect bearing. *In summa,* there was not a flaw about her to be criticized. Helen looked all around in the parlor with a right wanton mien, so that the students were violently inflamed with love for her, but since they took her to be a spirit they controlled their passion without difficulty, and she left the room again with Doctor Faustus.

After the vision had passed away, the young men begged Faustus to be so good as to have the image appear just once more, for they would fain send a painter to his house the next day to make a counterfeit of her. This Doctor Faustus refused to do, saying that he could not make her spirit appear at just any time, but that he would procure such a portrait for them. Later, he did indeed produce one, and all the students had it copied by sending painters to his house (for it was a fair and glorious figure of a woman). Now it is unknown to this day who got this painting away from Doctor Faustus.

As concerns the students, when they came to bed they could not sleep for thinking of the figure and form which had appeared visibly before them, and from this we may learn how the devil doth blind men with love—oh it doth often happen that a man goeth awhoring for so long that at last he can no longer be saved from it.

XXX

Concerning a Gesticulation Involving Four Wheels

Doctor Faustus was summoned and commanded to come to the town of Brunswick to cure a marshall there who had consumption. Now he used to ride neither horseback nor by coach, but was of a mind to walk wherever he was invited as a guest or summoned as a physician. When he was about a half a quarter from Brunswick and could see the town before him, a peasant with four horses and an empty wagon came clattering along. Doctor Faustus addressed the clown in all kindness, requesting that he be allowed to climb on and be driven the rest of the way up to the town gate, but the bumpkin refused to do this and turned Faustus away, saying he would have enough to haul on his return trip. Doctor Faustus had not been serious in his request, wanting only to prove the peasant, whether there were any love to be found in him, but now he repaid the clown's churlishness (such as is, after all, commonly found among peasants) in like coin, speaking to him thus:

"Thou bumpkin and worthless ass, since thou hast demonstrated such churlishness unto me, and since thou wilt certainly use others the same and probably already hast done so, thou shalt this time be paid for thy trouble. Thy four wheels shalt thou find one at each gate of Brunswick town."

Immediately the wagon wheels sprang away, floating along in the air so that each one came to a different gate, without being noticed by anyone there. The peasant's horses also fell down as if they had suddenly died and lay there quite still. At this was the poor clown sore affright, measuring it as a special scourge of God for his misanthropy. All troubled and weeping, with outstretched hands and upon his knees, he did beg Faustus for forgiveness, confessing himself indeed well worthy of such punishment, but vowing that the next time this would serve as a remembrance to him, so that he would never use such misanthropy again.

Doctor Faustus took pity upon the clown's humility and answered him, saying that he must treat no one else in this hard manner, there being nothing more shameful than the qualities of churlishness and misanthropy—and the wicked pride which accompanieth them. Now the man should but take up some earth and throw it upon the team, which would then rise up and live out its days. So it came to pass, Faustus saying as he departed from the peasant, "Thy churlishness cannot go altogether unpunished, but must be repaid in equal measure, inasmuch as thou hast deemed it such a great effort to take a tired man onto an empty wagon. Lo, thy wheels are without the town at four different gates. There wilt thou find all four of them."

The peasant went along and found them as Doctor Faustus had said, but with great effort, travail, and neglect of the trade and business which he had intended to accomplish. And thus will churlishness ever punish its owner.

XXXI

Concerning Four Sorcerers Who Cut Off One Another's Heads and Put Them On Again, Wherein Doctor Faustus, Attending Their Performance, Doth Play the Major Role

Doctor Faustus came to the Carnival in Frankfurt, where his spirit Mephostophiles did inform him that there were four sorcerers at an inn in Jews Alley who were attracting a great audience by chopping off one another's heads and sending them to the barber to be trimmed. Now that vexed Faustus, who liked to think that he were the only cock in the devil's basket. When he went to behold the thing, he found the sorcerers just getting ready to chop off their heads, and with them was a barber who was going to trim and wash them. Upon a table they had a glass cruse with distilled water in it. One among them, the chief sorcerer and also their executioner, laid his hands upon the first of his fellows and charmed a lily into this cruse. It waxed green, and he called it the Root of Life. Now he beheaded that first fellow, let the barber dress the head, then set it upon the man's shoulders again. In one and the same instant, the lily disappeared and the man was whole again. This was done with the second and the third sorcerer in like manner. A lily was charmed for each in the water, they were executed, their heads were then dressed and put back on them again.

At last it was the turn of the chief sorcerer and executioner. His Root of Life was blooming away in the water and waxing green, now his head was smitten off also, and they set to washing it and dressing it in Faustus's presence, which sorcery did sorely vex him: the arrogance of this *magicus princeps,* how he let his head be chopped off so insolently, with blasphemy and laughter in his mouth. Doctor Faustus went up to the table where the cruse and the flowering lily stood, took out his knife, and snipped the flower, severing the stem. No one was aware of this at the time, but when the sorcerers sought to set the head on again their medium was gone, and the evil fellow had to perish with his sins upon his severed head.

Afterwards they did find the stem cut, but they were not able to discover how this came to pass. This is the way the devil at last rewards all his servants, absolving them thus, the manner in which Doctor Faustus dealt with this man being entirely consonant with the shameful absolution which he did himself receive when he was repaid for his own sins.

XXXII

Concerning an Old Man Who Would Have Converted Doctor Faustus from His Godless Life

A Christian, pious, godfearing physician, a person zealous of the honor of God, was also a neighbor of Doctor Faustus, and, seeing that many students frequented Faustus's house, he considered such a den as bad as a brothel, for he did compare Faustus to all the Jews, who, so soon as they fell away from God also became His declared enemies, dedicating themselves unto sorcery for the sake of prophecy and deceit, seeking not only the bodily harm of many a pious child whose parents have devoted much effort to his Christian rearing, but also causing him to forget the Lord's Prayer. This old neighbor of Doctor Faustus had observed his rascality in such a light for long years and no longer doubted the devilish nature of his mischief, but he also knew that the time was not yet ripe for the civil authorities to establish these facts.

Considering thus above all the weal of the young men, he did in Christian zeal summon Faustus as a guest into his own lodging. Faustus came, and at table his old godfearing patron addressed him, "My sweet Lord, as a friend and as a Christian I ask you not to receive my discourse in rancor and in ill will, nor to despise these small victuals, but charitably to take and to be content with what our sweet Lord provideth us."

Doctor Faustus requested him to declare his purpose, saying he would attend him obediently. His patron then commenced: "My sweet Lord and Neighbor, ye know your own actions, that ye have defied God and all the Saints, that ye have given yourself up unto the devil, whereby ye are now come into God's greatest wrath and are changed from a Christian into a very heretic and devil. O why do ye deprave your soul! Ye must not heed the body, but your sweet soul, lest ye reside in the eternal punishment and displeasure of God. Look ye to it, my Lord, ye are not yet lost if ye will but turn from your evil way, beseech God for Grace and pardon, as ye may see in the example in Acts 8 concerning Simon in Samaria, who had also traduced many. They thought him to be a god, calling him the Power of God and *Simon Deus Sanctus*. But he was converted when he heard a sermon of St. Philip, was baptized, and did believe on our Lord Jesus Christ. It is particularly noted and praised in Acts how he did afterward much consort with Philip. Thus, my Lord, allow my sermon also to appeal to you. O, let it be a heartfelt Christian admonition! To sin no more is the penance wherewith ye must seek Grace and pardon, as ye may learn from the fine examples of the thief on the cross, as well as from St. Peter, St. Matthew, and Magdalena. Yea, Christ our Lord speaketh unto all sinners, 'Come unto me, all ye that labor and are heavy laden, and I will give you rest.' Or, in the Prophet Ezekiel, 'I have no pleasure in the death of the wicked; but that the wicked should turn from his way and live, for his hand is not withered, that he were no longer useful.' I beg you, my Lord, take my plea to your heart, ask God for pardon for Christ's sake, and abjure at the same time your evil practices; for sorcery is against God and His Commandment, inasmuch as He doth sorely forbid it in both the Old and the New Testaments. He speaketh, 'Ye shall not allow them to live, ye shall not seek after them nor hold counsel with them, for it is an abomination unto God.' Thus St. Paul called Bar-Jesus, or Elymas the Sorcerer, a child of the devil and an enemy of all righteousness, saying that such should have no share in the Kingdom of God."

Doctor Faustus attended him diligently and said that the speech had well pleased him. He expressed his gratitude to the old man for his good will and took his leave, promising to comply in so far as he was able.

When he arrived home he took the old man's counsel to heart, considering how he had indeed depraved his soul by yielding himself up to the accursed devil, and at last Faustus felt a desire to do penance and to revoke his promise to the devil.

While he was occupied in such thoughts, his spirit appeared unto him, groping after him as if to twist his head off his shoulders. The spirit then spake, rebuking him, "What is thy purpose with thyself?"

He reminded him of his motives in first consigning himself to the devil. Having promised enmity toward God and all mankind, he was not now fulfilling that pledge but was following after this old reprobate, feeling charity toward a man and hence toward

God—now, when it was already too late and when he was clearly the property of the devil.

"The devil hath the power, he spake, to fetch thee away. I am in fact now come with the command to dispose of thee—or to obtain thy promise that thou wilt never more allow thyself to be seduced, and that thou wilt consign thyself anew with thy blood. Thou must declare immediately what thou wouldst do, or I am to slay thee."

Sore affright, Doctor Faustus consented, sat down and with his blood did write as followeth (this document being found after his death):

XXXIII
Pact

I, Doctor Johann Faustus,
Do declare in this mine own hand and blood:
Whereas I have truly and strictly observed my first *instrumentum* and pact for these nineteen years, in defiance of God and all mankind;

And whereas, pledging body and soul, I therein did empower the mighty God Lucifer with full authority over me so soon as five more years be past;

And whereas he hath further promised me to increase my days in death, thereby shortening my days in Hell, also not to allow me to suffer any pain;

Now therefore do I further promise him that I will never more heed the admonitions, teachings, scoldings, instructions, or threats of mankind, neither as concerneth the Word of God nor in any temporal or spiritual matters whatsoever; but particularly do I promise to heed no man of the cloth nor to follow his teachings.

In good faith and resolve contracted by these presents and in mine own blood, etc.

Now just as soon as Faustus had executed this godless, damned pact, he began to hate the good old man so intensely that he sought some means to kill him, but the old man's Christian prayers and

Christian ways did such great offense to the Evil Fiend that he could not even approach him.

Two days after the events just recounted, when the old man was retiring, he heard a mighty rumbling in his house, the like of which he was never wont to hear. It came right into his chamber, grunting like a sow and continuing for a long time. Lying abed, the old man began to mock the spirit, saying, "Ah, what a fine bawdy music! Now what a beautiful hymn sung by a ghoul! Really a pretty anthem sung by a beautiful angel—who could not tarry in Paradise for two full days. This wretched fellow must now go avisiting in other folks' houses, for he is banished from his own home."

With such mockery he drove the spirit away. When Doctor Faustus asked him how he had fared with the old man, Mephostophiles answered that he had not been able to lay hold on him, for he had worn armor (referring to the prayers of the old man) and had mocked him besides.

Now the spirits and devils cannot suffer a good humor, particularly when they are reminded of their fall. Thus doth God protect all good Christians who seek in Him succor against the Evil One.

Doctor Faustus: His Last Tricks and What He Did in the Final Years of His Contract

XXXIV

How Doctor Faustus Brought About the Marriage of Two Lovers

A student in Wittemberg, a gallant gentleman of the nobility named N. Reuckauer, was with heart and eyes far gone in love with an equally noble and exceedingly beautiful gentlewoman. Of the many suitors (among them even a young knight) whom she turned down, this Reuckauer was privileged to occupy the least place of all. But he was a good friend of Doctor Faustus, having often sat with him at meat and at drink, so that when the acute affects of his love for the gentlewoman caused him to pine away and fall ill, Faustus soon learned of it. He asked his spirit Mephostophiles about the cause of this serious condition and, being told that it was the love affair, soon paid a visit to the nobleman, who was greatly astonished to learn the true nature of his illness. Doctor Faustus bade him be of good cheer and not to despair so, for he intended to help him win the affections of this lady so completely that she should never love another. And so it did indeed come to pass, for Doctor Faustus so disturbed the heart of the maiden with his sorcery that she would look upon no other man, nor heed any other suitor, although many gallant, wealthy noblemen were courting her.

Soon after his conversation with Reuckauer, Faustus commanded the young man to clothe himself sumptuously and prepare to accompany him to the maiden's house, for she was now in her garden with many other guests who were about to begin a dance, and there Reuckauer was to dance with her. Doctor Faustus gave him a ring, telling him to wear it on his finger during the dance with this lady, for just as soon as he might touch her with his ring finger she would fall in love with him and with no other. Faustus forbade Reuckauer to ask her hand in marriage, explaining that she would have to entreat him.

Now he took some distilled water and washed Reuckauer with it, so that his face presently became exceeding handsome. Reuckauer followed Faustus's instructions carefully, danced with the lady and, while dancing, touched her with his ring finger. Instantly, her whole heart and love were his, for the good maiden was pierced through with Cupid's arrow.

That night in her bed she found no rest, so often did her thoughts turn to Reuckauer. Early the next morning she sent for him, laid her heart and her love before him, and begged him to wed her. He gave his consent, for he loved her ardently. Their wedding was celebrated anon, and Doctor Faustus received a handsome honorarium.

XXXV

Concerning Divers Flora in Doctor Faustus's Garden on Christmas Day

In the midst of winter at the Christmas season, several gentlewomen came to Wittemberg to visit their brothers and cousins, all young gentlemen students there who were well-acquainted with Doctor Faustus. He had been invited to their table on more than one occasion, and, desirous now of repaying such social debts, he did invite these lords to bring their ladies to his domicile for an evening draught of wine. To come to his house, they had to trudge through a deep snow which lay over the town, but Doctor Faustus had used his peculiar sorcery to prepare a splendid marvel in his garden for them, and when they arrived there they beheld no snow at all, but a lovely summer day with all manner of flora. The grass was covered all over with many blossoms. Beautiful vines were growing there, all hung with divers sorts of grapes. There were roses, too, white, red, and pink, as well as many other sweet-smelling flowers, and it was all a great delight to behold.

XXXVI

Concerning an Army Raised Against My Lord of Hardeck

Doctor Faustus, being on a journey to Eisleben and about halfway there, did see seven horses riding in the distance. He recognized their leader, for it was that Lord of Hardeck upon whose forehead (as we have reported) he had charmed a set of hart's horns while at the Emperor's court. The lord, who knew Faustus quite as well as Faustus knew him, called his men to a halt, and when Faustus noticed this action he immediately retired toward a little hill.

The knight ordered a lively charge to intercept him, and also commanded the firing of a musket volley, but although they spurred their mounts hard to overtake Faustus, he achieved the higher ground first, and by the time the horses had topped the rise he had vanished from their sight. Here the knight called a halt. They were looking about, trying to catch sight of Faustus again, when they heard in the copse below a loud noise of horns, trumpets, and military drums, all tooting and beating. Some hundred horses came charging in upon them, and the knight with his men took to their heels.

They at first sought to slip home around the side of the hill, but they encountered a second great armed band all ready for the charge and barring their way. They turned about to dash away and beheld a third troop of horsemen. They tried still another route, but again found themselves faced with men ready for battle. The same thing happened five times, just as often as they turned in a fresh direction. When the knight saw he could nowhere escape but was threatened with a charge from every direction, he rode alone right into the main host, ignoring the danger to himself, and asked what might be the cause for his being surrounded and menaced on all quarters.

None would speak to him or say a word until at last Doctor Faustus came riding up to the knight (who was now restrained on all sides) and proposed that he surrender himself as a prisoner or taste the edge of the sword. The knight was convinced that he had encountered a natural army prepared for battle, and when Faustus now demanded their muskets and swords, then took their horses as well, it did not occur to him that it might be naught but sorcery. Presently, Doctor Faustus brought the men fresh, enchanted horses and new muskets and swords, saying to the knight (who no longer even knew him to be Faustus), "My Lord, the commander of this army hath bid me let you go this time—but upon a condition and probation. Will ye confess that ye did pursue a man who hath sought and received, and is henceforth shielded by, our commander's protection?"

The knight had to accept this condition. When they came back to his castle again, his men rode the horses out to drink, but once in the water the horses disappeared. The good fellows almost drowned, and had to ride back home afoot. When the knight beheld his men coming in all muddy and wet, and when he learned the cause of it all, he knew right away that it was Doctor Faustus's sorcery, even of the same sort as had been used to shame and mock him before. But since he had this time given Faustus his pledge, he would not break it. As for Faustus, he hitched the horses together, sold them and got some money in his pockets again. Thus did he heap coals upon the wrath of his enemy.

XXXVII

Concerning the Beautiful Helen from Greece, How She Lived for a Time with Doctor Faustus

Doctor Faustus would fain omit or neglect anything pleasant and good unto the flesh. One midnight towards the end of the twenty-second year of his pact, while lying awake, he took thought again of Helen of Greece, whom he had awakened for the students on Whitsunday in Shrovetide (which we reported). Therefore, when morning came, he informed his spirit that he must present Helen to him, so that she might be his concubine.

This was done, and Helen was of the following description (Doctor Faustus had a portrait made of her): Her body was fine and erect, well-proportioned, tall, snow-white, and crystalline. She had a complexion which seemed tinted with rose, a laughing demeanor, gold-yellow hair which reached almost to the calves of her legs, and brilliant laughing eyes with a sweet, loving gaze. Her nose was somewhat long, her teeth white as alabaster. *In summa,* there was not a single flaw about her body. Doctor Faustus beheld her and she captured his heart. He fell to frolicking with her; she became his bedfellow, and he came to love her so well that he could scarcely bear a moment apart from her.

While fond Faustus was living with Helen, she swelled up as were she with child. Doctor Faustus was rapturously happy, for, in the twenty-third year of his pact, she bore him a son whom he called Justus Faustus. This child told him many things out of the future history of numerous lands. Later, when Faustus lost his life, there was none who knew whither wife and child were gone.

XXXVIII

Concerning One Whose Wife Married While He Was Captive in Turkey, and How Doctor Faustus Informed and Aided Him

A fine gentleman of the nobility, Johann Werner of Reuttpueffel from Bennlingen, who had gone to school with Faustus and was a learned man, had been married for six years to an extremely beautiful woman, Sabina of Kettheim, when he was one evening through guile and drink brought to take an oath to go along to Turkey and the Holy Land. He kept his pledge and promise, saw many things, endured much, and had been gone almost five years when there came to his wife certain reports that he was dead. The lady mourned for three years, during which time she had many suitors, among them an excellent person of the nobility whose name we dare not mention, but whom she now accepted.

When the time was approaching for their marriage celebration, Doctor Faustus discovered it, and he asked his Mephostophiles whether this Lord of Reuttpueffel were still alive. The spirit answered yes, he be alive and in Egypt in the city of Lylopolts where he lay captive, having attempted to visit the city of Al-Cairo. This grieved Doctor Faustus, for he loved his friend and had not been pleased that the lady was remarrying so soon. He knew her husband had loved her well. The time for the marriage consummation and the subsequent ceremony being at hand, Doctor Faustus gazed into a mirror wherein he could see all things and by which means he was also able to inform the Lord of Reuttpueffel that his wife was about to be wed, at which the latter was much astonished.

The hour of consummation arrived. The nobleman disrobed and went out to cast his water. It was then that Mephostophiles did use his art, for when the man came in and leapt into Sabina's bed to enjoy the fruits of love, when they hoisted their shirts and squeezed close together, it was all to no avail. The good lady, seeing that he did not want on and was hesitating, did reach out herself for the tool, wishing to help him, but she could achieve naught, and the night wore on in mere grasping, wiggling, and squeezing. This did cause the lady to grieve and to think on her previous husband whom she thought to be dead, for he had rightly known how to tousle her.

On the very same night, Faustus had freed the nobleman and had brought him asleep back to his castle. Now when the good lady beheld her young lord she fell at his feet and begged his forgiveness, indicating at the same time that the other had had naught and had been able to accomplish naught. My Lord of Reuttpueffel, noting that her account corresponded with what Doctor Faustus had reported, did accept her back again. The other good fellow, who finally recovered his potency, rode hastily away, not wishing to be seen again because of what had happened to him. Later, he lost his life in a war. The husband, however, is still jealous, and the good lady must hear from him, even though he did not witness it, how she did after all lie with another, who felt her and grasped her and, had he been able to cover her, would have done that, too.

XXXIX

Concerning the Testament: What Doctor Faustus Bequeathed His Servant Christoph Wagner

Now during this whole time, right into the twenty-fourth year of his pact, Doctor Faustus had been keeping a young apprentice, who studied there at the University in Wittemberg and who became acquainted with all the tricks, sorcery, and arts of his master. The two were cut from the same piece of cloth. Wagner was a wicked, dissipated knave who had gone about begging in Wittemberg but had found no kindness with anyone until he had met Faustus, who took the stripling in as his famulus and even called him his son, letting him enjoy his ill-gotten gains. Neither troubled himself with the price of them.

When his twenty-four years were all but run out, Faustus called unto himself a notary together with several magisters who were his friends. In their presence he bequeathed his famulus his house and garden, which were located on the Ring-Wall in Scherr Alley, not far from the Iron Gate and indeed right beside the houses of

Ganser and of Veitt Röttinger (since that time, it has been rebuilt, for it was so uncanny that none could dwell therein). He also left him 1,600 guilders lent out on usury, a farm worth 800 guilders, 600 guilders in ready money, a gold chain worth 300 crowns, some silver plate given him by a man named Kraffter, as well as such other things as he had taken away from various courts—those of the Pope and of the Turk, for example. All these items together were worth many hundred guilders. There was not really much household stuff on hand, for he had not lived much at home, but at inns and with students, in gluttony and drunkenness.

XL

The Discourse Which Doctor Faustus Held with His Son Concerning the Testament

The testament being drawn up, Faustus summoned his famulus, explained to him how he had made that person beneficiary of his estate who had been a trusty servant throughout his life and had never revealed any of his secrets, and how he would, in addition, like to grant this person one further request, if he would but name it. Wagner asked for Faust's cunning, but this fine father reminded his pretty son (who should have been named Christ*less* Wagner) that he would after all inherit all his books, and that he must diligently guard them, not letting them become common knowledge, but taking his own profit from them by studying them well (this route to hell).

"As to my cunning," spake Faustus, "thou canst win it if thou wilt but love my books, heed no man else, and follow in my footsteps. Hast thou none other request?—That thou be served by my spirit? This cannot be, for Mephostophiles oweth me no further debt, nor doth he bear affinity to any other man. But if thou art fain to have a spirit as servant I will help thee to another."

Three days later, Faustus again called his famulus unto him, asking whether he were still of a mind to possess a spirit, and, if so, in what form he would have him.

"My Lord and Father," answered Wagner, "in the form of an

ape let him appear, for even in such a manner and form would I have him."

A spirit immediately came bounding into the parlor in the figure of an ape, and Doctor Faustus said, "Lo, now seest thou him, but he will not obey thee until I be dead. At that time my Mephostophiles will vanish forever, and thou shalt never see him more. Then, if thou wilt perform what is necessary—this being thine own decision—then canst thou summon thy spirit unto thee by calling upon Urian, for this is his name. In return, I do beg of thee not to publish my deeds, arts, and adventures before the time of my death, but then to write all these matters down, organizing and transferring them into a *Historia* and compelling Urian to help thee by recalling unto thee whatever thou canst not remember, for men will expect these things of thee.

XLI

What Doctor Faustus Did in the Final Month of His Pact

His days ran out like the sand in an hourglass, and when only one month remained of the twenty-four years which he had contracted of the devil (as ye have read), Doctor Faustus became faint-hearted, depressed, deeply melancholic, like unto an imprisoned murderer and highwayman over whose head the sentence hath been pronounced and who now in the dungeon awaiteth punishment and death. Filled with fear, he sobbed and held conversations with himself, accompanying such speeches with many gestures of his hands. He did moan and sigh and fall away from flesh. He kept himself close and could not abide to have the spirit about him.

XLII

Doctor Faustus: His Lamentation, that He Must Die at a Young and Lusty Age

Sorrow moved Doctor Faustus to set his grief in words, lest he forget it. Here followeth one such written complaint:

Alas, thou reckless, worthless heart! Thou hast seduced the flesh round about thee, and my fate is fire. The blessedness which once thou didst know is lost.

Alas, Reason and Free Will! What a heavy charge ye do level at these limbs, which may expect naught else than rape of their life!

Alas, ye limbs, and thou yet whole body! It was ye let Reason indict Soul, for I might have chosen succor for my soul by sacrificing thee, my body.

Alas, Love and Hate! Why abide ye both at once in my breast? Your company hath occasioned all mine anguish.

Alas, Mercy and Vengeance! Ye have caused me to strive after glory and rewarded me with infamy.

Alas, Malice and Compassion! Was I created a man that I might suffer those torments which now I see before me?

Alas, alas, is there aught in the wide world that doth not conspire against this wretch?

Alas, of what help is this complaint?

XLIII

Doctor Faustus Lamenteth Yet Further

Alas, alas, wretched man, o thou poor accursed Faustus, now in the number of the damned! I must wait the inestimable pains of a death far more miserable than any tortured creature hath yet endured.

Alas, alas, Reason, Willfulness, Recklessness, Free Will! O, what a cursed and inconstant life hast thou led! How unseeing, how careless wast thou! Now become thy parts, soul and body, unseeing and ever more unseen.

Alas, Worldly Pleasure! Into what wretchedness hast thou led me, darkening and blinding mine eyes!

Alas, my timid heart! Where were thine eyes?

And thou my poor soul! Where was thy knowledge?

All ye senses! Where were ye hid?

O miserable travail! O sorrow and desperation forgotten of God!

Alas, grief over grief, and torment upon woe and affliction! Who will release me? Where am I to hide? Whither must I creep? Whither flee? Wherever I may be, there am I a prisoner.

The heart of Doctor Faustus was so troubled that he could speak no more.

XLIV

Doctor Faustus: His Hideous End and Spectaculum

His twenty-four years were run out. As he lay awake in the night, his spirit came unto him to deliver up his writ, or contract, thus giving him due notice that the devil would fetch his body in the following night, and allowing him to make any necessary preparations for that event.

This occasioned such a renewed moaning and sobbing into the night that the spirit returned, consoling him, and saying, "My Fauste, be not so faint of heart. Thou dost indeed lose thy body, but thy time of judgment is yet far distant. Why surely thou must die—even shouldst thou live for many hundreds of years. The Jews and the Turks must also die expecting the same perdition as thou—even emperors die thus, if they be not Christian. After all, thou knowest not yet what it be that awaiteth thee. Take courage, and despair not so utterly. Dost not remember how the devil did promise thee a body and soul all of steel, insensitive to the pain which the others will feel in Hell?"

This and such like comfort and consolation he gave him, but it was false and not in accord with the Holy Scriptures. Doctor Faustus, having none other expectation but that he must absolve his debt and contract with his skin, did on this same day (in which the spirit had announced that the devil was about to fetch him) betake himself unto the trusted friends with whom he had spent many an hour, the magisters, baccalaureates, and other students, entreating them now to go out to the little village of Rimlich with him, about a half mile removed from the town of Wittemberg, there to take a repast with him. They would not turn him away, but went along and ate a morning meal with many costly courses both of meat and of drink, served by the host at an inn.

Doctor Faustus joined in their merriment, but he was not merry in his heart. Afterward, he requested all his guests to do him the great kindness of remaining to eat supper with him, too, and to stay the night here as well, for he had something important to tell them. Again they agreed, and they took the evening meal with him also.

It was finished, and a last cup had been passed. Doctor Faustus paid the host, and addressed the students, saying that he wished to inform them of some things. They gave him their attention, and Doctor Faustus said unto them, "My dear, trusted, and very gracious lords: I have called you unto me for this good and sufficient cause. For many years now, ye have known what manner of man I be, the arts and the sorcery I have used. All these things come from none other than from the devil. I fell into such devilish desires through none other cause than these: bad company, mine own worthless flesh and blood, my stiff-necked, godless will, and all the soaring, devilish thoughts I allowed in my head. I gave myself up unto the devil and contracted with him for a term of twenty-four years, setting my body and soul in forfeit. Now are these twenty-four years run out. I have only this night left. An hourglass standeth before mine eyes, and I watch for it to finish.

"I know that the devil will have his due. As I have consigned my body and soul unto him with my blood in return for certain other costly considerations, I have no doubt that he will this night fetch me. This is why, dear and well-beloved, gracious lords, I have summoned you here just before the end to take one last cup with me, not concealing from you the manner of my departure. I entreat you now, my dear, gracious brothers and lords, to bring my cordial and brotherly greetings to my friends and to those who do honor my memory, to bear no ill-will toward me but, if ever I have offended you, to forgive me in your hearts. As regardeth my *Historia* and what I have wrought in those twenty-four years, all these things have been written down for you.

"Now let this my hideous end be an example unto you as long as ye may live, and a remembrance to love God and to entreat Him to protect you from the guile and the deceit of the devil, praying that the Dear Lord will not lead you into temptation. Cling ye unto Him, falling not away from Him as I, damned godless mortal, have done, despising and denying baptism (Christ's own sacrament), God, all the heavenly host and mankind—such a sweet

God, who desireth not that one shall be lost. Shun bad company, which would lead you astray as it hath me, go earnestly and often to church, war and strive constantly against the devil with a steadfast faith in Christ and always walking a godly path.

"Finally, my last request is that ye go to bed and let nothing trouble you, but sleep on and take your rest even if a crashing and tumult be heard in this house. Be not afraid. No injury shall befall you. Arise not out of your beds. Should ye find my corpse, convey it unto the earth, for I die both as a bad and as a good Christian. Contrition is in my heart, and my mind doth constantly beg for Grace and for the salvation of my soul. O I know that the devil will have this body—and welcome he is to it, would he but leave my soul in peace. Now I entreat you: betake yourselves to bed. A good night to you—unto me, an evil, wretched, and a frightful one."

Faustus needed great resolve and courage to make this confession and to tell his tale without weakening and becoming fearful and faint. As for the students, they were cast into great wonderment that a man could be so reckless as thus to imperil body and soul for no more profit than knavery, knowledge, and sorcery. But, as they loved him well, they sought to console him.

They said, "Alas dear Fauste, how have ye imperiled yourself! Why remained ye so long silent, revealing none of these things to us? Why, we should have brought learned *Theologi* who would have torn you out of the devil's nets and saved you. But now it is too late and surely injurious to body and soul."

Doctor Faustus answered, saying, "Such was not permitted me. Often was I amind to seek counsel and succor of godfearing men. Indeed, once an old man did charge me to follow his teachings, leave my sorcery, and be converted. Then came the devil, ready to put an end to me (even as he will this night do), saying that in the moment of my conversion—nay, even in the instant of such an intent on my part—all would be over with me."

Upon hearing these words, and understanding that the devil would surely dispatch Faustus this night, the students urged him to call upon God, begging Him for forgiveness for Jesus Christ's sake, saying, "O God, be merciful unto me poor sinner, and enter not into judgement with me, for I cannot stand before Thee. Although I must forfeit my body unto the devil, wilt Thou preserve my soul!"

Faustus agreed to do this. He tried to pray, but he could not. As it was with Cain, who said his sins were greater than could be forgiven him, so was it with Faustus also, who was convinced that in making his written contract with the devil he had gone too far. But the students and good lords prayed and wept for Faustus. They embraced one another and, leaving Faustus in his chambers, retired to bed, where none could rightly sleep, for they lay there awake, waiting the end.

And it came to pass between twelve and one o'clock in the night that a great blast of wind stormed against the house, blustering on all sides as if the inn and indeed the entire neighborhood would be torn down. The students fell into a great fear, got out of their beds, and came together to comfort one another, but they did not stir out of their chamber. The innkeeper went running out of the house, however, and he found that there was no disturbance at all in any other place than his own. The students were lodged in a chamber close by those of Doctor Faustus, and over the raging of the wind they heard a hideous music, as if snakes, adders, and other serpents were in the house. Doctor Faustus's door creaked open. There then arose a crying out of Murder! and Help! but the voice was weak and hollow, soon dying out entirely.

When it was day the students, who had not slept this entire night, went into the chamber where Doctor Faustus had lain, but they found no Faustus there. The parlor was full of blood. Brain stuck to the walls where the Fiend had dashed him from one to the other. Here lay his eyes, here a few teeth. O it was a hideous *spectaculum*. Then began the students to bewail and beweep him, seeking him in many places. When they came out to the dung heap, here they found his corpse. It was monstrous to behold, for head and limbs were still twitching.

These students and magisters who were present at Faustus's death gained permission afterwards to bury him in the village. Subsequently, they retired to his domicile where they found the famulus Wagner already mourning his master. This little book, *Doctor Faustus: His Historia*, was already all written out. Now as to what his famulus wrote, that will be a different, new book. On this same day the enchanted Helen and her son Justus Faustus were also gone.

So uncanny did it become in Faustus's house that none could dwell there. Doctor Faustus himself walked about at night, making revelations unto Wagner as regardeth many secret matters. Passers-by reported seeing his face peering out at the windows.

Now this is the end of his quite veritable deeds, tale, *Historia,* and sorcery. From it the students and clerks in particular should learn to fear God, to flee sorcery, conjuration of spirits, and other works of the devil, not to invite the devil into their houses, nor to yield unto him in any other way, as Doctor Faustus did, for we have before us here the frightful and horrible example of his pact and death to help us shun such acts and pray to God alone in all matters, love Him with all our heart and with all our soul and with all our strength, defying the devil with all his following, that we may through Christ be eternally blessed. These things we ask in the name of Christ Jesus our only Lord and Savior. Amen. Amen.

Translated and adapted
by Harry G. Haile

ACKNOWLEDGMENTS

All reasonable efforts have been made to locate the parties who hold rights to previously published translations reprinted here. We gratefully acknowledge permission to reprint the following material:

The History of Doctor Johann Faustus, translated by H. G. Haile. Copyright © 1965 by the Board of Trustees of the University of Illinois. Reprinted by permission of the University of Illinois Press and Professor Harry G. Haile.

The Legend of Duke Ernst, translated by J. W. Thomas and Carolyn Dussere. Copyright © 1979 by University of Nebraska Press. Reprinted by permission of University of Nebraska Press.

Unfortunate Heinrich, translated by Frank Tobin reprinted from *Allegorica* 1, no. 2 (Fall 1976), Arlington, Texas.